Captain
W.W. Withenbury's
1838–1842

Red River Reminiscences

Captain W.W. Withenbury's 1838–1842 *Red River Reminiscences*

Edited and Annotated by Jacques D. Bagur

University of North Texas Press

Denton, Texas

Printed in the United States of America.

10 9 8 7 6 5 4 3 2 1

Permissions:
University of North Texas Press
1155 Union Circle #311336
Denton, TX 76203-5017

The paper used in this book meets the minimum requirements of the American National Standard for Permanence of Paper for Printed Library Materials, z39.48.1984. Binding materials have been chosen for durability.

Library of Congress Cataloging-in-Publication Data
Withenbury, W. W. (Wellington W.), 1815–1880, author.
Captain W.W. Withenbury›s 1838/1842 Red River reminiscences / edited and annotated by Jacques D. Bagur. -- First edition.
pages cm
Includes index.

Summary: A selection of letters written to the Cincinnati Commercial newspaper from 1870–1871 about steamboat travel on the Red River in 1838–1841.
ISBN 978-1-57441-547-6 (cloth : alk. paper) -- ISBN 978-1-57441-557-5 (ebook)
1. Withenbury, W. W. (Wellington W.), 1815–1880--Travel--Red River (Tex.-La.) 2. Withenbury, W. W. (Wellington W.), 1815–1880--Correspondence. 3. Inland navigation--Red River (Tex.-La.) 4. Inland navigation--Southwest, Old. 5. Steam-navigation--Southwest, Old. 6. Steam-navigation--Red River (Tex.-La.) 7. Red River (Tex.-La.)--Navigation--History. 8. Southwest, Old--Description and travel. I. Bagur, Jacques D., editor. II. Cincinnati commercial. III. Title.
F377.R3.W58 2014
976.6›6--dc23
2013041982

The electronic edition of this book was made possible by the support of the Vick Family Foundation.

For Jesse M. "Duke" DeWare IV,
who has been a constant source of
encouragement for my historic work.

Contents

Preface

During the late 1860s and early 1870s, steamboats from the midwestern commercial centers of St. Louis and Cincinnati began to enter the trades of the Red River and one of its major tributaries, the Ouachita, in direct competition with New Orleans. Midwestern boats had traditionally operated through New Orleans, but began bypassing New Orleans and dealing directly with the Red River ports and landings, particularly Shreveport, which was the center for trade activities in the upper portions of the river. The change began with import freights and quickly moved to cotton.

New Orleans was losing one of its major trade areas. There was much discussion about how to block these changes among the commercial entities and organizations of New Orleans, including the Red River Pilots' Association and the Board of Underwriters of the Port of New Orleans. The New Orleans *Daily Picayune*, which defended the interests of the city, brought the issue before the public through a series of editorials. These editorials were read by someone in Cincinnati, who published in the October 7, 1870, *Cincinnati Commercial* an objection to the *Picayune*'s statement that "When the outside Westerners come with the view they now plainly indicate to share that moiety of business which is due only to our home boatmen, they will find in the Association a power quick and potent to defend our legitimate carrying interests against the encroachments of the stranger. We have before told the boatmen of the West that there is nothing for birds of passage, either in Red or Ouachita Rivers. They had better be advised."

The letter of objection was signed "Bird of Passage" and challenged the *Picayune* on the boats and people who were instrumental in the development of the Red River trade, pointing out that almost all of the boats had been built in the Midwest (which was then called the West). The letter was read by another Cincinnati resident, W. W. Withenbury, who had been a Red River captain, but was then retired. Withenbury had been reading the *Picayune*, becoming increasingly irritated by its assertions, and was prompted by the letter to begin a series of letters to the *Cincinnati Commercial* demonstrating the importance of midwesterners like himself to the development of the Red River trade. These letters came to be known as Withenbury's "Red River Reminiscences."

Wellington W. Withenbury was born in Hartford, Connecticut, on June 25, 1815, the fifth child of Benjamin Withenbury from Sheffield, England, and Elizabeth Clark. For obvious reasons, he was never referred to by his first name in steamboat circles. His older sister Harriet came to Cazenovia, New York, in 1831 and married James Parsons in 1834. Withenbury was apprenticed to the Cazenovia cabinet maker Benjamin Clarke (a half brother by his mother's first marriage to Joseph Clarke), where he produced extant pieces dated 1832 and 1833. He married (date unknown) Sarah Swain, daughter of Roland Swain, with whom he had five children, only two of whom lived to maturity, with the first born in March 1840 and dying in May 1841. Sarah died in October 1868 at the age of 46, and Withenbury married Mary Cranley in December 1872, with whom he had one child (in 1874) who died at the age of four.[1]

Withenbury was a longtime Cincinnati resident and died on July 15, 1880, at his Walnut Hills residence. His obituary in the July 15, 1880, *Cincinnati Commercial* states that he had been stricken with paralysis (apparently a stroke) a few years before, that he had retired from steamboating about ten years before, and that he had been a Northern sympathizer during the Civil War and was during that time under sentence of death in Louisiana.

Withenbury published a brief sketch of his life as a boatman in the July 10, 1878, *New Orleans Daily Democrat*, stating that he began his career in 1839 as cook on a flatboat from Cincinnati to New Orleans; that he was second clerk on the *Southerner* (Capt. F. C. Swain) bound for Mobile, Alabama, in the fall of 1840; that he remained on the *Southerner* operating from New Orleans to Vicksburg, Mississippi, until the summer of 1841; and that he shipped as clerk of the *Relief* from Cincinnati in the fall of 1841, resulting in his first trip to the Red River in December of that year.

Summarizing his career, he stated that "During my experience on the river I have been on and (the greatest number) commanded the following boats: Southerner in Mobile and one trip to Tensas; Relief, Little Ben Franklin, Ohio river; Waverly, Lama, J. E. Roberts, Enterprise, Monterey, Echo, W. R. Douglas, P. F. Kimball, Rosa, Union, B. E. Clark, all in the order named, in Red river; Franklin Pierce, Ohio river; Reub White, Swamp Fox, Red river; Susquehanna, Ohio river; Texana, formerly the Franklin Pierce, St. Louis and the Yazoo; Lecompte, Vigo, Homer, Robt. Fulton, and last in 1863, the Eleanor, all in Red river." The referenced name change of the *Franklin Pierce* to the *Texana* referred to the fact that President Franklin Pierce had become immensely unpopular; Withenbury was losing money operating a boat by that name and appealed to the Federal Congress, which granted his request with the approval of the president.[2]

Withenbury was particularly proud of the fact that he had taken the first steamboat, the *Lama*, to Jefferson,Texas, in 1845 and that he had pioneered (also on the *Lama*) in Saline Bayou (a branch of the Little River, which enters the Red a short distance above Fulton, Arkansas) to a point later known as Ground's Landing, seven miles higher up than any boat had gone before. Withenbury's statement that he ended his steamboat career in 1863 is in tension with the obituary, which places his retirement around 1870; but the latter was apparently referencing an unconsummated plan by captains Withenbury, his nephew James Wellington Parsons (Harriet's son), and W. Daniels to purchase the *Shannon* and operate her in the Cincinnati and Red River trade, as reported in the December 28, 1871, *Daily Shreveport Times.*

Withenbury was running the *Homer* at New Orleans when it fell to Union forces in May 1862, and he and his boat were impressed into Confederate service. He was paid for his services in cotton that was legally but not physically transferred. The cotton was seized as a prize of war during Nathaniel Banks' Union campaign in the Red River area, to which Withenbury provided assistance.[3] After the war, Withenbury sued for this cotton in the United States admiralty court, which rendered an unfavorable judgment in November 1865.[4]

I became aware of the existence of the "Red River Reminiscences" while completing *A History of Navigation on Cypress Bayou and the Lakes*, in which Withenbury and the *Lama* played an important role. A notice of his death appeared in the July 19, 1880, *New Orleans Daily Democrat* mentioning that he had written a number of letters several years before to the *Cincinnati Commercial* under the title "Red River Reminiscences." The letters in microfilm copy were obtained for me by M'Lissa Kesterman with the Cincinnati History Library and Archives on the basis of sparse information about year and content. Acquisition of the letters was particularly fortuitous because they were published anonymously under the name "Outsider." It is obvious that knowledge of the author's identity was widely known at the time they were being published and that Withenbury maintained the convention as a gibe at the *Picayune*. That the letters were written by Withenbury is known from internal evidence and confirmed by the August 24, 1871, *Cincinnati Commercial*.

It was Withenbury's original intent, as stated in the first letter, to provide a systematic account of the men and boats that operated on the Red and Ouachita rivers from the late 1830s up to the present. The Ouachita River soon dropped from the picture, and after the first few letters the title "Red and Ouachita River Reminiscences" was replaced by "Red River Reminiscences." The systematic account was also discarded, and Withenbury concentrated on four voyages by three boats on the Red River above Shreveport. This is fortunate because the names of the boats and captains are readily available from period newspapers; and Withenbury's strong suit is in character and incident, making his reminiscences unique among those that were becoming common during the 1870s and 1880s as the railroads captured the various trades that had been dominated by steamboats.

Withenbury published 54 letters from October 1870 to July 1871. Of these, 39 are concerned with the activities of the *Concord*, the *Hunter*, and the *Relief* on the Upper Red River and are used in the following rendition of the reminiscences. Others concerning Withenbury's quarrels with the *Picayune*, the Pilots' Association, and the Board of Underwriters have not been used, including portions of some letters that have been used dealing with similar matters. Still others covering matters of historic importance have not been used. The deletions were made because they distract from the central stories. It is extremely difficult to follow the movements of the boats and to enter into the tempo of the voyages in the context of Withenbury's lengthy asides, a problem that he recognized in the constant refrain: "but I have almost lost sight of the Relief."

The disposition of all of the letters in relation to the present rendition is covered in an appendix. The 39 letters that have been used fall into four parts:

1. An introductory letter in which Withenbury makes a few fundamental points and lays out his plan of response to the *Picayune*.
2. Two letters concerning the voyage in 1838 of the *Concord* under Capt. Jonathan Hildreth, in which Withenbury did not participate.
3. Two letters concerning the voyages in 1840–1841 of the *Relief* under Capt. Joseph Ross and the *Hunter* under Capt. Benjamin Crooks, in which Withenbury did not participate.
4. Thirty-four letters concerning the voyage in 1841–1842 of the *Relief* under Capt. Joseph Ross, in which Hildreth served as pilot and Withenbury served as clerk.

All of these voyages were to what then was called the Upper Red River, which referred to the area above the Great Raft, an immense logjam on the river that extended from slightly above to far below the site that eventually became Shreveport. This raft was removed by Capt. Henry Shreve of the Corps of Engineers in 1838, allowing the *Concord* to become the first steamboat to reach the upper river by way of the river. The raft soon reformed at the place where its head had been, which forced the *Relief* and *Hunter* to use a western bypass around the raft; and, in spite of intermittent, temporary removals, it continued to grow upward until nearly reaching the Arkansas line when it was permanently removed in 1873.

The letters come to an abrupt end in the July 20, 1871, *Cincinnati Commercial* with the *Relief* at Pecan Point in northeast Texas on its second upward trip. The search for additional letters ended with the December 7, 1872, issue, in which Withenbury's remarriage was announced. The August 24, 1871, issue in which Withenbury is noted as the author of the reminiscences indicates that he had just returned from a Western tour and was meeting with Capt. W. D. Bateman concerning the growing trade between Cincinnati and the Red River region. This one-month trip was the proximate cause of the end of the letters.

Withenbury was ill for two months after his return, went to Washington in November 1871, contemplated acquisition of the *Shannon* in December, was confined with rheumatism in the first two months of 1872, went to Washington and the East in hopes of improving his health in May (from which he wrote a letter signed "Outsider" but not concerned with the Red River, which appeared in the June 14 *Cincinnati Commercial*), and married in December and left for Jacksonville on a honeymoon. The 1878 sketch of his life as a boatman ends with the statement: "My memory of steamboat life is full of reminiscences which would doubtless be interesting to many, but I am in such wretched health that it is a task to recount them, though I will endeavor to continue them at some future period."

With respect to the letters themselves, it should be noted that the observations on persons were derived by Withenbury from encounters over many years and that the profiles are not intended as biographical (for example, three signers of the Texas Declaration of Independence are described, but this fact is not mentioned). Most of the important ports and landings on the upper river are at least mentioned, but little is said about facilities or about Fulton, which was the most important port. The letters make it clear that many of the ports and landings were heavily dependent on the liquor trade with the Choctaw, which was outlawed in the Indian Territory.

The hand-drawn maps showing the western bypass through Black and Red bayous are based on a detailed 1855 Corps of Engineers map by Charles Fuller titled *Map of Red River with its Bayous and Lakes in the Vicinity of the Raft*. The hand-drawn maps showing the locations of the ports and landings on the upper river are based on online topographic maps of the region using contemporary political boundaries. The locations of the ports and landings can be known with a high degree of specificity from Withenbury's accounts, land records, General Land Office survey maps, and period maps. Some of the landings have been placed off-channel to give a better idea of their historic location.

Withenbury's letters are primarily commentaries on people and places in northwest Louisiana, northeast Texas, southwest Arkansas, and southeast Oklahoma (then the Indian Territory) in the late 1830s and early 1840s. Almost all of the places along the Red River mentioned by Withenbury that were of sufficient importance to be designated ports, as well as places in the interior, are shown on maps available online in the David Rumsey Historical Map Collection. Greater specificity with respect to the location of a few of the ports is available in the historic maps for Bowie and Red River counties on the Texas General Land Office website.[5]

Many of the persons mentioned in the letters were planters with large property holdings and their own landings. Property ownership in the Indian Territory was tribal; but this is not a problem because most of the people mentioned in the letters in the Indian Territory were non-planters connected with Doaksville and Fort Towson. Land in Texas was allocated as headrights, with the name of the owner shown on the property in various county maps.[6] Louisiana and Arkansas used a township and range system for property allocations, with townships numbered north and south and ranges numbered east and west.[7] Each township-range is six square miles, which is divided into 36 one-square-mile sections of 640 acres, with Section 1 beginning in the northeast corner and Section 36 ending in the southeast corner. Property owners, the land they owned (location and acreage), and date of acquisition are identified in the Land Patents section of the U. S. General Land Office website,[8] but it should be kept in mind that occupancy preceded ownership and that the southwest Arkansas counties changed dramatically over time. The planters mentioned in the letters had large landholdings with dispersed properties. Probable locations of plantations and landings were identified by mapping the properties on contemporary topographic maps, which also use the township and range system.[9]

A great deal of information on the Upper Red River, particularly in relation to navigation activities, was drawn from the early Shreveport, Louisiana; Clarksville, Texas; and Washington, Arkansas, newspapers. The Shreveport newspapers covered all of the boats going to and coming back from the Upper Red River and are particularly valuable because they identify the highest port or landing reached by each boat on each voyage. Although an interior town, Clarksville provided fairly substantial coverage of navigation because Roland on the Red River was its primary import and export point. Also an interior town, Washington provided a great deal of information on what was happening in Fulton on the Red River to the southwest, which was its primary import and export point. Statements about the relative importance of the various ports and landings reflect a systematic analysis of the information in the newspapers through the 1870s.

Introductory paragraphs and footnotes are provided as guides to the reader and to demonstrate that Withenbury was referring to real persons in real places. Most of the information was obtained from the Internet, from regional newspapers available on microfilm, and from published resources available at the Louisiana State University library. The presented information is limited because this is Withenbury's story. Almost all of the cited sources are available online, including many of the newspapers, which are rapidly being converted to electronic format through such programs as the "Portal to Texas History."

Notes

1. There are no profiles of Withenbury. Basic information on Withenbury, including his wives and children, was supplied to me by M'Lissa Kesterman in Cincinnati. On Withenbury and related families, see Richard Withenbury's *The Withenbury Heritage*. The Parsons-Withenbury relationship is covered in Henry Parsons' 1920 *Parsons Family*. Sarah's death notice is in the October 20, 1868, *Cincinnati Commercial*. Interment records for Withenbury, Sarah, and all of Withenbury's children are available on the Spring Grove Cemetery website. Mary's birth and death dates are unknown.

2. See "Repudiating His Own Name" in the March 7, 1855, Shreveport *South-Western*.

3. Withenbury provided extensive testimony on this assistance in the investigation of the Red River Expedition in the *Report of the Joint Committee on the Conduct of the War* (Senate Report 142, 38th Cong., 2d Sess.), which is available online.

4. This case was of sufficient significance to be reported on by the *New York Times* in 1865 in its October 28 ("Prizes of War") and November 14 ("A Great Cotton Case") issues. A local perspective that mentions Withenbury is provided in the November 29, 1865, Shreveport *South-Western* in "The Great Cotton Case."

5. It should be noted that all of the ports with the exception of Fulton were settlement areas that never developed into towns in the modern sense, and none of them contained port-related infrastructure such as wharves. On the other hand, some of them (Jonesboro, Roland, Berlin, and Spanish Bluff) developed and implemented town plans, which is known from town lot assessments in the county tax rolls. This means that information on their development can be obtained from their respective county deed records.

6. Because of their clarity, the 1933 map for Bowie County and the 1934 map for Red River County (both of which are available on the Texas General Land Office website) were used to identify the location of headrights. The surveys for the headrights, which are also available on the website, provided information of value.

7. For example, Township 21 North, Range 16 West, which is abbreviated as T21N R16W.

8. RootsWeb provides convenient summaries of the information contained in these documents.

9. The agricultural fields of some of the planters mentioned in the letters are shown in the Survey Plats section of the U.S. General Land Office website. Most of the early surveys were conducted during the late 1830s and early 1840s.

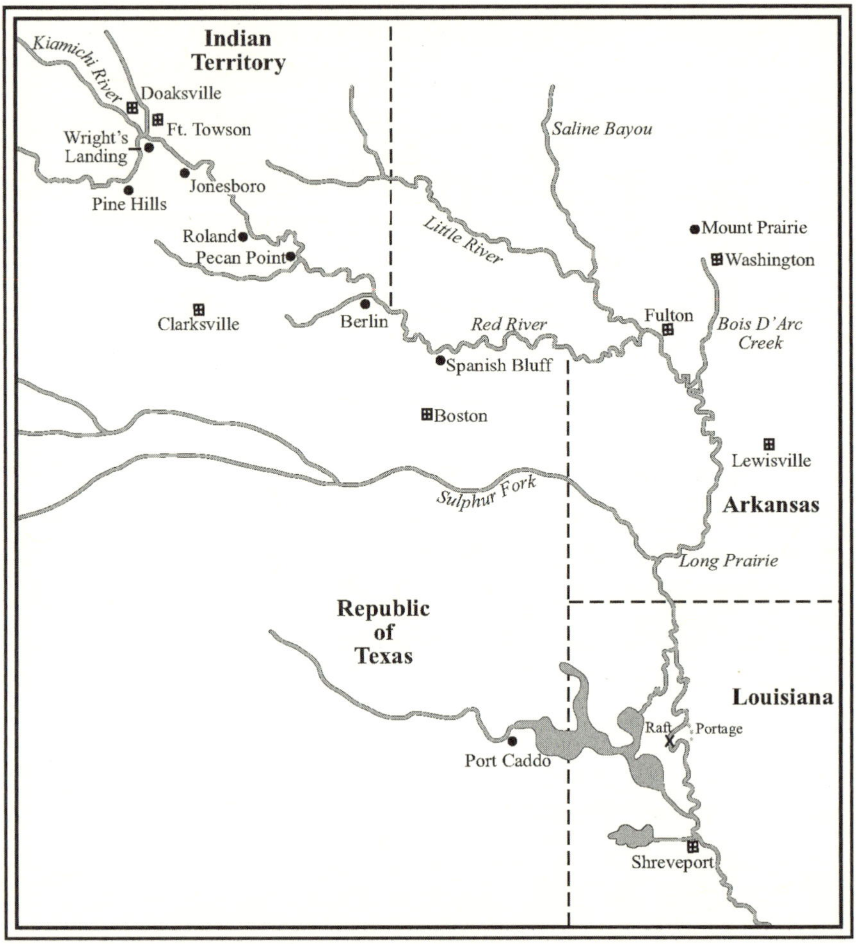

FIGURE 1: UPPER RED RIVER REGION

Introduction

Most of Withenbury's letters, and all that have been selected, are concerned with trips to the Upper Red River. The term referred to the portion of the Red River above the raft in which boats operated (first keelboats and flatboats and then steamboats) and also to the region serviced by those boats (Figure 1). The term did not encompass the entire river above the raft, whose headwaters extend into eastern New Mexico. The theoretical limits of navigation reached as far as Preston (north of Dallas and across from the mouth of the Washita River in the Indian Territory), but boats seldom went that far. The practical limits for commercially successful boat operations extended only up to Pine Hills in the northwestern corner of Red River County, Texas; however, most freight contracts did not extend above Wright's Landing (usually called Kiomatia), which served Paris, Bonham, and Sherman and was also in the northwestern corner of Red River County, but about 25 miles by river below Pine Hills.

The Upper Red River region was the area serviced by those boats, primarily through import freights of farm and plantation supplies and export freights of cotton. The region included large portions of southwest Arkansas, northeast Texas, and southeast Oklahoma (then the Indian Territory) and a small portion of northwest Louisiana. The size of the trade area was enhanced in southwest Arkansas through its penetration by Little River (a major tributary of the Red that entered immediately above Fulton) and in northeast Texas through its penetration by Sulphur Fork (a major tributary below Fulton that extended far to the west).

The Red River is an alluvial river that meanders across a broad floodplain of fine soils of its own making between distant bluffs. The alluvial soils provided ideal conditions for cotton agriculture and the bluffs a location out of the floodplain for plantation homes. The river usually stayed within its banks, which were high, but sometimes broke out, always replenishing the soils and sometimes destroying crops and facilities.

The river is shallow and convoluted, with numerous sandbars and shoals; and it cuts into its own banks and forms numerous bends that are eventually cut off. It contained a great deal of debris from bank cutting into forested areas that lodged downstream, causing the raft to grow upward; and it was festered with snags and stumps, many of which were produced by steamboatmen clearing obstacles or securing fuel. It was usually not navigable during the summer, and there were times of drought when it was not navigable for long periods. When it was navigable, boats were often able to get only as far as Fulton. The river was subject to rapid and dramatic rises and falls. The primary danger was getting stuck above, because steamboats were commercial operations that lost money through delays. Fulton became the place at which captains "read" the river to determine whether they should proceed upward.

The Upper Red River region did not begin to be developed[1] until after the United States purchased the Territory of Louisiana from France in 1803. The purchase included most of the region. The exception was the portion in Texas, which remained under Spanish or Mexican jurisdiction until the formation of the Republic of Texas in 1836. The boundary between the United States and Spanish possessions (and later the Republic of Texas) was uncertain until 1841. In any case, the land assumed to be within the jurisdiction of the United States was occupied by the Caddo Indians, whose claims were enforced to some degree by the government, which established an Indian agency (or factory, at a time when factor meant agent) at the mouth of Sulphur Fork in 1818. The Caddo sold these lands to the United States in 1835, and Texas entered the Union in 1845.

Settlers began arriving in Arkansas shortly after the Louisiana Purchase, and it had sufficient population to achieve territorial status in 1819. Some of the settlers went overland to the southwest corner along the Southwest Trail, an old Indian trail that ran through the Little Rock area on the Arkansas River to the Fulton area on the Red River. Many of these persons were slaveholding cotton planters from older southern states who were seeking new opportunities in the fertile valleys of the Red River and its tributaries. Settlements were established prior to 1819 at Mount Prairie on the Southwest Trail five miles northwest of Washington and at Long Prairie downriver from Fulton on the east side of the river,[2] with an advertisement for the sale of town lots in Fulton appearing in the December 11, 1819, *Arkansas Gazette*.

Others passed farther on into the area north of the Red River that was to become Oklahoma and south of the river that was to become Texas. This area included the old Miller County, Arkansas, including portions of what is now Texas and Oklahoma, which was possible because of the immense uncertainties concerning boundaries. One of the main routes into Texas was Trammel's Trace, which was blazed by Nicholas Trammel about 1815 and ran between Fulton and Nacogdoches, Texas, to the south. There was another trail that ran west out of Washington and cut south across the Red River slightly below its confluence with the Kiamichi River. Jonesboro was established at this crossing on the south side of the Red River, with the first settlers arriving in 1816. It was joined during the same year by Pecan Point about 30 miles downstream at the mouth of Pecan Bayou.

The second factor contributing to the development of the area was the decision of the United States government to relocate the Indians east of the Mississippi River to the Indian Territory in what is now Oklahoma. This process began with the Choctaw in the early 1830s, which were relocated from Mississippi and Alabama to southern Oklahoma. They were joined in the same area by the Chickasaw from northern Mississippi in the late 1830s, who later established a permanent residence for themselves farther to the west. Some of the Choctaw and Chickasaw were mixed-blood slaveholding cotton planters in their homelands and were quick to seize the new opportunities afforded by the Red River Valley. One of the most notable of these was the Choctaw Robert Jones, who became a multiple plantation owner and among the wealthiest persons in the South.

The third factor in the development of the area was the establishment of forts to protect Arkansas settlers and the resettled Indians from the Indians to the west. These forts included Fort Gibson in east-central Oklahoma and Fort Towson slightly north of the Red River and east of the Kiamichi River, both of which were established in 1824. They were joined in 1842 by Fort Washita farther to the west on the Washita River. The forts took on a secondary role as administrative centers for the newly relocated Indians.

Many of the earliest arrivals in the region were by keelboat. The first keelboat penetrated the Upper Red River to the Fulton area in 1816 under the command of Matthew Moss,[3] who was followed in 1818 by his brother James and his nephews James, William, and Matthew. The Mosses settled in the Washington area. Claiborne Wright brought his family, including his sons George and Travis, to Pecan Point in September 1816 aboard the keelboat *Pioneer.*[4]

Keelboats ran to the Indian agency on Sulphur Fork; and military records indicate the movement of more than one keelboat to Fort Towson almost every year at least through the late 1830s.[5] A notable trip involving boats of special design was the 1806 Freeman and Custis expedition, which was intercepted by Spanish troops at a place later known as Spanish Bluff that became an important keelboat and steamboat landing.[6]

Upstream movements of keelboats and downstream movements of keelboats and flatboats was primarily from and to Alexandria, Louisiana, on the lower Red River during the first few years, because that point had been reached by steamboats operating out of New Orleans in 1818. These activities shifted to Natchitoches above in early 1820, which was regularly served by steamboats from that year on. Upstream boat movements carried settlers, farm and plantation supplies, military personnel, and military provisions. Downstream boat movements carried cotton and Indian trade goods such as hides, pelts, skins, and bear oil, which were usually offloaded at Natchitoches and sent downstream to New Orleans. There were also substantial movements between points on the Upper Red River.

Flatboats were common and continued to be used during the steamboat period, particularly when the river was low. Persons known to have been regular operators of keelboats and flatboats on the Upper Red River include Travis Wright (Claiborne's son), Richard Finn, Abraham Block, George Alban, and James Gamble; and the Caddo Lake recluse and bee hunter Hiram Bails served as guide for many keelboat passages.[7] Referring to the keelboating activities of Travis Wright and Richard Finn in 1831, the February 5, 1881, *New Orleans Daily Democrat* says "The crews at this time were made up of a wild set composed of renegade whites and Indians."

The best indication of the extent of keelboat and flatboat traffic on the Upper Red River is a list of landings published in the December 9, 1854, Clarksville *Standard* that was prepared by Capt. J. E. Hopkins during the period in which keelboat navigation prevailed on the Upper Red River and originally included all of the plantations. The keelboat landings, moving upstream and on both sides of the river, were Caddo Prairie, Diggs' Bluff, Sulphur Fork, Conway, Abrams', Chicaninny Cutoff, Col. Winn's Fishers Prairie, Little's Prairie, Hamilton's Lost Prairie, Dooley's Ferry, Buzzard Bluff, Fulton, Glass Landing, White Oak Shoals, Pine Prairie, Shaw's Landing, McKinney's Landing, Paxton's Bluff, Spanish Bluff, Smith's Landing, Lanesport, Mill Creek, Pecan Point, Rowland, Albion, James Bluff, Jonesborough, Fort Towson, Kiamichi, Wright's, Pinehills, and Slate Banks. Most of these became important steamboat landings.

Navigation from and to the Upper Red River was not by way of the river, which was choked with raft materials from a point above Natchitoches to a point above the site that eventually became Shreveport.[8] The route used was on the east side of the river and was constituted by a maze of bayous and lakes, with the upper outlet to the river through Willow Chute. This outlet was closed in 1821 by the upward movement of the raft. Canals were constructed back into the river farther up, but by 1828 the raft had reached Hurricane Bluffs (immediately above Shreveport) and the eastern raft bypass was inaccessible.

Under the pressures of military needs and Upper Red River planters, the Federal Government instructed Lt. Washington Seawell of the Corps of Engineers to develop a navigation route on the west side of the river. Seawell's project, which was conducted from 1829 to 1831, involved the cutting down of cypress trees (but leaving the stumps) on Red Bayou and Black Bayou, construction of a canal (what came to be designated "Sewell's Canal") linking Red Bayou and Black Bayou, and construction of a small canal in what is now downtown Shreveport linking the route to Bayou Pierre, which paralleled Red River on the west.

The only steamboat to use the full Seawell route (including Bayou Pierre) was the *Bolivar*, which went to Jonesboro in 1836. The importance of the Seawell route was in its upper portion, which became (along with upward extensions as the raft moved upstream) the permanent route for boats from and to the Upper Red River, with the exception of brief periods when the raft was removed. That route ran from Twelvemile Bayou (which enters the Red at Shreveport) through Soda Lake (now extinct), Stumpy Bayou, Clear Lake (now extinct), Black Bayou, Sewell's Canal, and Red Bayou.

The existence of the upper portion of the Seawell route enabled the first steamboat, the *Enterprise*, to reach the Upper Red River in 1831.[9] This boat was owned by Benjamin Milam, who was later to become an important figure in the Texas Revolution. The trip was made in May-June during an extreme low-water period from Natchitoches to Long Prairie and could only have been accomplished by a very small boat such as the *Enterprise*, which drew 20 to 24 inches when loaded. The route out of Natchitoches was the old route on the east side of the river. The *Enterprise* emerged from this route through Mack's Bayou, which connects with the Red River at Shreveport, moved through a portion of the Red River between two raft segments, and entered into Twelvemile Bayou.

Henry Shreve removed the Red River raft from 1833 through 1838, with clearance up to the mouth of Twelvemile Bayou in 1835, which enabled boats to use the main river rather than the eastern bypass out of Natchitoches. Boats taking the Seawell route during this period included the *Indian* to Fort Towson in 1834, two trips by the *Compromise* to the Choctaw Nation in 1835, the *Bolivar* and *Native* to Jonesboro in 1836, and the *Rover* to Fort Towson in 1836. The *Compromise* carried out cotton, snakeroot, bear skins, coon skins, tallow, beeswax, bear oil, and beaver pelts. The *Indian* under Capt. Benjamin Crooks made improvements to the route, beginning the process of transforming it from a passage for small keelboats to a passage for mid-sized steamboats.

When Shreve completed removal of the raft in March 1838, steamboats had direct access to the Upper Red River. The first boat through was the *Concord*, followed by the *Indian*, *Black Hawk*, *Brian Boroihme*, *Revenue*, *Heroine*, *Livingston*, *Mariner*, and *Cochuma*. The *Black Hawk* and *Revenue* wrecked on their down trips in an area that had not been completely cleared of raft debris. However, the first true Upper Red River wreck was the *Heroine*, which struck a snag a short distance from the Fort Towson landing, which was on the Red River a few miles downstream from the Kiamichi River.[10]

Raft segments formed and were removed periodically in 1839 at the old raft's head about 15 miles above Shreveport. Boats that ran to the upper Red when the river was open included the *Mariner*, *Columbian*, *Manchester*, *Cochuma*, *Brian Boroihme*, *Florida*, and *M. Tarver*. The *New York* wrecked a short distance above Jonesboro. When a new raft segment formed at the old raft's head in late 1839, a four-mile ox-wagon portage was established between Hurricane Bluffs and Phelps' Bluff (now Carolina Bluffs) to carry freight overland around the raft. The settlement of teamsters at Phelps' Bluff connected with the portage was referred to as Fogleville (Cheatsville[11]) and the Dead Fall (for the number of killings). The teamsters were under the nominal control of George Alban, who was to become a famous Red River pilot and captain.

Boats could use the western bypass to reach the upper river as an alternative to the portage, but it was dangerous, expensive, and ill-suited to steamboats that operated on the river out of New Orleans. The portage required two sets of boats. The larger set ran from New Orleans to the foot of the raft. The smaller set, which in 1840 included the *Mariner*, *Relief*, and *Hunter*, ran back and forth between the raft and points on the upper river. The *Mariner* wrecked at Pecan Point early in 1841. The *Relief* and *Hunter* continued to run on the upper river, operating in conjunction with 16 arrivals at the foot of the raft from New Orleans during that year. Thomas Williamson received a contract for raft removal in late 1841 and was assisted by the *James Ross* and *Napoleon*, which broke through the head of the raft and proceeded to the upper river. The *James Ross* used the Seawell route on its down trip because the raft had reformed. The *Napoleon* wrecked on a tributary to Little River.

The *Relief* and *Hunter* continued to operate on the upper river in 1842. The raft was removed early in the year and reformed in the summer. During the interval, the *Caddo*, *Houma*, *Star*, *Waverly*, *Harrisburg*, *Vermillion*, *Mechanic*, *Odessa*, and *Glide* reached the upper river on commercial ventures; and the *Gen. Brooke*, *Sarah Ann*, *Mungo Park*, and *Chippewa* transported troops to Fort Towson. The *Caddo* wrecked below Spanish Bluff and the *Houma* at Chicaninny Prairie. The machinery from the *Mariner* was used to build the *Red River Planter* on the upper river, which was one of the first steamboats constructed in Texas.

This brief introduction brings us through the year 1842, encompassing the period in which the voyages of the *Concord*, *Hunter*, and *Relief* were conducted. The *Concord* was a 58-ton sidewheeler built in Wheeling, Virginia, in 1835. The *Hunter* was a 157-ton sidewheeler measuring 130 feet by 23 feet built in Pittsburgh,

Pennsylvania, in 1840 with a single engine out of the *Virginia*. With a 900-bale capacity and drafting 7½ feet loaded and 3½ feet light, she was considered a large boat for the Upper Red River trade in those years. The *Relief* was a 90-ton single-engine sidewheeler 19 feet wide built in Portsmouth, Ohio, in 1840 with a 500–600 bale capacity and drawing 4½ feet loaded and 20 inches light.[12]

Of the 39 letters that follow, all but two are concerned with the activities of Captain Joseph S. ("Uncle Joe") Ross[13] and the *Relief*, whose voyages serve as the foundation for Withenbury's reminiscences. The *Relief* was named after an engine of the Cincinnati Fire Engine and Hose Company (Cincinnati's second, founded in 1815), for which Ross was one of the operators. Ross was born in Brunswick, New Jersey, on March 5, 1803, and was brought to Cincinnati when he was three and Cincinnati was in the wilderness. He became an apprentice carpenter in 1817, worked one year as a journeymen, married Rhoda Bradstreet, and went into business on his own account. He lost his shop to fire in 1828, resumed business with success, and opened a feed store in 1832. During that year he was elected to the city council.

When the *Relief* left Cincinnati in October 1840, Ross apparently had no experience as a steamboatman. His friends did not consider him suited to such a life and refused to endorse the notes for insurance on the boat. It is unlikely that the *Relief* would have been built and the voyage taken to the Upper Red River had not Ross' friend Capt. Jonathan Hildreth made a similar voyage in 1838 (with the *Concord*) and agreed to accompany Ross on the *Relief*. The career of the *Relief* lasted only from 1840 to 1843, and with its demise the career of Ross as a steamboatman ended.

Notes

1. The Upper Red River has not been addressed as a region. For the general development of the area, see Grant Foreman's *Advancing the Frontier, 1830–*

1860; Rex Strickland's 1937 University of Texas dissertation "Anglo-American Activities in Northeast Texas" (largely published as three articles in 1940 and 1941 in the *Chronicles of Oklahoma* and now available as an e-book under the title *Red River Pioneers*); Skipper Steely's *Six Months from Tennessee*; Arrell Gibson's *Oklahoma*; and S. Charles Bolton's *Arkansas, 1800–1860*.

2. Thomas Nuttall mentions Mount Prairie on the Southwest Trail in his *Journal of Travels into the Arkansas Territory During the Year 1819*. W. B. Dewees, who arrived by keelboat from Tennessee, wrote a letter from Long Prairie in March 1819 that appears in his *Letters from an Early Settler of Texas* and mentions Mount Prairie.

3. Joseph Paxton, "Letter in Relation to the Raft of Red River" (Sen. Doc. 78, 20th Cong., 2nd Sess.). In writing *A History of Navigation on Cypress Bayou and the Lakes*, I incorrectly assumed that Paxton was referring to a military figure when he says that the boat was conducted by a Major Moss. In Goodspeed's 1890 *Biographical and Historical Memoirs of Southern Arkansas*, James Moss states that his Uncle Matthew brought the first keelboat to the Upper Red River in 1814. However, Paxton was writing an official report (to A. H. Sevier, Delegate to Congress from the Territory of Arkansas) in 1828 from Mount Prairie, Paxton and Matthew Moss were neighbors, and Sevier was acquainted with Moss.

4. Wright is covered by Skipper Steely in *Six Months from Tennessee*.

5. Grant Foreman, "River Navigation in the Early Southwest," *Mississippi Valley Historical Review*, June 1928.

6. The account of the Freeman and Custis expedition is presented by Dan Flores in *Jefferson and Southwestern Exploration*.

7. All of these persons are mentioned in the letters.

8. Early routes and improvements are covered in my *A History of Navigation on Cypress Bayou and the Lakes*.

9. This and subsequent boat movements through 1842 were derived from the *Arkansas Gazette*, the *New Orleans Price Current*, the *New Orleans Commercial Bulletin*, the New Orleans *Daily Picayune*, the *Washington Telegraph*, and the Clarksville *Northern Standard*. On the voyage of the *Enterprise*, see Muriel Wright, "Early Navigation and Commerce Along the Arkansas and Red Rivers of Oklahoma," *Chronicles of Oklahoma*, March 1930.

10. June 6, 1828, *Arkansas Gazette*.

11. A "fogle" was a silk handkerchief and "fogle hunter" a slang term for "pickpocket."

12. The standard source for steamboat data is William Lytle's *Merchant Steam Vessels of the United States, 1807–1868*. Additional information on these boats was provided by the letters. The standard source on steamboat structure and operations is Louis Hunter's *Steamboats on the Western Rivers: An Economic and Technological History*.

13. For a profile of Ross, see *In Memoriam: Cincinnati 1881.* Ross is listed in connection with the fire engine *Relief* in Charles Cist, 1841, *Cincinnati in 1841.* Further information on Ross, particularly in relation to his later activities as a Cincinnati councilman in the acquisition of the first steam fire engine (the *Uncle Joe Ross*), is provided in Kathleen Kiefer, "Flying Sparks and Hooves: Prologue" (*Cincinnati Historical Society Bulletin*, Summer 1970) and John White, "The Steam Fire Engine: A Reappraisal of a Cincinnati 'First'" (*Cincinnati Historical Society Bulletin*, Winter 1970).

The Reminiscences

1 ✦ Taking the Challenge

In this first letter, Withenbury takes up the challenge of responding to the *Picayune*'s attacks on westerners (that is, midwesterners) as intruders in the trade of the Red and Ouachita rivers, as suggested by the letter signed "Bird of Passage." Withenbury lays out an ambitious plan of response, which is never fulfilled. The intent was to start with the steamboats that began using the Red River from the time that the raft was first removed, rather than going back to the beginning (although Withenbury will make some valuable comments on activities during the keelboat/flatboat period). The letter uses as initial examples of the importance of midwesterners in the development of the Red River trade Capt. Jonathan Hildreth (unnamed) of the *Concord*, Capt. Benjamin Crooks of the *Hunter*, Capt. Joseph Ross of the *Relief*, Capt. John Smoker of the *Brian Boroihme*, and himself (unnamed) as captain of the *Lama*.

⁂

I was pleased to see in your issue of this morning that somebody has seen fit to review the New Orleans Picayune on the point as to who has the right to navigate the "Red and Ouachita Rivers" and share in the results of legitimate competition for the fast increasing business of those two rivers of the South.

I have frequently of late read articles from the Picayune breathing the same spirit as the one reviewed by your correspondent, and have wished that someone would take up the gauntlet so often of late thrown down by this mouth-piece of the New Orleans Association and the self-constituted exclusives who would shut out Western men and capital from participating in legitimate trade and commerce. And now, with your indulgence, I propose to take part in this discussion, as I know a few things of the past history of the navigation of Red and Ouachita Rivers, which, if brought to light, may serve to enlighten the Picayune and some of these newly fledged steamboatmen who seem to think the Southern rivers of the United States were made for their special use and benefit.

I will first refer to the date when Shreveport was only known as Coat's Bluff,[1] when Captain Shreve, with the United States snagboats, penetrated the great Red River raft to that point, and finally succeeded in forcing a passage entirely through it to the clear and unobstructed navigable waters of a thousand miles in extent, and which, up to that time, had never been disturbed by the wheels of a steamboat. I will not raise the question as to whether Captain Shreve was a "Westerner" or a Southerner, inasmuch as he was employed by the Government, and had an undoubted right to go to Red River. But I will tell the Picayune the name of the first steamboat which followed in the wake of the Government snag-boat through the Red River raft. That was the Concord, officered by "Westerners" and commanded by a citizen of Cincinnati; and here I will simply suggest that if any credit belongs to the enterprising pioneer of a trade which to-day assumes such proportions as to attract the attention of the whole people of the country, West and South, it certainly falls to the lot of "Westerners." But for fear of making this communication too long, I would enter minutely into the history of those who followed close upon the heels of the Concord, and thus show conclusively that to Western men alone is that region of country indebted for its thrifty condition of to-day. I can not leave this interesting part of the history of the early navigation of Red River, without giving the names of a few of the adventurers who risked and well nigh lost their all in the experimental undertaking. Among those most prominent was Captain Benjamin Crooks, who spent more than a score of the best years of his life, and built and wore out a number of steamboats in the upper Red River, thus doing much to develop the resources of the country, and finally died leaving to his family nothing but his fame,[2] on the banks of the Ohio, near Gallipolis; but to the South, all the benefits resulting from his perseverance in striving to establish a steamboat communication between the wilderness of upper Red River and the great commercial mart of the Mississippi Valley—New Orleans. But Capt. Crooks was a "Westerner." Among the early "birds of passage" in the Red River steamboat lines, was found in 1840–41, a citizen of Cincinnati, Joseph S. Ross—yes, our own "Uncle Joe;" and the writer of this well remembers the hardships and losses he suffered before he was forced to quit his hazardous undertaking, and return to this city with the few remaining fragments of his fortune. He surely deserves some credit as a Red River pioneer, for he carried on his little "Relief" the first bale of cotton ever moved by a steamboat from Port Caddo, Texas. But "Uncle Joe" is still alive and among us, and can speak for himself. He will never deny, I am sure, that he was and is a "Westerner." During these early days, we find foremost among the steamboat men in Red River Captain John Smoker, and could the remains of the Charleston, the Brian Boroihme, the Bois d'Arc, and the Express Mail rise from their watery graves and speak, they would not fail to tell us that this bold adventurer, this most extraordinary good steamboat man, their Master, however thoroughly Southernized he may have since become, was a Pennsylvania Dutchman,[3] hailing from Lancaster, Pennsylvania. Was Captain Smoker a "Westerner?" In the year 1845, the people of Eastern Texas, seeking an outlet for their produce, and a means of communication with New Orleans via Red River, subscribed liberally of their means to "clean out and make navigable" Cypress Bayou, from Jefferson to Caddo Lake, thus hoping to find their way to Shreveport; and when the work of cutting down trees and pulling up stumps was all done "according to contract," they looked about for some adventurous spirit among the Red River steamboatmen who would undertake the doubtful project of reaching Jefferson with a steamboat. They found their man,[4] but strange to say, he was a "Westerner." None else at that day would undertake the job, but he succeeded, and with the little "Llama"[5] brought the first shipment of cotton from the now large and prosperous city of Jefferson, Texas, which, according to statistics, shipped more than sixty thousand bales of cotton last year. The Captain of that little pioneer steamer is still a citizen of Cincinnati, and from his log book of those early days, as well as from the lips of A. Bird Holabird, Esq., who was his engineer, I gather many interesting facts concerning this period in the history of the settlement of the country contiguous to Red River, and which now pours its millions into the lap of the great city where is domiciled the Picayune, crying out lustily against "Western" men running steamboats in the "Red and Ouachita Rivers." But I propose at another time, with your permission, to continue this subject, following, step by step, the history of steamboating in the Red and Ouachita Rivers from the early dates mentioned in this to the present day, giving the names of the principal boats and men who have been engaged therein, and leaving the Picayune and the people of the South to judge whether without the aid of "Westerners" in former years, the commercial importance, now so justly claimed for the Red River Valley, would have been attained at this day. The "Steamboatmen's Associations" of New Orleans, I propose also to discuss, for I have known them from their earliest organization, and I can show that many of the very members who are now crying out through the Picayune against "Western men" and "outsiders," were, long since the dates I have given in this, quietly digging potatoes on the banks of the Ohio River—on the Ohio side—and had not then learned that there was a Red or Ouachita River in the South, where their services were so much needed. "OUTSIDER."

Notes

1. The first bluff downstream from the bluff that became the nucleus of Shreveport. On the early development of Shreveport, see Holice Henrici, *Shreveport: The Beginnings*.

2. Corrected to "farm" in next letter (not used).

3. Corrected to "descended from a Pennsylvania Dutchman" in next letter (not used).

4. Withenbury is referring to himself.

5. Registered as *Lama* according to William Lytle's *Merchant Steam Vessels of the United States*.

2 ✦ Up Trip of the *Concord*

A number of steamboats had positioned themselves to go to the Upper Red River in the wake of Shreve's raft removal efforts. The *Concord* was the first to go through (on March 7, 1838, according to Shreve's official report in the 1838 Report of the Secretary of War) and arrived at Conway, Arkansas, on the ninth (according to the *Arkansas Gazette* of the 21st). This letter is concerned with the trip of the *Concord* from the raft area to John Nunnely's landing in what is now Little River County, Arkansas (with Figure 2 showing the features mentioned beginning at the Arkansas line, which was 20 miles above the raft area). Withenbury was not on this trip. Information on the trip was obtained from Erasmus Philley, the *Concord*'s pilot.

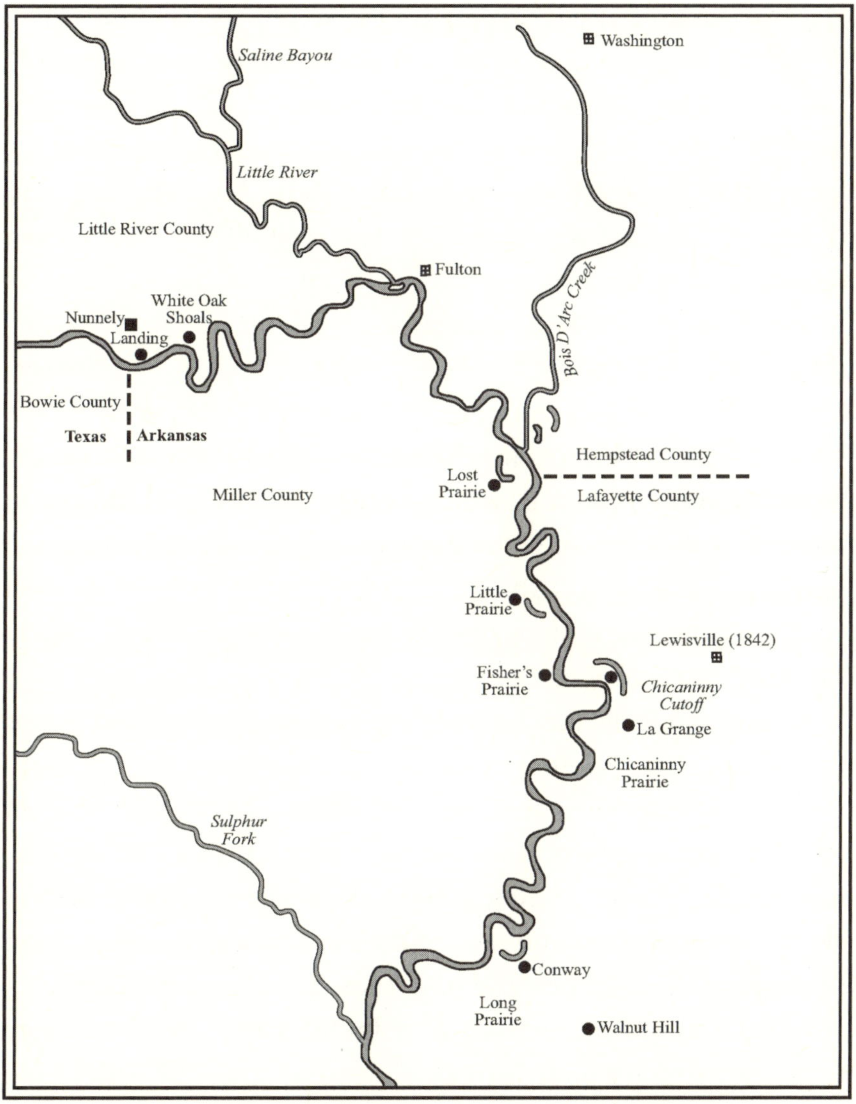

FIGURE 2: ROUTE OF THE *CONCORD*

⁂

I find that by "digging up the reminiscences" of "Coat's Bluff," the Red River Raft and the steamboat "Concord," I have brought to life, as it were, the very man who piloted (if feeling one's way in unexplored waters can be called piloting) the "Concord" on her first trip above the Raft. This man is Erasmus Philley, brother of Mr. Henry Philley, a well known citizen moving daily among the real estate and money sharpers of Third street.[1] Mr. Philley's head is so full of confused recollections of those early days that he insists upon relating anecdote after anecdote, and incident upon incident, that I can hardly decide which to select from his inexhaustible store, as bearing most directly upon my subject or which would prove of most interest to those who now clamor so loudly against "Westerners" coming to Red River, and who, at the same time, know so little of the men who took the initial steps towards opening to the whole people this great channel of commerce.

Mr. Philley tells me that the Concord was pushed and pulled through the little opening made by the snagboat in the raft, until she found herself free and above all obstructions. Then she cut loose, and away up the broad, smooth river she ran with uncommon speed, without coming in sight of a single clearing or human abode, until near the mouth of Sulphur, some sixty miles above the head of the raft, then and now known as Hurricane Bluffs.[2]

At the mouth of Sulphur they found a high bluff, called in those days Factory Bluff. Here lived the pioneers—the Kelleys, the Blantons, and the Scotts[3]—who planted the first cotton in that region. In the Sulphur River, or as it was then called Sulphur Fork, they supplied themselves with clear water for drinking and culinary purposes, exchanged civilities with the few settlers, and went on their way without stopping again until the neighborhood of Conway,[4] a little village at the head of Long Prairie.[5] At this point they found quite a settlement of planters, among whom were the Lowes, the Crabtrees (Lotta descended from them), the Warners, the Cryers, the Conways and the Perkins.[6]

The next settlement reached by the adventurers was "Chicaninna Cut-off,"[7] and here at the head of a beautiful prairie was located the county site[8] of Lafayette County, Arkansas, with quite a gathering of wealthy planters in the vicinity, who, in addition to their cotton crops, had "made more corn than would do them," for which they had no market.

After leaving Chicaninna, they found the country better settled, and at Little Prairie,[9] Fisher's Prairie,[10] and Lost Prairie,[11] they met with the Hamiltons, the Garlands, the Wynns and the Finns,[12] all families who hailed the advent of the little steamboat with joy, nor did they stop to inquire whether the Captain and crew were "Westerners," "birds of passage," or "outsiders," for they were content to know that their coming was an earnest of a glorious future for their country,[13] and the writer of this well knows that they were not mistaken, for many of those old settlers lived to see in their own day the hundred fold fruits of the venturesome spirit which prompted these early explorers, and of the "far seeing faith" which, pointing upward and onward, led them still further on their untried and doubtful way. And I am well assured that there are many of the descendants of those old settlers who hailed with joy the coming of the first steamboat upon Upper Red River, who to-day are ready to welcome the coming of Western men among them, well knowing that thus are their profits of planting and their comforts of living increased. The New Orleans "Association," nor the croaker of the Picayune, will find it in their power to drive the common sense out of this people.

But I had almost lost sight of the "Concord." About twenty-five or thirty miles above the upper part of Lost Prairie is Fulton,[14] in Hempstead County, Arkansas. Here, where the land was quite above overflow, had settled a number of merchants, and the neighborhood as far back as Washington,[15] fifteen miles in the interior, was called "rich."

From Fulton the little boat proceeded to "White Oak Shoals,"[16] some twenty miles. Here some difficulty was encountered, but having succeeded in getting over the shoals, she went on as far as "Squire Nunnaley's landing,"[17] five miles beyond White Oak Shoals, where the old Squire greeted them, "birds of passage," as they were, with a "God bless you all, gentlemen," which this writer has heard him repeat a hundred times since, when grasping the hands of a whole boat's crew of "Westerners."

The Concord, Captain Jonathan Hildreth, from Cincinnati, never went above this point, on Red River, being advised by Squire Nunnaley that the river was too low. So they remained a few days, partaking of the Squire's hospitality, and then turning her head down stream, she began to retrace the two hundred and twenty miles she had come above the raft. But I will reserve the history of her down trip till another time,[18] trusting that I have not trespassed too much upon your space in this prosy sketch of the Concord's first trip above the Red River Raft. "OUTSIDER."

Notes

1. Cincinnati's financial center.

2. Withenbury means that the head of the raft was at Hurricane Bluffs in 1838.

3. U.S. General Land Office land records indicate that Readick Kelley, Richard Blanton, and John Scott were large early property owners on the west side of the river below Sulphur Fork, with Blanton in Arkansas, Scott in Louisiana, and Kelley in both, but mainly in Louisiana. Goodspeed's *Biographical and Historical Memoirs of Southern Arkansas* says that Richard Blanton moved to Lafayette County in 1837 and to Miller County in 1839 and broke the first soil west of the Red River. Blanton's Landing is shown immediately above the

Arkansas line on Lt. Eugene Woodruff's 1872 *Map of the Red River Raft Region and Cypress Bayou* in the National Archives.

4. The landing for the plantation of James Conway, first governor of Arkansas, on the floodplain of the river in Lafayette County. A small settlement coalesced around the landing, which was located on a river bend that has since been cut off. Conway's plantation house was at Walnut Hill to the southeast on high land. See the article on James Conway in the *Encyclopedia of Arkansas History and Culture*. Walnut Hill and Conway are shown as towns on Sidney Morse and Samuel Breese's 1845 *Arkansas*. The nearly exact location of the landing can be determined because Conway owned land in Section 30 of T18S, R25W, which is now occupied by the Dixon Bend Cutoff.

5. So named because of its shape. John Sibley, the Indian Agent in Natchitoches, in his 1805 "Account of the Red River and Country Adjacent" (*American State Papers: Indian Affairs*) describes it as "a handsome rich prairie, twenty-five miles long … and four or five miles wide, bounded by handsome oak and hickory woods, mixed with some short leaved pine, interspersed with pleasant streams and fountains of water."

6. U.S. General Land Office land records indicate that James, John, and William Crabtree, Morgan Cryer, and James Conway were large early property owners near Conway. Esma Lowe is listed in the 1840 Lafayette County census and was the county judge from 1836–1840 according to the *Biographical and Historical Memoirs of Southern Arkansas*. Franklin Warner is listed in the 1840 Lafayette County census, but owned land far north of Conway. Milton Perkins was appointed postmaster in Conway according to the June 10, 1840, *Arkansas Gazette* and is shown as a gun smith in the 1850 Lafayette County census. Lotta Crabtree was a famous actress during the 1800s, but born in New York in 1847 and not descended from them. Claimed relationships to Lotta were probably so common at the time that Withenbury is invoking a cliché.

7. A river bend cutoff named for the adjacent prairie. (Caddo "Chakanina," means "Place of Crying," the earliest of the Caddo historic settlements according to Dan Flores in *Jefferson and Southwestern Exploration*.) The cutoff was of an eastward-tending bend as shown on A. J. Johnson's 1860 *Arkansas, Mississippi and Louisiana* and occurred just prior to 1822 according to Frank Schambach and Frank Rackerby in *Contributions to the Archeology of the Great Bend Region of the Red River Valley, Southwest Arkansas*. The relict channel is shown as Spirit Lake on present-day maps. A landing in Lafayette County (at the lower end of the cutoff according to Schambach and Rackerby) that is usually referred to as "Chickaninny Cut-off" or simply "the Cut-off" had been a keelboat landing and was a major steamboat landing.

8. The first seat of Lafayette County, which was replaced by Lewisville to the northeast in 1842. According to the online county history in the "Lafayette County Arkansas Genealogy Trails," the original courthouse was a log struc-

ture erected on the Chicaninny Prairie property of a man named Wright. This was apparently Moorhead Wright, who owned property below Spirit Lake in Section 35 of T16S R25W. The Lafayette County courthouse on Red River is shown on David Burr's 1835 *Arkansas*, with a road leading directly west to the old Miller County courthouse in Texas.

9. On the west side of the river in what is now Miller County and so named because of its size in relation to Long Prairie, with John Sibley describing it in his 1805 "Account of Red River and Country Adjacent" as about five miles long and four or five miles wide. The landing related to the prairie is usually rendered "Little's Landing" in newspaper records under the misapprehension that it was named for a person. The landing, which had been a keelboat landing and was a minor steamboat landing, was on the property of Robert Hamilton on a river bend that has since been cut off. Little Prairie and the field in which the landing was located are shown on the 1842 U.S. General Land Office survey plat for T15S R25W.

10. On the west side of the river and below Little Prairie, usually called Col. Wynn's Fisher's Prairie after the landholder William Wynn. The landing in relation to the prairie had been a keelboat landing and was a minor steamboat landing. Fisher's Prairie is shown on the 1842 U.S. General Land Office survey plat for T16S R25W with about two-thirds occupied by Col. Wynn's cotton plantation and the other third by Col. Garland's cotton plantation. The landing was to the southeast on a separate piece of property owned by Wynn.

11. On the west side of the river and above Little Prairie, usually called Hamilton's Lost Prairie after the landholder Robert Hamilton. The landing in relation to the prairie had been a keelboat landing and was a minor steamboat landing located on a river bend that has since been cut off. Lost Prairie is shown on the 1842 U.S. General Land Office survey plat for T15S R26W, with the land occupied by the plantations of Robert Hamilton, Richard Pryor, and Isaac Jones. Lost Prairie appears as a town on David Burr's 1835 *Arkansas* connecting with the Lafayette Courthouse on the south.

12. U.S. General Land Office land records indicate that Robert Hamilton, Josiah Garland, William Wynn, and Richard Finn were large early property owners in these areas. A January 25, 1854, *Washington Telegraph* estate sale advertisement for Hamilton's Little Prairie and Lost Prairie plantations includes 105 slaves plus farm equipment, mules, horses, stock, and fodder. Hamilton also owned plantations in Louisiana and Texas. Withenbury will have more to say about Hamilton in letters 15 and 19.

13. Country usually referred to region in this early period.

14. The primary port on the Upper Red River. Jack Jackson in "Nicholas Trammell's Difficulties in Mexican Texas" (*East Texas Historical Journal*, Fall 2000) says that Stephen Austin and his son-in-law James Bryan operated trading posts at Fulton and Long Prairie, but does not give dates. The December

11, 1819, *Arkansas Gazette* advertisement for town lots in Fulton characterizes it as the principal landing for the import and export freights of Hempstead County and the principal entrance to Texas from the Missouri Territory. William McClintock in "Journal of a Trip through Texas and Northern Mexico in 1846–1847" (*Southwestern Historical Quarterly*, July 1930) arrived at Fulton in September 1846 and says that it consisted of two warehouses, three groceries, one blacksmith shop, and four cabins. The dimensions of the town prior to the Civil War are best represented by Jeremy Gilmer's 1864 *Vicinity of Fulton, Ark's*, which can be seen online in the digital maps collection of the University of North Carolina Library.

15. The seat of Hempstead County to the northeast of Fulton. According to an article on the town in the *Encyclopedia of Arkansas History and Culture*, Washington was established as the county seat in 1824, with a land auction in 1826 creating the structure of the town.

16. A shoal and adjacent landing in Arkansas three overland miles and five river miles east of the Texas line that was a navigation impediment. With a rock and gravel bottom, it was the first place on the upper river that was suitable for fording according to Dan Flores in *Jefferson and Southwestern Exploration*. The landing by that name had been a keelboat landing and was a major steamboat landing. White Oak Shoals is addressed in Letter 34.

17. John Nunnely had a home at present-day Ogden, Arkansas, and extensive landholdings to the south and southwest. The landing, which was to the south, is not mentioned in newspaper accounts of boat movements. Nunnely is addressed in Letter 34.

18. See Letter 34.

3 ✦ Down Trip of the *Concord*

The *Concord* left Nunnely's Landing and proceeded downstream to Shreveport, with a delay caused by accumulation of raft materials.

⁂

In my communication of yesterday, I left the Concord and her crew in the hands of Squire Nunnaley, where they enjoyed his hospitality until their exhausted larder had been bountifully replenished from the abundance found at this well conducted Arkansas plantation, and the "wood-pile" filled up from the neighboring hills, where pine knots were found in profusion, only requiring the aid of the Squire's teams and negroes to place them within reach of the crew.

When the boat had turned her head down stream, Mr. Philley says he looked toward the shore, and there stood the old Squire, with his hat in his hand and his "silvery locks uncovered to the breeze," waving a good-bye to the friends he had met for the first time and so soon parted from, perhaps forever; and as the Concord turned the point and was just closing the gap between the Squire and herself, his voice was distinctly heard, as he pronounced his wholesale and heartfelt benediction: "God bless you all, gentlemen," emphasizing the last word, till its echoes seemed to reverberate from shore to shore.

As the commerce of Red River was then in its infancy, there was nothing for the Concord to do at Fulton. Still she lingered there long enough for the crew to extend and receive the hand of fellowship, and I am not in error when I assert that out of the acquaintance formed on that occasion has grown many a transaction of importance, and mutual benefit to the country which sent out this little band of adventurers, and to those sensible men who bade them "welcome."

I find it hard to leave the vicinity of Fulton without introducing the reader more formally to some of the then prominent citizens of Hempstead County, Arkansas, as well as to some few occupying humble positions at the time of which I write, but who subsequently have loomed up into wonderful importance among steamboatmen, and a still later day among the New Orleans underwriters.

At Washington lived the venerable Abraham Block, an Israelite, possessing the shrewdest business traits ever implanted in man.[1] He was rabbi, merchant, auctioneer, politician, speculator and flatboatman, ready for any undertaking that was honorable, and always a genial companion; when traveling, full of fun and anecdote, and at his home, which was the abode of plenty, always hospitable and entertaining. His sons and sons-in-law, I am happy to say, are now numbered among the best and most prosperous business men at New Orleans and at the East; and, to their credit be it said, they have never yet refused a fair share of their patronage to any steamboatman because he happened to come from the North or West.

At Washington, too, lived that autocrat of the New Orleans Board of Underwriters[2] of later years; but as he was then quite a young man it is hardly to be presumed that he had then even dreamed of his coming greatness. He owes his introduction to commercial matters to his friend, Mat. Moss, the best fiddler in that part of Arkansas in those days. The Messrs. Mat. and William Moss,[3] of Washington, at an early day, (say 1841 or 1842,) built a little boat for the upper Red River trade and called her the Hempstead,[4] and on her, our embryo steamboat inspector accepted a clerkship, and a number one clerk he was; as a proof of which I will refer to his rapid advancement from the clerkship of the little Hempstead, step by step, to the Annie Crocker,[5] the Houma, the Vermilion, the Compromise, and the New Latonia.[6] His next step was to the position of steamboat inspector for the Board of Underwriters of New Orleans, to which place he was recommended by his old friend Phil. Shaw, who had held the place for a number of years, and abdicated in his favor.

But I am losing sight of the Concord. In due time she resumed her course down the river, and on reaching "Chicaninna Cut-off" and Conway, where the thrifty planters had corn "enough and to spare," she took on a load for the poorly supplied people at Shreveport. At the head of the raft she found some difficulty; but after a number of days of perilous work, and by the aid of the snag-boats Eradicator and Archimedes, she finally reached Shreveport, where the hungry people were right glad to welcome her return with her cargo of the "staff of life."

Here I propose to leave the Concord and her Cincinnati crew for the present, as her subsequent career has no particular interest in it; but as the different members of her crew were identified with other boats at a later day, I may have occasion to call them up again.

In a former communication, I said I would not raise the question as to whether or not Captain Shreve was a "Westerner;" but upon the principle of "rendering unto Caesar the things which are Caesar's," I must tell for the benefit of the Picayune and the "Association," if for no other reason. He came from Steubenville, Ohio, that "Western" town on the banks of the Ohio, where there is a long iron bridge spanning the "beautiful river," and right where the "Pan Handle" Road starts for the Atlantic shore. Come up, Mr. Picayune, and look at it, and don't be afraid of being contaminated by coming in contact with an OUTSIDER.

Notes

1. According to an article on Block in the *Encyclopedia of Arkansas History and Culture*, he was born in Bohemia in 1780 and established his first store in Washington by 1825. Block and his wife Frances had 14 children, 12 of whom lived to maturity, and are considered the first Jewish family to immigrate to Arkansas. Block's primary line of business was dry goods and groceries. His business activities and those of his sons in Washington, Fulton, and Paraclifta can be followed in the *Washington Telegraph*. The first extant advertisement is for A. Block & Son, with Augustus as the partner, in the November 17, 1841, issue.

2. The Board of Underwriters was responsible for setting boat and freight insurance rates. As indicated in Letter 32, the person referred to was L. W. Cooper, who captained the boats mentioned later in the paragraph. A brief profile of Cooper in the October 2, 1880, *New Orleans Daily Democrat* indicates that he became inspector before the Civil War and resigned from that position in 1879.

3. The brothers William, Matthew, and James Moss appear in the 1850 Hempstead County census as born in Virginia in 1804, 1807, and 1810, respectively. They were sons of James Moss (1773–1833), who arrived at Fulton with his family in 1818 and was Hempstead County judge from 1827 to 1832 according to the *Biographical and Historical Memoirs of Southern Arkansas*, and nephews of Matthew Moss (1776–1859), who brought the first keelboat to Upper Red River in 1816. The three brothers were farmers according to the census, and Matthew and William began operating the portage around the raft in 1846 according to an advertisement in the March 18, 1846, *Washington Telegraph*. On the genealogy of this family, see M. D. Myers' "Descendants of Matthew Mark Moss I."

4. An advertisement in the October 30, 1844, *Washington Telegraph* indicates that this boat was captained by Matthew Moss.

5. Corrected to *Annes Crocker* at end of next letter.

6. Corrected to *New Latona* at end of next letter.

4 ✦ The *Relief* and *Hunter* Go Up

This letter concerns the trips of the *Relief* and *Hunter* to the Upper Red River in 1840, where both stayed through 1841 (the subject of the next letter). Withenbury was not on this trip of the *Relief.* Capt. Hildreth of the *Concord* had returned to Cincinnati and told Joseph Ross that the river was open and that the commercial possibilities were great, which Ross responded to by building the *Relief.* The *Relief* left Cincinnati in October 1840. On reaching Shreveport, Capt. Ross found that the raft had reformed and took the western bypass (Figure 3), followed by the *Hunter* under Capt. Benjamin Crooks, who had taken this route to Fort Towson with the *Indian* in 1834 and the *Rover* in 1836. Capt. Jim Gamble of the *Mariner* was immediately before them, attempting to block their passage so he could monopolize the Upper Red River trade.

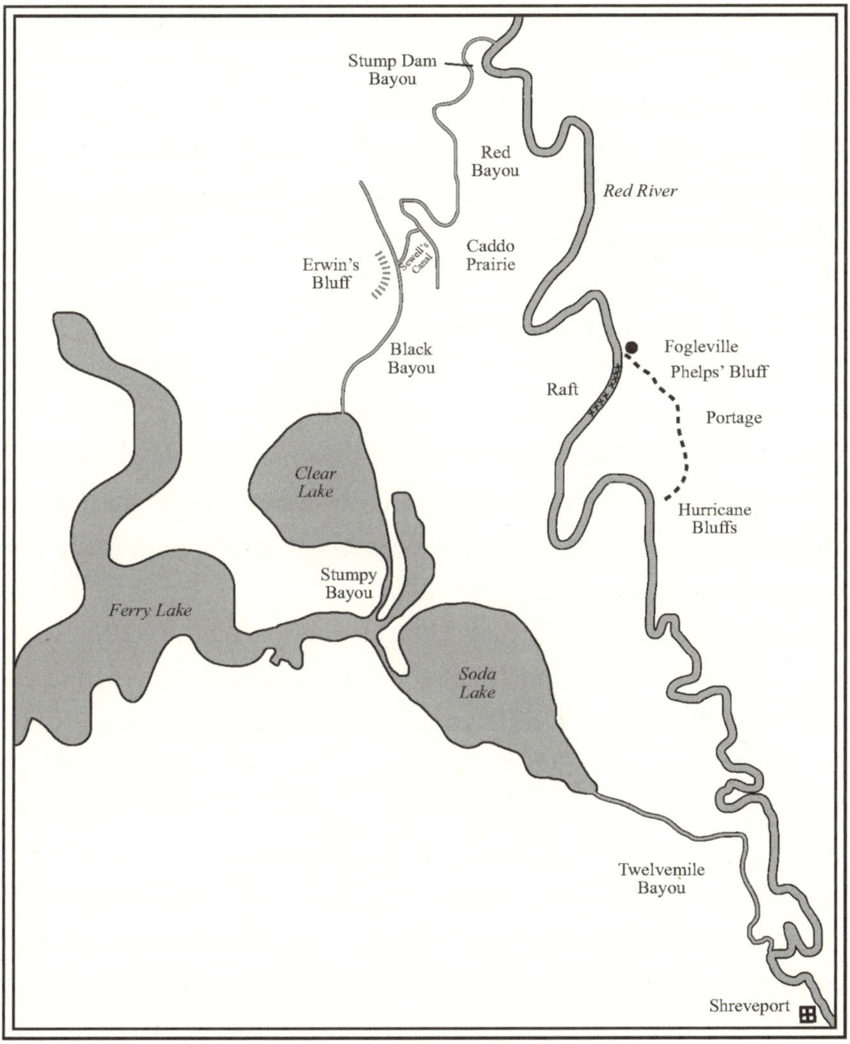

FIGURE 3: WESTERN BYPASS

⁂

Having done with the Concord and her day in Red River, I will "drop down" to the days of the Relief, and after having, from the recollection of others, given a few notes of her first year's history, I will quote from the "log-book" of an old Western friend[1] who spent the season of 1841–42 on board of her with Uncle Joe Ross, Jonathan Hildreth, E. Philley and other "birds of passage," who in those days knew no better than to go to Red River expecting to share in the profits (?) of the business in proportion as their merits, when compared with others engaged in the same calling, should entitle them.

The Relief was built at Brush Creek, Ohio, in the year 1840. The necessary capital in cash was advanced by Uncle Joe, others having promised to contribute and failing made the burden fall rather heavy on him, and he left this city a little short. But the picture of prospective profits having been beautifully painted by the Concord's crew, Uncle Joe bade good bye to home, family and friends, and "shoved out" hopefully.

After many tedious days of toil and peril, the little Relief reached Shreveport, and there the fact became known that the Raft had closed and a different route or channel must be taken in order to reach the waters of Upper Red River. This route was by way of Twelve mile Bayou, which empties into Red River four miles above Shreveport, thence through Sodo Lake twenty miles to Stumpy Bayou, (two miles long, and often two days' run,) thence through Clear Lake six miles to Black Bayou, thence seven miles to Erwin's Bluff and Caddo Prairie, where Black Bayou and Red Bayou were connected by an artificial canal of three quarters of a mile in length, and as "crooked as a ram's horn," and through Red Bayou fully twenty long, weary, crooked miles to Red River. The point at which Red Bayou connects with Red River is about thirty-five miles above Hurricane Bluff, by way of the river, which in those days was the head of the Raft.

The whole distance of this route from Shreveport to Upper Red River is about seventy-five miles, and a more hazardous piece of steamboat navigation, I will venture to say, has not been tried, in the whole Mississippi Valley, than was this, at the time I am writing of, and if I know myself, it is not very easy yet.

Well, Uncle Joe (I suppose I ought to call him Captain Ross,) and his crew nerved themselves for the undertaking, and after many days of exploration and hard labor, the recital of which would be too tedious for this article, they found themselves at "Stump Dam,"[2] a point in Red Bayou five miles below its entrance into, or rather its debouchure[3] from the river. At this point the Bayou was so narrow that it was necessary to "strip the wheels," that is, take out all the arms projecting down below the boat's guards,[4] and pull the boat by the capstan[5] as long as the power of the crew was sufficient; and when that failed, by applying steam and using the main shaft.

Here I will state that the Relief was but nineteen feet beam,[6] and in many parts of this last five miles of Red Bayou it was necessary to dig away the banks to render it wide enough to enable the boat to be pulled through by the aid of steam and the main shaft. While the carpenter[7] was engaged, stripping the wheels, Captain Ross and several of his officers started on foot up the banks of the Bayou reconnoitering, when all at once they heard a loud noise like the falling of trees, and soon they heard a shout of human (?) voices, and next the puffing of a steamboat. They hurried on as rapidly as the tangled undergrowth of vines and briars and the tall, thick canebrake would allow, and when about two and a half miles from the boat the whole affair was explained, for here, piled one upon another, were a dozen or more huge cotton wood and cypress trees, which had just been cut and had fallen in every conceivable shape of entanglement across the Bayou.

Now for the interesting part of the history of "Uncle Joe's" first trip to Red River.

The steamboat Mariner, Captain Jim Gamble,[8] had preceded the Relief through the intricate route I have just described, some two days, and Captain Gamble, having heard that Captain Ross was building the Relief, and Captain Ben. Crooks was also building the Hunter for the Upper Red River trade, concluded to steal a march on these "Western birds of passage," and, after working the Mariner throughout the Bayous, cut all the big trees above Stump Dam, and fell them across the Bayou, thus securing to himself a monopoly of the trade, and leave all competitors outside. But how little poor Jim Gamble knew of these "Westerners," who were so close upon his heels, will appear as I proceed with this narrative. Captain Ross and his crew nothing daunted immediately manned every axe and saw, and all other available implements (and all the boats in those days carried a good supply), and long before the Relief had reached the barricades, the sound of the axe and the grating of the cross-cut saw was heard ringing through the woods and echoing from the hills some five miles distant on the opposite side of the river. If ever Westerners showed their true grit, it was on this occasion, when the miserable, narrow-minded, self-styled Southerner had resorted to this contemptible means of shutting out honorable competition. And I need not tell my readers that these outsiders did not remain idle—they did not come to Red River to be frightened or driven away, but they associated themselves together, and proved that with them there was a "power quick and potent," and that "to will was to do," and in the course of three short days all obstructions were effectually cleared away, and the Relief was running at her best speed on the bosom of the broad and beautiful river above the Raft for the first time.

Here I will leave the Relief, and return to Red Bayou to see how Captain Crooks and the Hunter[9] get along, and I find it necessary to go to the canal I have spoken of, called Sewell's Canal, which connects Red and Black Bayous, thus forming a continuous navigation (and the only one to this day) from Shreveport to the upper river.

This canal was cut a few years prior to the date I am writing of, for the purpose of a keel-boat route to Fort Towson, in the Choctaw Nation, and it was the only route by which the United States Government sent the supplies to the fort and to the Indians.

The difference in the level of Black and Red Bayous at this point was some six or seven feet, and as a consequence there was a rapid current through the canal and for some distance above it, which in very low water, made it very difficult to overcome it with any sort of water craft.

Captain Crooks was so unfortunate as to arrive at this canal when the water was very low, and most men would have faltered and laid up for a rise before undertaking the difficult passage—but not so Captain Crooks; there was too much of the "Westerner" about him for that. He at once set to work and built a dam across the canal at the stern of the Hunter, thus creating a pool sufficient to float her a length or two, and repeated the operation (building four dams in all) until the Hunter was above the falls in Sewell's Canal. From this point he went on without much difficulty, until he came to the very narrow part of the bayou at "Stump Dam," and when the process of "stripping wheels" was gone through with, he dreamed of no further trouble in the bayou; but when he came to the fallen trees which the Relief had cut, and found that the Hunter was fully six feet too wide to pass through, it is said the woods rang with the old man's imprecations upon the head of the selfish scoundrel who had undertaken to keep honest competition from interfering with his coveted monopoly.

Poor Captain Crooks was obliged to cut all the logs again before the Hunter could get through, but the work was soon accomplished; and long before Jim Gamble with his Mariner had picked up his first load he met both the Relief and the Hunter in the field with him.

Here was the spirit of selfishness and proscription in part suitably rewarded. But it was reserved for the two "Western" Captains and their crews to see, before the season was over, the carcass of the Mariner, lying sunk at Pecan Point,[10] hundreds of miles above the barricade her crew had thrown up against "free trade and sailors' rights." Which, in those early days, were the benefactors of the people to whom they were looking for patronage—the exclusive Jim Gamble or the persevering "outsiders," who brushed away all obstacles, and whose descendants are yet keeping open, these same channels of commerce, I leave the Picayune and the "Association" to answer, and much oblige an OUTSIDER.

Notes

1. Withenbury is apparently referring to himself because of the mention of a person who was aboard the *Relief* in 1841–1842. The information conveyed in the letter could easily have been acquired by Withenbury during the second trip.

2. A bayou that enters Red Bayou shortly before Red Bayou connects with Red River.

3. Red Bayou was a distributary of the Red River, meaning that water flowed out of the river into the bayou.

4. Parts of the deck that extended beyond the hull. The wheels on sidewheel steamers projected below the guards. The arms of the wheels were removed to enable easier pulling through tight places.

5. A rope was tied to a tree and wrapped around a rotating drum with handles on the bow of the boat that was turned manually by the crew, pulling the boat forward.

6. Hull width.

7. Boat crews usually included a carpenter or a person with carpentry skills, particularly for replacing damaged paddles.

8. Texas General Land Office land records indicate that in 1838 James Gamble purchased the headright of Robert Gamble, which fronted on the Red River and was bisected by Pine Creek. Gamble appears in the 1840 Red

River County tax rolls. Gamble had been a keelboatman using the eastern route around the raft according to the March 21, 1872, *Daily Shreveport Times.* The *Mariner* under Capt. J. W. Gamble advertised in the January 14, 1841, *Shreveport Intelligencer and Caddo Beacon* that she would run regularly during the boating season from the raft to Fort Towson. Gamble was no longer a resident of the state by 1846 according to a court summons in the May 13, 1847, Clarksville *Northern Standard.*

9. The voyage of the *Rover* under Capt. Crooks through this area in 1836 is described in detail in the March 1, 1836, *Arkansas Gazette.* The *Hunter* under Capt. B. Crooks advertised in the January 14, 1841, *Shreveport Intelligencer and Caddo Beacon* that she would run regularly during the boating season from the raft to Fort Towson.

10. The *Mariner* was snagged at Pecan Point on March 10, 1841, according to William Lytle's *Merchant Steam Vessels of the United States, 1807–1868.* The machinery was used by John Dyer at Berlin on the Upper Red River to build the *Red River Planter,* on which Dyer served as captain and Gamble as pilot, as indicated in Letter 18.

5 ✦ The *Relief* and *Hunter* Above

The *Relief* and *Hunter* remained on Upper Red River through 1841, operating upriver from the head of the raft in conjuction with boats from New Orleans to the foot of the raft, with the portage serving as the point of transfer for up and down freights.

⁂

Passing without comment the first season of the Hunter and Relief, after their success in having overcome the varied obstacles met with before reaching

Upper Red River, I leave them quietly in possession of the entire field, (after the sinking of the Mariner,) and will only say, that before the season was over, the planters and merchants of the country had learned to look with anxiety for their coming and going, trip after trip; and as Captains Crooks and Ross, each for himself in his own peculiar manner, had made his own special friends, the whole people learned to regard as a "Special Providence" the coming among them of these two Western boats, and their crews of sober, earnest business men. The trade proper of Upper Red River at this period of its history was from the "Pine Hills,"[1] Texas—which are twenty-five miles above Fort Towson, to the head of the Raft, a distance (computed at that early day[2]) of about six hundred miles. From the head of the raft to the foot of the same, where the New Orleans boats came regularly to exchange freights with the Hunter and Relief, and the passage through it by the Concord, which was in the spring of 1839,[3] the Government work on it had been suspended for the time, and the accumulation of drift wood had filled it up again, increasing its length some eight miles, up to Phelps' Bluff, but leaving the river in a navigable (?) condition from Hurricane Bluff (the head of the raft in 1839, but in 1841 the foot) to Shreveport, so that at the date I am writing of, the raft was confined between these two points, Hurricane Bluff the foot, and Phelps' Bluff or "Fogleville" the head.

At Fogleville, *alias* the "Dead Fall," were congregated a number of teamsters with their oxen and carts, ready and willing to do their part in the transportation business, thus forming the connecting link between the Lower and Upper Red River boats.

The teamsters who were located temporarily at the "Dead Fall" were of the rougher sort, as might be expected, while those of the planters' resident in the neighborhood, who willingly took a part whenever there was a "rush of business," were quiet, industrious men, and seemed disposed to perform their part promptly, and when their services were not required, return to their homes, holding themselves in readiness to come again when called upon.

The rougher element at Fogleville required a head, and as every man was "working on his own hook" the conflicting interests were liable to come in collision. Accordingly, by unanimous consent, one man was agreed upon as a sort of arbitrator. This man, it seems, had come to this place providentially, for, by his excellent administrative and executive talent, he was able to keep tolerable "good order in camp," which I do not believe any other man among them could have done. But whether his strength lay in the quality and quantity of the rations he dispensed among them, or in his natural talent for governing the masses, I will not pretend to say; but judging from his subsequent success in his undertakings directly connected with the navigation of the Upper Red River, I am inclined to the opinion that he is a man of no ordinary caliber, and I freely accord much credit to the itinerary population of Fogleville for having unanimously voted George Alban Mayor of the "Dead Fall."

Captain George Alban[4] has passed by regular gradation from the head man among the teamsters at the raft to his present position as explorer and part owner of the "last link" in the present route around the raft, the upper portion of which being an artificial canal, is vulgarly known in those parts as "Alban's Gut."[5] But George don't care what they call it, so long as he is allowed to levy and collect a tax of fifty cents per bale on all the cotton and twenty-five cents per barrel on all "up-freights" which pass through his "gut" (and there is no other route to Upper Red River to-day).

Captain Alban, as I have already said, was early upon the ground, and no one will deny that he has devoted his working hours exclusively to the development of the Red River country, taking every position from teamster to keel-boatman, and pilot and Captain of many steamboats. He piloted the first steamboat (the Llama) that went of Jefferson, Texas, and for a long time was the only real reliable pilot through the lakes and bayous around and above Shreveport, and at this time he would rank No. 1 in the profession, were he to turn his attention to it. But he has a better thing in his "gut."

Your readers will not wonder at the diversity of innate talent developed in Captain Alban from time to time, as the often changing circumstances and continued progress in the navigation of Red River seemed to call them forth, when I tell them that he, too, was a "Westerner," hailing from the vicinity of Wellsville, Ohio.

But I find that the romance of the days of 1840 to 1844 has almost caused me to forget for the moment the realities attending the career of the Hunter and Relief; and now, as I have wandered so far, I must economize space and barely mention that the two boats continued to work harmoniously together throughout the season, doing all the work which fell to their lot at satisfactory prices, and extending to the people every facility in their power in the way of credit, relying upon the "good crops of next season" for their ability to pay, never in those times doubting their will to do so.[6]

But the last trip down of the Relief,[7] she met the Hunter bound up, aground on White Oak Shoals,[8] and Captain Crooks, having lost faith in the "June rise," thought it prudent to pay off and discharge most of his crew,[9] and he hailed Captain Ross to come along side and take them to Shreveport. This "Uncle Joe" did, and, to use his own words spoken to day, "never charged a mother's son of them a red cent for passage."

The Relief passed down through Red Bayou and the Lakes to Shreveport, and finally[10] flew back to Cincinnati like any other "bird of passage," and on her arrival here "Uncle Joe" sat down to count up the result of the season's work, and he tells me that if his recollection serves him right, the balance was on the wrong side. But then he had a good deal owing to him, which, if he ever collected, would make it all-right.

During the summer of 1841 the Relief was put in tip-top repair in this city, with a view to another season's work in Red River, and, strange to say, the Picayune did not raise its voice of warning to frighten this "bird of passage" from "coming to share that moiety which is due only to our home boatmen,"[11] nor did any "association" threaten to call into use its "quick and potent power to defend our legitimate carrying interests against the encroachment of this stranger." But on her reaching New Orleans late in November, 1841, the Picayune quietly pocketed the pay for advertising her for Upper Red River and never said a word about her being a "Westerner." Truly this is the age of progress, and the scales of ignorance are falling from the eyes of the people, and we are all waking up to "our legitimate carrying interests," and we will defend them against the stranger and the OUTSIDER.

Notes

1. In the northwest corner of Red River County, as shown on Jacob De Cordova's 1867 *Map of the State of Texas.*

2. Using an old steamboat notation that was greater than actual river miles.

3. Should be 1838.

4. Alban had been a keelboatman using the eastern route around the raft according to the March 21, 1872, *Daily Shreveport Times*. A brief profile of Alban in the October 2, 1880, *New Orleans Daily Democrat* says that he came to the Red River at the time that Shreve was removing the raft; that in 1845 he was captain of the *Little River* and afterwards of the *Alida*, *White Cliffs*, *Corinne*, *Marion*, *William Terry*, and others; that he had steamboated little after the war

but superintended improvement of the route to Jefferson; and that he was then living on a farm near Shreveport.

5. A late raft bypass on the east side of the river through Posten Lake, with a canal built by Alban connecting with Red River. The lake, which was bisected by the Arkansas-Louisiana line and is now extinct, resembled a stomach. A description of this project along with a Corps of Engineers map showing the configuration referred to by Withenbury can be found in my *A History of Navigation on Cypress Bayou and the Lakes*. The removal of the raft in 1873 eliminated the need for the bypass.

6. Most financial transactions were conducted on credit at this time, with debts cleared by the subsequent cotton crop.

7. The July 15, 1841, *Daily Picayune* indicates that the *Relief* had gone up as far as Fort Towson.

8. The *Hunter* was aground north of present-day Texarkana.

9. It was common to discharge crews when long delays were anticipated. The Fulton merchant William Street advertised in the December 8, 1841, *Washington Telegraph* that he had just received goods from the *Hunter*. The *Hunter* continued to operate above the raft in subsequent years.

10. The *Relief* arrived in New Orleans in the middle of July with Hildreth as captain, as recorded in the July 15, 1841, *Daily Picayune*.

11. Withenbury is quoting the *Picayune*.

6 ✦ The *Relief* at Shreveport

This is the first of 32 letters concerning the trip of the *Relief* to Upper Red River in 1841–1842, when Withenbury was 26. The *Relief* had spent much of the second half of 1841 being refurbished in Cincinnati, went back to New Orleans, and advertised in the November 30, 1841, *Daily Picayune* for above the raft, Fulton, Fort Towson, and all intermediate landings, with J. S. Ross as captain. The advertisement

was modified the next day to say by way of Soda Lake, emphasizing that the western route would be taken, rather than the main river. On reaching Shreveport, the *Relief* was met with a request to carry freight to a merchant in Port Caddo (on Cypress Bayou, which enters Caddo Lake west of Shreveport) on the way to Upper Red River.

In its previous trip, the *Relief* had gone west of Shreveport through Twelvemile Bayou and Soda Lake, but then proceeded north through Stumpy Bayou rather than heading farther west into Caddo Lake, which was then called Ferry Lake. Only a few trips had been made by steamboats into Caddo Lake, and this was largely uncharted territory (Figure 4). A guide was found in the person of Hiram Bails,[1] a Caddo Lake recluse who had lived in the area long before Shreve arrived and was known locally by the sobriquet "Bails the bee hunter." Bails was intimately acquainted with the intricate maze of lakes and bayous on the west side of the river through many years of hunting bees and game and served as a contract guide for keelboats and steamboats, including the *Enterprise* (the first steamboat to the Upper Red River).

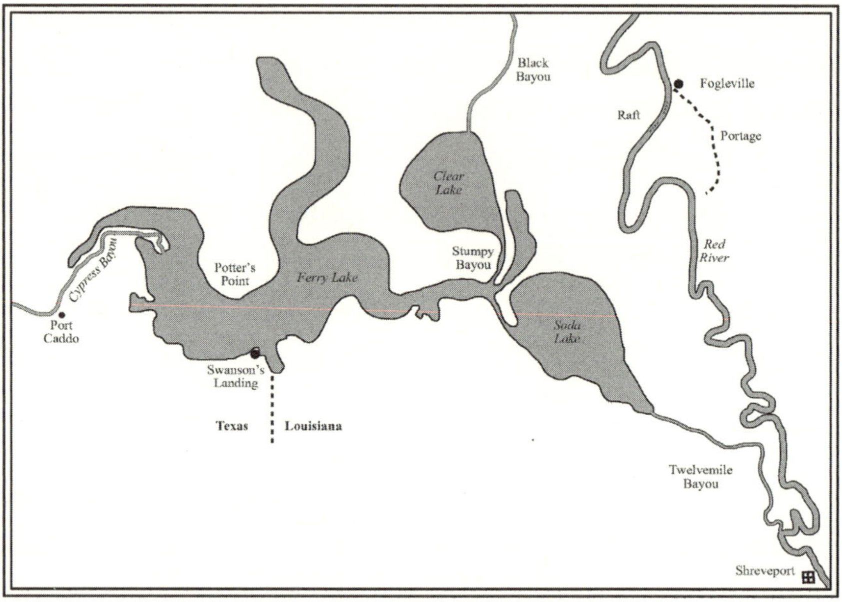

FIGURE 4: FERRY LAKE

⁂

[First part not used.]

Having arrived at Shreveport on the 8th of December, 1841, after dark, Captain Ross did not attempt to do any business that night, but gave himself up wholly to the entertaining of old friends and the "new-comers" who had settled there since the close of the last season, and to receiving congratulations for the safe return of his little boat to the scene of her former usefulness; and I will leave my readers to judge of the "*entente cordial*"[2] which was that night renewed and cemented between the people of Shreveport and the Captain and crew of the Relief, and also, to surmise what kind of "cordial" was used for the cementing process. "Uncle Joe" can tell if he chooses.

On the following morning Captain Ross received proposals for a trip to Port Caddo, Texas.

This new town was situated on Cypress Bayou, sixty miles from Shreveport, and the route lay through Twelve-mile Bayou and Sodo Lake,[3] thence through Ferry Lake[4] to the mouth of Cypress Lake,[5] and nine miles up the same. As this route, after leaving the head of Sodo Lake, was an entirely new one[6] to Captain Ross and his pilots, he hesitated in regard to the undertaking until he could be assured of finding a pilot who knew the way. Finally, the man who was anxious to make the principal shipment produced a man who was said to be familiar with the lakes and bayous. This man was old Hiram Bale, the bee hunter, but if I remember rightly, he was not exactly "in trim" for bee hunting; he didn't seem to "walk a bee line" as he came on board. On questioning him, Captain Ross became satisfied of his ability to show the way to Port Caddo, particularly after he stated with much earnestness that he knew "every catfish and alligator in the lake, and what's more," said Bale, "they all know me."

Accordingly, the Relief was loaded, and on the morning of December 10 started on the trip. Mr. Bale having taken a few "cat naps" on the forecastle[7] the night before to cool off, was ready for his part of the work. When fairly into Sodo Lake, where the view for some ten miles was unobstructed,[8] a steamboat was in sight; and as the Relief gained steadily on her, it soon became apparent that she was aground. On coming alongside, Captain Ross was surprised to see foremost in the ranks of the anxious faces on the deck, the familiar face and long gray beard of old man Rees,[9] the street preacher, who, as the Relief backed out from the wharf at Cincinnati on the 12th of November, was preaching from a pile of salt barrels. How he had managed to get into that country we did not stop to inquire, but pushed on, leaving the "Rochester" and

"Father Rees" stuck in the mud. The Rochester abandoned the trip and never reached Port Caddo.[10] The Relief crossed the line into Texas[11] just before dark, and fired a big gun,[12] and then came to the shore for the night at "Swanson's Landing," where the people came from the neighboring settlements and gave a warm welcome to the unexpected "Stranger" from the United States, which Captain Ross says was exceedingly gratifying, as this occurred long before the annexation of Texas, and for that reason he would not have been surprised had he been looked upon and treated as an OUTSIDER.

Notes

1. The February 5, 1881, *New Orleans Daily Democrat* provides a profile of Bails under the title "The First Pilot to Upper Red River": "'Bails, the bee-hunter,' as he was known and called, was a strange character. He emigrated to North Louisiana some years before Capt. H. M. Shreve opened a way through the great raft and founded Shreveport. He took up his abode among the Caddo and Kickapoo tribe of Indians, which inhabited the country around the lakes. Bails became a great hunter of wild game, and also took particular pleasure in hunting bees. He had an eye like an eagle, and would follow them for long distances until he would find the tree where they made their hives, and then capture their honey. On his excursions through the lakes he found every channel that could be navigated by a craft, and upon the appearance of keel-boats was employed as pilot, as he was the only white man who knew the intricate windings through the bayous and lakes to upper Red river. He also piloted the first steamboat that went above Shreveport. When the boating season closed, he would take his rifle and canoe and start again into the wilderness to hunt game and bees, and would then disappear for six months at a time. He did not care to live among civilized people, and finally died on one of the small islands in Caddo lake, among the Caddo tribe. He was a quiet, unassuming man, a good pilot, and was known to nobody about Shreveport except by his sobriquet, 'Bails, the bee hunter.'"

2. A friendly relationship between parties.

3. Soda was a variant of Sodo, which more appropriately renders the Caddo word. This and the following water and water-related features are described in my *A History of Navigation on Cypress Bayou and the Lakes*.

4. The old name for Caddo Lake derived from the operation of a ferry across the lake by James Shenick from at least 1824 to at least 1841.

5. Cypress Bayou was sometimes referred to as a lake because it provided slackwater navigation up to a few miles from Jefferson.

6. It had only been necessary for the *Relief* to go to the head of Sodo Lake to take the western bypass in its previous trip.

7. The front of the upper deck.

8. Soda Lake formed in a shallow floodplain depression.

9. Apparently Rees E. Price, head of a prominent Cincinnati family, an abolitionist, and a religious eccentric. An example of his views can be found in J. R. Buchanan's 1855 *Buchanan's Journal of Man*.

10. The *Rochester* was apparently not headed to Port Caddo. The March 22, 1856, Clarksville *Standard* reports that the *Waverly* from Cincinnati spotted the *Rochester* coming out of Sulphur Fork carrying a load of cotton in early 1842.

11. The Republic of Texas until 1845, with the international line running through Caddo Lake.

12. To alert the people at Swanson's Landing that the *Relief* was arriving.

7 ✦ At Swanson's Landing

Swanson's Landing[1] was on the south shore of Caddo Lake a short distance past the Texas line and served as a shipping and receiving point for the adjacent Swanson plantation and those of neighbors. Peter Swanson, his wife Elizabeth Amelia ("Milly"), and their family were among the earliest settlers on the lake. Swanson arrived in Texas in February 1838, and the first steamboat to penetrate Caddo Lake (the *Manchester*, in June 1838) brought freight to Swanson's Landing before making a side trip across the lake to Potter's Point. The landing inadvertently became the starting point

of the Southern Pacific Railroad in 1857, developed a significant infrastructure for the export of cotton and the import and sale of dry goods and groceries, and intended to become a town named Petersburg—an objective that came to naught when the rails were removed during the Civil War for use elsewhere.

⁂

[First part not used.]

The Relief, as I have stated, lay all night of December 10, 1841, at "Swanson's Landing." This fact of itself would seem to have no particular significance, but to the few remaining rivermen of those days, and to the landsmen who have "kept the run of things," it may not be uninteresting to look back to Swanson's Landing of 1841, to old Peter Swanson and his hospitable, provident wife, and their sociable sons and daughters, who never failed to visit the boats which landed at their place, when engaged in the exploration in their new field of labor. We boatmen all remember the butter, the sausages, the head-cheese, in fact all the choice edibles which a well regulated farm could produce, and a thrifty, cleanly housewife prepare; and when our mouths water now at the recollection of these good things, we are carried back to Swanson's Landing of the early days, and the picture of welcome to the "stranger" is only made complete by the images still fresh in our memories, of "Uncle Peter" as he sat on the shore leaning upon his rifle and at regular intervals sending up little curling wreaths from his pipe, only removing it from his mouth long enough to cry out "Captain, your boat's right on a stump;" of the good old lady in the back-ground, with her baskets, her crocks, her jugs (of buttermilk, of course); an old negro or two, with mules loaded with bags of sweet potatoes, cow-peas and hominy, and a few strings of chickens dangling across their backs, who, seeming to realize their impending doom, improvised the chorus "Gone up in a balloon;"[2] and the sons—one, two, three—of these old folks at home, who, at the sight of a "steamboat on the lake,"[3] seemed to foresee the future importance of their landing, the first available point after crossing the line into Texas, and their young eyes seemed to twinkle with pride as they fancied themselves standing there upon their own soil, and dispensing the commerce of Texas among the many "birds of passage" who, in time to come, would alight at this favorite spot, and already they began to run their hands away down to the very bottom of their pockets, hoping to feel the cash results of their anticipated profits.

But to return to the Relief. After making her fast for the night, all hands went ashore, each anxious to be the first to place his foot on a "foreign shore." Here was a little shed,[4] called in those days a "warehouse," and as it was empty the crew of the Relief took possession of it at once, and I need not say that in the twinkling of an eye all distinction of rank among them was forgotten, and "Uncle Joe" came down from his high position of commander to the level of the humblest deck hand of the crew—but this was on shore, and I must not forget to say that as soon as the effervescing joy at standing on the soil of Texas had subsided, order was restored and discipline resumed, and "each in his proper station moved." There was nothing "rotten in Denmark," for "Uncle Joe" was Captain again.

Well, among us was a fiddler, and so of course there was a dance; yes, sort of a dance. The few among us who could "cut the pigeon wing"[5] did their level best, and the palm was freely accorded to Philley; in fact, I have never seen him excelled since, except by General Banks[6] at New Orleans. It is needless for me to say that we had every variety of the Irish jig, for among us were many of "the boys who could do that." The young negroes of the plantation at the sight and sound of all this found it impossible to keep their feet on the ground, and as the bar-keeper had brought out a jug full of the great "human leveler," the whole party allowed the little darkies, by common consent, to sidle up and take part in the dance, and it was genuine enjoyment to sit there in the light of the great bonfire we had built, and witness the pranks of these dark skinned urchins, and see the eyes of the old negroes glisten with pride as they "patted" for the little ones to dance; and at last one old crooked-legged patriarch came hobbling into the ring, declaring, "Fo God, massa, I can't go home till dis nigger shoes dese white folks what he could do when he was a boy, and dis ole crooked leg didn't had de roomatiz," and in he went, and accompanying his gyrations with his voice, "joined in the chorus" by all the little negroes, he soon brought cat-gut to a discount[7] and had the whole field to himself. When the old negro had exhausted himself with dancing, and his audience, with violent laughter, were begging for quarters, the frolic for the night came to a close. Captain Ross ordered "all the hands aboard," and the crew of the Relief retired for rest, hoping to spend their next night in Texas, at Port Caddo, still some twenty-five miles distant.

The negroes camped in the warehouse and around the fire, which they so bountifully replenished with pine knots that it was burning briskly when the Relief left her moorings at the first crack of daylight on the morning of the 11th December, 1841.

And now having done with the festivities and the hospitalities attending this first landing of the Relief at Swanson's landing, I must say a few words of the importance of this point in the subsequent history and development of the country, and also the commerce of the lakes between Shreveport and Jefferson.

When the first charter of the "Southern Pacific Railroad" was obtained there were certain conditions imposed upon the company, which if not complied with, would bring about a forfeiture of their charter. Among these conditions was one that they should construct within a specified length of time, twenty-five miles of the road within the State of Texas. Now, the Texas line leaving the Sabine River, where the thirty-second degree of longitude crosses it, thence running due north until it strikes Red River, passes some twenty miles back of Shreveport and crosses Ferry Lake about one-fourth of a mile east of Swanson's landing, and not touching Red River until it reaches a point some miles above White Oak Shoals. And so to avoid the expense of transporting the materials over the twenty miles from Shreveport to the line where they must begin the road, the company wisely decided to make Swanson's Landing the initial point of the Southern Pacific Railroad, and right there on the very identical spot where "Uncle Joe" and his friends met for the first time in Texas, was the first rail laid and the first spike driven.[8] The descendants of old Peter Swanson, who was now dead, christened the place "Petersburg," in honor of their father, and they freely donated land for the use of the road.

The railroad company, I believe, succeeded in completing the twenty-five miles within the State of Texas in time to secure the charter,[9] and after operating the road a few years, from Marshall to Petersburg, the track from Swanson's Landing was taken up, and the initial point of the Southern Pacific Railroad was transferred to Shreveport, and thus was Swanson's Landing shorn of its honors and robbed of much (nearly all) of its commercial importance. The two sons of old Peter Swanson, James and Thomas, who managed the shipping business at Petersburg, are both dead, and so have been saved the chagrin and disappointment they would have felt had they lived to see the change I have described, and the patronymic they had bestowed upon this favored spot fallen into disuse.

So much for the history of Swanson's Landing; and as I find my scribblings are exceeding my limits, I will leave the Relief once more, not, however, without a promise that in my next I will stick to her until I have brought her away from Port Caddo, showing some of the peculiarities of the navigation of the Lakes in those days, and telling, also, how it has since been improved by more than one OUTSIDER.

Notes

1. On Swanson's Landing, including development of the railroad, see my *A History of Navigation on Cypress Bayou and the Lakes.* On the first steamboat on Caddo Lake, see my *Antebellum Jefferson, Texas*, which incorporates the information contained in Withenbury's letters.

2. This popular ballad of the 1800s contains a warning about eating too much, lest one fall out of bed as a result of dreaming about going up in a balloon. For the full lyrics, see the "Broadside Ballad Entitled 'Up In A Balloon'" on "The Word on the Street" website.

3. This was only the fourth trip of a steamboat to Caddo Lake.

4. Sheds used primarily for the protection of cotton were probably the typical facilities, replaced by enclosed structures only at the largest landings.

5. A fancy dance step performed by jumping and striking the legs together.

6. Nathaniel Banks, a commander of occupying Union forces during the Civil War.

7. The pace of the dance is likened to a reduction in the value of the cat-gut (sheep or horse intestine) that was used for the strings of the fiddle.

8. The Southern Pacific was intended as an east-west line within Texas that would be constructed from the state line, connecting with a rail from Shreveport that would carry the construction materials. The rail from Shreveport had not been built, and it was necessary to construct the Southern Pacific from a point where materials could be brought in by water.

9. This was done.

8 ✦ On Ferry Lake

The *Relief* moved west on Caddo Lake (then called Ferry Lake) from Swanson's Landing to Port Caddo on Cypress Bayou.[1] The lake was formed in 1800 in the valley of Cypress Bayou by the raft-induced diversion of Red River water to the west. The valley had been forested with cypress, oak, and pine, most of which were killed by the lake waters. The oak and pine deteriorated quickly, producing submerged stumps. The cypress deteriorated more slowly, producing at the time the *Relief* was passing through Caddo Lake many erect trunks with dead branches.

⁂

Leaving Swanson's Landing on the morning of the 11th December at early dawn, we felt our way cautiously among the stumps, the tall dead cypress trees which stand there in the water often fifteen or twenty feet deep, silent witnesses of an age when this lake was dry land—and the green cypress and willows which are struggling for life where the water covers their roots fully two-thirds of the year—in many places not able to see a boat's length ahead of the course we were to go.

Here we began for a moment to doubt the ability of Mr. Bale, the bee hunter—now our pilot—to show us the way, but his apparent confidence in himself as he stood beside Mr. Philley at the wheel, directing him to "steer around that old dead tree to the right thar, and then haul her short to the left by that clump of green bushes, and then you'll see an opening for a few rods, which will lead you along side of that tall dead cypress with the eagle's nest[2] in the top of it," &c., partially reassured us; but just as "Uncle Joe" began to have faith in the man who swore he "knew all the alligators and catfish in the lakes," the Relief struck a stump which threw her out of the track Bale had pointed out, and instead of going "to the right of that dead tree thar," we found ourselves going head on to it, and before the engine could be reversed "she struck it fair in the face," and down came a half a cord of dry cypress limbs rattling on the decks and splashing in the water.

Here I will state that in this part of the lake we did not attempt to run more than about two miles an hour, on account of the myriads of stumps under the water, and which it was impossible to avoid as there is no current to "make a break" or ripple over them. Mr. Bale did not express the least astonishment at this *contretemps*,[3] but coolly remarked: "You may look out for a good many of that sort, for they are all along here." By the time the confusion was over and the Relief ready for another start, Mr. Philley found it difficult to "go to the right of that tall dead tree, thar," and so Bale said, "let her go to the left then, damn the odds, it don't make much difference along here anyhow." And so we found it, for the water was about of a uniform depth all over this part of the lake, and the stumps seemed to be about as equally distributed as were the trees, which were thickly scattered everywhere.

Captain Ross "weakened," and said he to Dr. Scott,[4] a passenger, and citizen of Port Caddo: "I'll be dod durned if this ain't more'n I bargained for, and if I ever get out of this you don't catch me here again." But we soon got used to the bumps, and as Bale was intent upon spinning his bee-hunting yarns, as well as giving us something in the way of the history of the settlement of the country bordering on these lakes, and the character of the first settlers—most of whom were personally known to him—we all soon became so thoroughly absorbed in the novelty of the scenery, and so completely imbued with the quaint sayings of Bale, and the romance of his historical reminiscences, that we lost all our fears for the safety of boat and cargo, and kept creeping along slowly among the stumps and trees, occasionally coming to a portion of "the bayou" where the Relief could bound off at full speed for half a mile or so,[5] and then into the woods she must go again, where in a few minutes she would be perfectly lost to "the naked eye" of any adventurer who might chance to be within a quarter of a mile of her.

This peculiarity of navigation holds good from Swanson's Landing to the mouth of Cypress Bayou, a distance by the circuitous route of those days of twelve or fifteen miles, which distance has been materially shortened since then[6] by the venturesome spirit and perseverance of the "birds of passage," who, year after year, have visited these waters and woods, aided also by the liberal contributions of the New Orleans merchants and the people of Texas; but as this aid has been of comparatively recent date, I will not enter into its history or discussion until some future time, but will continue to tell how the Relief got through with this, (all but one,) the pioneer trip by steamer to Port Caddo.

In a northwesterly direction from Swanson's Landing, and about three miles distant by an air line, rises a bold promontory known as Potter's Point; and as our route carried us within three-fourths of a mile of its base, and it was pointed out to me by Mr. Bale as one of the "land marks" to guide the mariner on his doubtful way in all future time, we naturally enough asked, "Why was it called Potter's Point?," and the answer of our guide (the only man among us, except Dr. Scott, who had ever seen it before) only served to excite our curiosity to know more of the people whose names are so indispensably connected with the celebrity of this point. His answer was: "Up on that hill yonder old Bob Potter[7] settled, and right out there on the right, about one hundred yards from the shore, he was shot by ______ Scott, while trying to make his escape by swimming from the Scotts, who were his mortal enemies." Here followed an interesting narration of the antecedents of both Potter and the Scott family, the cause of the feud which for a long time existed between them, and which culminated in the death of Potter; but the story, although full of thrilling incidents, is quite too long to be entitled to a place in the history of this short trip of the Relief.[8]

In passing, I will just mention that "old Bob Potter" was, in his better days, a citizen of North Carolina, and if all traditions of his career are correct, he was a member of Congress from that State; at any rate, he was a very talented man, and at one time occupied a high place politically in his own state, if not in the Congress of the United States. Being driven to frenzy by the suspicion of his young wife's infidelity to him, and coupling the person of an old preacher (her uncle, I think,) with his wife as the partner of her guilt, he enticed the old man to a secluded spot on a by-road, and there committed an outrage upon him of a character meriting capital punishment, and then left for Texas; and wandering from place to place, he finally settled on the shores of Ferry Lake, where he met the fate I have described, leaving his name attached to that particular locality where it has long since become "familiar as household words."

We were about five hours making the run from Swanson's to the mouth of the Bayou, and here it seemed we had reached the *ultima thule* [9] of our tiresome and hazardous trip, and were never to reach Port Caddo; for the mouth of the Bayou was completely blockaded with drift, (known in those parts as "raft,") as far as the eye could reach. "Uncle Joe," turning to our guide said, "How now, Mr. Bee-hunter; ain't you lost? Do you think there's any catfish here that will know you, or any alligators that you know?" "Oh, I'm all right," says Bale; "I've pulled my dugout over this raft many a time; it ain't more'n a half mile long, and the logs are loose; we can worm our way through here right soon." And so we found it; Bale was "all right."

Captain Ross ordered the yawl[10] brought forward, and in a few minutes all hands were at work clearing out the "raft;" the most active ones of the crew were at once out upon the mass of drift, and foremost among them, with axe in hand and skipping from log to log, was Mr. Philley. He showed us very soon that he could cut a cypress log almost as quickly as he could cut the "pigeon wing" at the dance on the preceding night, and apparently with equal relish. With the saws and axes in the hands of men as anxious as we were to get our feet upon the land before night should overtake us, it was an easy job to cut away the principal logs, and while Mr. Bale and myself were pushing and pulling the yawl through the openings between the trees, in order to reach the clear water of the bayou above the "raft," the Relief, by the aid of her steam began to work her way through it. We, by taking "short cuts," got above the raft fully an hour ahead of the Relief, and as Bale had taken the precaution to bring "Old Bet" (his rifle) with him, as soon as we struck the clear water he said to me, "Now you just lay low while I pull carefully round that pint[11] yander, and I'll show you perhaps the biggest alligator you ever hearn tell on. I've know'd him here these three years, and have put mor'n one ball into his skin, but somehow I can't fetch him."

I remained quiet and watchful, and sure enough, there he lay apparently asleep on a log, but the noise of the Relief had disturbed him, and just as we came in sight of him he began to move, and as quick as I can write it "Old Bet" had sent a bullet after him, but he only quickened his movements a little, just to acknowledge the presence of his visitors.

Bale, in his chagrin, cried out, "Damn his old hide, he always sleeps with one eye open," and by the time "Old Bet" was loaded again the Relief came around the point below us, and we hastened on board, for now we were assured by our reliable man, who knew all the alligators, that our troubles were over.

The fires were filled up, and the steam raised, till the safety [text missing]. We ran, it seemed to me, faster than ever before. The word beautiful falls far short of expressing the character of Cypress Bayou from its entrance into Ferry Lake to Port Caddo. There is no current, and the dark, clear water is from twenty to sixty feet deep and from one hundred and fifty to two hundred feet wide, and we were not long in reaching our destination.

Our big gun was loaded ready for a salute, and at a word from Bale, as we were rounding the "last pint," its "thud" told the anxious citizens of the approach of the "strangers;" and as we hove in sight, while echo was still answering the echo from the distant hills, to the shore where stood an anxious, *thirsty* crowd, a shout of welcome went up from the multitude: welcome to the "Bird of Passage" and to the OUTSIDER.

Notes

1. On the details of this route, including the improvements mentioned (but not described) by Withenbury, see my *A History of Navigation on Cypress Bayou and the Lakes*.

2. The location of this permanent fixture is shown on Lt. E. A. Woodruff's 1872 *Map of the Red River Raft Region and Cypress Bayou*.

3. Embarrassing mishap.

4. Withenbury will have more to say about Scott in the next letter.

5. The *Relief* was running intermittently in the submerged channel of Cypress Bayou.

6. Withenbury is referring particularly to the creation of a cutroad at the northern end of the lake by Capt. Robert Martin in 1855.

7. Robert Potter was in the North Carolina Legislature and the U.S. Congress, emasculated two men to justify a claim of infidelity against his wife, served time in jail on a misdemeanor charge, came to Texas in 1835, signed the Texas Declaration of Independence, was first secretary of the Texas Navy, established a bond marriage with Harriet Moore in 1836, built a home at Potter's Point in 1837, served in the Republic of Texas Legislature, and was killed on Caddo Lake in March 1842 by a posse led by William P. Rose. See the article on Robert Potter in the *Handbook of Texas Online*.

8. Bails' account of Robert Potter's death is placed aboard the *Relief* in December 1841; but Potter was not killed until March 1842. Withenbury probably inserted information concerning Potter's death into his original logbook account of Bails' speech. William P. Rose, his son Preston, and his son-in-law John W. Scott were arrested, but the case was dismissed for lack of evidence. See the article on William Pinckney Rose in the *Handbook of Texas Online*. Although there were a number of people in the posse, it can be assumed that John W. Scott was the person who killed Potter because he was one of the persons arrested and because Harriet Potter in her "The History of Harriet A. Ames During the Early Days of Texas" says that Potter was shot by a man named Schott.

9. Farthest limit.

10. The boat's skiff.

11. Devil's Elbow, where Cypress Bayou turns sharply to the west.

9 ✦ At Port Caddo

Port Caddo[1] was a few miles upstream on Cypress Bayou from Caddo Lake and was the primary outlet for the cotton of Harrison County, which was one of the largest cotton producers in Texas. The town was laid out in 1838 and was used late in the year as a base for Republic of Texas troops

in an altercation with remnants of the Caddo tribe. This was the occasion for the first steamboat to Port Caddo (the *Echo* in December 1838), apparently to bring supplies to the troops. The *Echo* made another trip to Port Caddo in April 1839. These were the only arrivals prior to the *Relief*, and neither involved the export of cotton. Withenbury indicated in his sketch of his life as a boatman and in the first letter that the December 1841 trip of the *Relief* was the first to take cotton from Port Caddo by steamboat, but this is not mentioned in this letter.[2]

⁂

I left the Relief just landed at Port Caddo, on the 11th December, 1841, and did not even take time to introduce to my readers, as I should have done, the crowd who came rushing on board, eager, many of them, to place their feet for the first time on the decks of a steamboat, while others, who had been more highly favored and who knew what to look for, came with the hope of appeasing their appetites for something better than they got every day ashore. In the scramble to get on board, two men were knocked into the bayou before more than a single plank could be got out,[3] and there came well nigh being blood spilt before the lines were fairly made fast; as it was, Captain Ross found it very difficult to satisfy the two wet individuals, that Hines, the deck hand, who was running out with a head line, and in haste had butted one of them off and tripped the other overboard with the bight of the line, "meant no harm," and that the "safety of the boat required quick movements of the men in such case;" and as these two men had never been on a steamboat before, they accepted the Captain's explanation, and without much urging they accepted also an invitation to "take a little something" with the Captain, but not until Hines had been invited up to join them, when they buried the hatchet and, slapping the deck-hand on the back, swore he was "a noble fellow and welcome to Texas." Captain Ross gave Hines the wink and he went below.

The multitude were so overjoyed at the arrival of the boat that there was no use in trying to discharge her freight until the next day.

Dr. Scott, our passenger, had sent a messenger overland from Shreveport to assure the people that by the joint efforts of himself and Mr. English,[4] the merchant who owned the freight, the coming of a boat was a certainty; consequently, everybody was on the *qui vive* [5] for her arrival, and they had abandoned all thoughts of business until they should have celebrated the occasion in one big spree.

This town was established at this particular point because here was high land, and from here a good road to Marshall[6] (sixteen miles) could be more easily constructed than from any other point on the lake or bayou. The distance from Swanson's Landing to Marshall is but a trifle greater, but the country through which the road must be made was not so favorable. Port Caddo, then, must needs be, for all time, "the head of navigation," notwithstanding the bayou was perfectly beautiful for six miles further; but no one in those days dreamed of a steamboat ever attempting to go further up the bayou than these six miles. Little did these owners of town lots in Port Caddo dream that so soon as the 5th day of March, 1845, the scene of rejoicing at the success of the Relief in reaching their new city, would be re-enacted, and that, too, in a largely increased ratio, at another new city not yet thought of, forty miles further up the bayou; but the spirit of pioneering had this day been awakened among the crew of this little steamboat, and it was reserved for one of the number, Captain W. W. Withenbury, to land the Llama, the first boat, at Jefferson, which to this day is the head of navigation of Cypress Bayou. But more of Jefferson and the trip of the Llama hereafter.[7]

The people who had settled at Port Caddo were a strange mixture; Dr. Scott was an educated man and talented, but the love of adventure and the associations of frontier life in Texas had apparently wrought a sad change in the man. When sober, he was a gentleman; but when drunk, a desperado. His brother, who lived also at Port Caddo, was a rough and dangerous man drunk or sober, and we had no little difficulty in keeping on the right side of the two[8] while we remained there. Mr. English, the merchant, was a man of good sharp sense; had been a steamboat Captain; "knew what was what;" but being now an adventurer in Texas, he was not over-scrupulous in his dealings with his fellow craftsmen, and the then clerk of the Relief is willing to this day to admit that, in collecting his freight bill from Captain English, he learned something of human nature as it was frequently met with in those days in Texas; and he took a lesson which he tried not to forget.

Among the planters in this region were many estimable men, and of their number was one who, though he did not visit the boat at the time I am writing of, was often mentioned as *the* planter above all others in those days. This man was Colonel S. M. Haggarty.[9] He came from some one of the Southern States, and was in some way connected with the affairs of the Creek Indians, and from that tribe he chose his wife, who lived near Port Caddo to a good old age, a most exemplary woman, leaving behind her at least two daughters,[10] who were educated ladies, one of whom, if she is still living, is the wife of Captain "Jim" Scott (no relation to the Doctor), whom everybody on Red River knows as a correct business man and a good fellow. The other daughter, if still living, is Mrs. Samuel McFarland, of Jefferson, Texas, whom none know but to love and respect.

Colonel Haggarty was a successful planter, and did much in his day to improve the condition of the country, and made his mark, which others following will find leads to success.

Close to the water's edge were encamped some straggling Indians, of the Caddo and Quapaw tribes, and they had associated so much with the whites that, according to my impressions at the time, they were sadly demoralized. Among these poor wanderers, I must, at the risk of being tiresome, speak of one family, consisting of an old squaw and her children, who claimed Larkin Edwards,[11] a white man, for their father.

Of course I can not be expected to give their precise history, having had but a few hours to learn it in, and in speaking of them I may be in error slightly. The old woman who could speak tolerable English, told me that "Edwards" was the father of her children, one a girl of about fifteen, a bright little boy of eleven or twelve, his little sister, and a babe in arms, as near as I can recollect made up the family.

Captain Ross, Mr. A. W. Bently,[12] (formerly a merchant tailor in this city and who came with us from New Orleans,) and myself went out to the tent occupied by these squaws and half-breed children, to learn something of their habits of living. On our approach the oldest girl, "Polly," ran away to the woods, but the old women and the young children remained, and when satisfied that we were friendly they soon forgot their timidity and offered us a part of the repast of which they were then partaking. It was a sort of boiled hominy which they called "Spohkee." We all partook, though not very freely, and were just getting cleverly acquainted with these poor people, when into the tent burst Dr. Scott and his drunken brother, and the poor Indians fled like a flock of quails on the approach of the hunter, and in a moment the tent was vacated and we returned to the boat, sorrowing for the fate of these victims of white men's passions and brutality. Mr. Bently now lives at New Albany, Indiana, and is largely engaged in the Insurance business, and no doubt well remembers all I have related of this memorable trip of the Relief, the narration of which I fear I am stringing out to an unreasonable length.

Thus was Port Caddo settled and peopled, and strange to say it "flourished like a green bay tree" for a number of years, and at one time had half a dozen or more quite large mercantile establishments and several large warehouses from which were shipped in former days many thousand bales of cotton. Among the merchants of Port Caddo at a later day, say in 1845–46, was the firm of Todd & Brander, a branch from the old house of Brander, Williams & Co., of New Orleans, and Rawlins & Wingfield. Colonel "Jim" Wingfield is still living and holds an important office in the N. O., J. & G. N. R. R.,[13] and as he was a good business friend of mine in former years, both at Port Caddo and New Orleans, he may recognize the hand which is scribbling at these memories of olden time.

But Port Caddo felt a precursor of its doom in 1845, when the Bayou was found to be navigable to Jefferson, and again it drooped when the Southern Pacific Railroad was commenced at Swanson's Landing, and to-day there is but little remaining of its former greatness. It is a neighborhood shipping point, with a store or two, and no more. Steamboats pass it almost daily during the business season, "loaded to the guards and black with people" bound for Jefferson, its successful rival.

The Relief having finished her business left Port Caddo on Sunday, December 12, 1841, at noon, bound for Upper Red River, and only reached Swanson's Landing before dark. Here she lay, "wind bound," two days, which is one of the vexatious delays often happening in this Lake.[14] Our delay of two days gave us ample time and opportunity to renew our acquaintance with the people, and to see new faces who came from different points on the opposite shore of the lake to look at the "Bird of Passage," and to welcome the OUTSIDER.

Notes

1. On Port Caddo, see my *A History of Navigation on Cypress Bayou and the Lakes* and V. H. Hackney's *Port Caddo—A Vanished Village and Vignettes of Harrison County*. On prior boat movements to Port Caddo, see my *Antebellum Jefferson, Texas*, which incorporates the information contained in Withenbury's letters.

2. Withenbury's sketch of his life as a boatman in the July 10, 1878, *New Orleans Daily Democrat* indicates that the cotton was owned by John Kitchen and transported by the *Relief* to the head of the raft: "We took a few bales of cotton belonging to a man named Kitchen, this being the first shipment of cotton from Port Caddo by steam. It was destined to New Orleans by a circuitous route, viz: Down the bayou through the lakes, through Red and Black bayou, to Red river, above the raft, and thence hauled from the head to the foot of the raft, where it was reshipped on a New Orleans boat. The reason for the cotton taking such a roundabout course was that rumor said that Kitchen had received a hint that a Texas sheriff was hunting for his cotton, and he said he didn't care a d__m what route it took so we got it out of Texas quick, and he got a bill of lading for it as consigned to his New Orleans merchant. We had a tedious trip from Port Caddo to the head of the raft, and the cotton was a long time getting to its destination."

3. Freight and passengers moved on a plank that was laid by hand between the boat and the shore.

4. Capt. William English ran the *Nick Biddle* to Coates' Bluff in 1836 and 1837 and appears in the 1841–1842 Harrison County tax rolls.

5. On the alert.

6. The seat of Harrison County southwest of Port Caddo. Harrison County was established in 1839. Marshall was founded in the 1841 and became the county seat in 1842. Port Caddo was within Harrison County.

7. Withenbury does not fulfill this promise.

8. The identity of the Scott brothers is indeterminable on the basis of readily available documents. None of the many Scotts in the 1850 Harrison County census is designated a doctor, and no Scotts are shown among the 50 residents of Port Caddo. V. H. Hackney in *Port Caddo* indicates that John S. Scott and Joseph Scott owned property (which would have been town lots) in Port Caddo. Town lot ownership was not necessarily an indicator of location, and in any case these names do not appear in the early 1840s Harrison County tax rolls.

Withenbury may be referring to William T. Scott and his older brother John W. Scott (sons of Thomas Scott and Mary Keller), both of whom came to Texas in the spring of 1840 according to Texas General Land Office land records. An article on William Thomas Scott in the *Handbook of Texas Online* indicates that he was a legislator in the Republic of Texas and in the state, an owner of multiple plantations (including one at Scottsville southwest of Port Caddo in Harrison County), and a railroad promoter and investor. Texas General Land Office land records indicate that John W. Scott acquired the John A. McKinney headright north of Jefferson, Texas, in 1846, establishing the Refuge Plantation. Withenbury's characterization is compatible with the participation of John W. Scott in the killing of Robert Potter and the appearance in the July 10, 1839, Houston *Telegraph and Texas Register* of a proclamation by the State of Mississippi offering a reward for the apprehension of John W. Scott, William T. Scott, and their younger brother James C. Scott on a charge of murder. On the other hand, there is nothing to indicate that any of the brothers was a doctor, and Withenbury states that James C. Scott was not related to the Scott brothers he is describing.

9. Spire Hagerty was from Alabama and operated a plantation called Phoenix northeast of Marshall. This was part of an extensive estate that included more than 7,000 acres, as well as two town lots and a warehouse in Port Caddo. In 1838, Spire married Rebecca McIntosh Hawkins, whose husband, Benjamin, had been killed in 1836. Rebecca was born in Georgia, the daughter of the half-Scottish chief of the Lower Creek Nation and a full-blooded Creek mother. Rebecca and Spire had five children, three of whom died in infancy. The marriage was reportedly an unhappy one, and they separated in 1848. After Spire died in 1849, Rebecca came under control of two plantations and was one of the wealthiest persons in Texas. The second plantation, which was the main residence, was the one called Refuge that had been established by John W. Scott in 1846. It was purchased by Rebecca (along with other family members) in 1849, with James C. Scott acting as the administrator of the estate of John W. Scott. On these families, see Judith McArthur, "Myth, Reality, and Anomaly: The Complex World of Rebecca Hagerty," *East Texas Historical Journal*, Fall 1986 and Charles Steger, "Rebecca McIntosh Hawkins Hagerty: The Richest Woman in Texas," *Stirpes*, September 2007.

10. Rebecca's daughters by Benjamin Hawkins were Louisa and Anna. Charles Steger indicates that Louisa married James C. Scott in 1850 and lived into the next century; Anna married Samuel McFarland in 1859 and died during the Civil War.

11. Larkin Edwards was from Tennessee, came to Texas, apparently with his children, when his wife died in 1820, served as interpreter for the Caddo, and married a daughter of the chief. He was granted 640 acres at Bennett's Bluff by the Caddo that became the nucleus of Shreveport and died at his Coates' Bluff

home in 1842. On Edwards, see my *A History of Navigation on Cypress Bayou and the Lakes*, which mentions the marriage to the daughter of the chief, but without any information on the composition of this family. Edwards' death in 1842 explains why this family was in Port Caddo without protection.

12. A. W. Bently was an 1838 incorporator of the Emigrants Friend Society of Cincinnati, which was involved in the education of emigrants, according to *Acts of a Local Nature, Passed at the First Session of the Thirty-Sixth General Assembly of the State of Ohio*. He located in New Albany, Indiana, in 1850 and entered the insurance business in 1868 according to D. P. Robbins' 1892 *The Advantages and Surroundings of New Albany, Indiana.*

13. New Orleans, Jackson & Great Northern Railroad.

14. Boats were often delayed by wind because Caddo Lake is broad and shallow.

10 ✦ To Black Bayou

The wind died, and the *Relief* left Swanson's Landing and headed towards Black Bayou near the foot of Caddo Lake, but not before Withenbury recounts a fish story at Swanson's Landing.

⁂

[First part not used.]

Well, now, as the wind has nearly ceased blowing, I will try and get the Relief out of the lake and up Black Bayou, into new scenery. While she lay at Swanson's, the crew and our passenger, Mr. Bently, improved the opportunity and made many little excursions into the country, visiting the Swanson plantation, which lies nearly three miles from the lake. There we were always hospitably and pleasantly entertained. We generally had a gun or two in each party which went out from the boat, and while there we got several fine deer and turkeys. The forests abounded in game, and we had no trouble in getting a good supply of provisions wherever we landed.

Mr. Bently was very fond of fishing, and on the first morning from Port Caddo he arranged his tackle, and took a skiff which was lying at the shore, and pulled out into the lake about one hundred yards, tied to a tree, and commenced fishing; and soon he discovered, a little way off, a line tied to an old dry stump, just above the water; and as he was getting no bites, he concluded to examine the "trot line," and there he found a number of very fine bass, of the "goggle eye" species, and any quantity of big catfish. He quietly took the "goggle eyes" and left the "cats." He came to the boat in the full and sole possession of his secret, but it was too good to keep. We had the fish for dinner, and just before it was ready, the owner of the "trot line" came on board, swearing that he had had the worst luck, yes " the "d__dest luck he ever had, for he hadn't a fish on his line but these d__d cats." Mr. Bently expressed much astonishment, and asked him in what part of the lake his line was set? "Why, right out thar," said he as he walked to the door and pointed in the direction of his line. "Why, that's strange," said Bently, "for I went out in that direction this morning and in less than an hour I got a fine mess, and our dinner is just ready; come, sit down and join us." The fisherman did not wait for a second invitation, but joined us, and during the meal he entertained us with many a "fish story;" but we knew one worth them all.

"Uncle Joe" thought this would be a good lesson for Bently's Sunday school boys at Cincinnati, and Bently thought it was a good joke on the fisherman.

Our first day's run from Swanson's brought us into the mouth of Black Bayou,[1] a distance of about eighteen miles, and just at sunset we found our "boat right on a stump," and we made her fast to a tree; and as we were all tired out with a hard day's work, Captain Ross said: "Now boys, all turn in, and let 'er rip till daylight." And there we spent the night in a dreary wilderness, out of sight of land.

We were a little inclined to melancholy, for the novelty of the trip had begun to wear off, and from appearances, Mr. Bale told us we would not get beyond Caddo Prairie[2] until a rise in the bayou came to our relief. But he assured us we would have no lack of amusement, for at Caddo Prairie lived one of the best men in the whole country, who had any quantity of dogs and guns, and was very fond of company; and "more'n that, right up on the bayou here, about three miles, you come to a pint of dry land, and, a few hundred yards out, there's the biggest kind of a bee tree, and if you say so, Cap'n, we'll stop and cut it; won't take long."

Captain Ross said anything for variety, and so we all went to rest and dreamed of honey. OUTSIDER.

Notes

1. Withenbury does not describe the entrance to Black Bayou from Caddo Lake, which involved a run through Stumpy Bayou and Clear Lake. The *Relief* is in Clear Lake at the mouth of Black Bayou, where low-water conditions were a constant problem for steamboats.

2. The broad prairie constituted by the Red River floodplain northwest of Shreveport.

11 ✦ Up Black Bayou

The *Relief* proceeded up Black Bayou, which is located on the Red River floodplain, but ran fairly close to a line of bluffs on the west, and arrived at Erwin's plantation (Figure 5). The plantation was owned by James Erwin, but run by his brother Leander and Leander's son Albertus. The plantation house was located on the bluff across from the entrance to Sewell's Canal, and the cotton fields were on Caddo Prairie on the east side of the bayou. The plantation and fields were connected by a bridge over the bayou.[1]

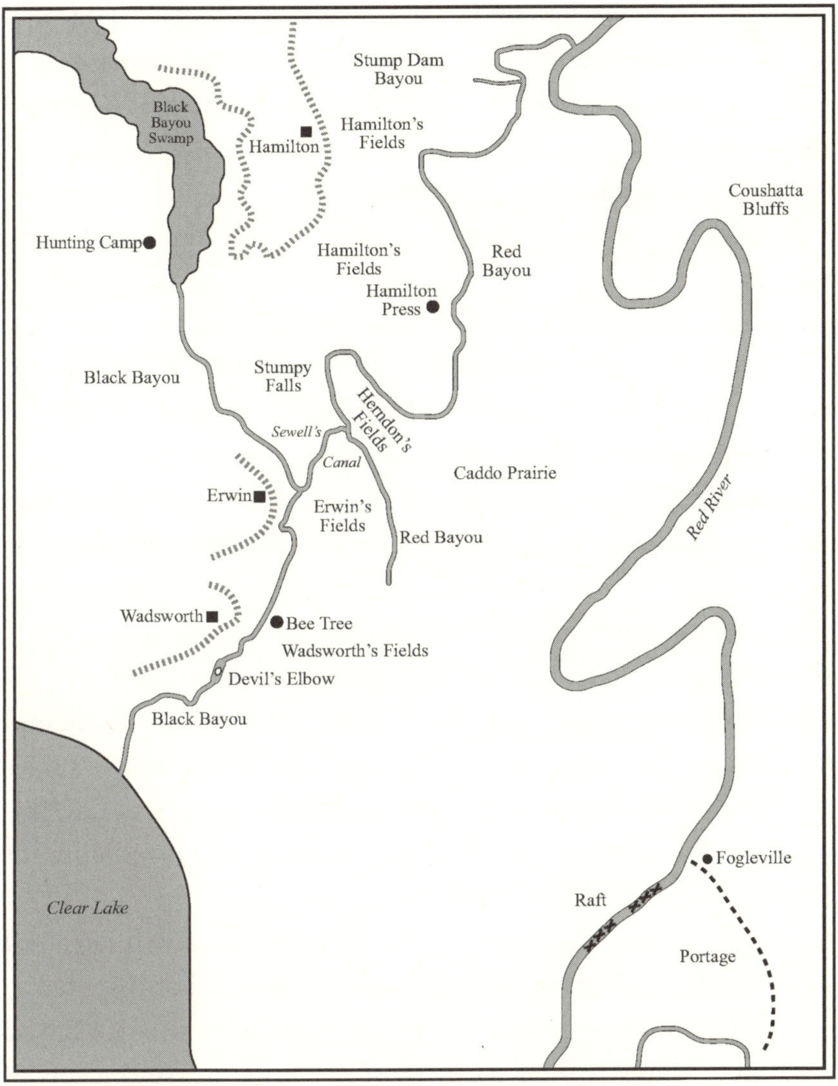

FIGURE 5: ROUTE OF THE *RELIEF*

⁂

It was hardly fair for me to leave the Relief "right on a stump" and "all hands turned in" for the night, as it is not doing "Uncle Joe" justice to suppose that he would allow himself "or any other man" to go to sleep while his boat was in any sort of jeopardy. So I must be allowed to amend my statement and say that the Relief was pulled off the stump and a line run across the bayou to a tree, which held her in the middle of the stream, thus guarding against the wind which sometimes rises very suddenly, and would damage the boat among the overhanging tree tops. Capt. Ross never left his work half done.

Morning came and found us all ready for a start. Not a man had strayed away, for there was not a foot of dry land nearer than the "pint," three miles up the bayou, where we were promised the bee tree.

I wish it were possible to describe the navigation of Black Bayou as it was in those early days when none but "Birds of passage" visited its waters with steamboats. I ought not to attempt it, for were the one-quarter of its perplexities and dangers told, and the description compared with the Black Bayou of to-day, this "scribbler" would only get the credit of having a fruitful brain for creating unreasonable fictions.

But luckily there are a few of the old stock living who can attest to the truth of all I write, should it ever be doubted or disputed.

At the time I am writing of, the first two miles of Black Bayou was but a little streak of water twisted among dense thickets of underbrush, the branches of which were a mere tangled mass of crooked, thorny, wirey twigs, and unlike any growth I have ever seen elsewhere; and scattered throughout this "patch of brush," as Bale called it, were many tall, dead cypress trees, and some living ones. These last, where they stood near enough to the edge of the Bayou for the boat's guards to rub against them, were a perfect

"God send" to us, for their straight, smooth trunks, only branching out near their tops, served us as fenders, and kept the boat from burying herself in the craggy brushwood, and tearing her light, upper works to pieces.

The dead cypresses, however, were quite a different thing, for let the weight of the Relief when flanking, or "cannoning" from a tree on the opposite side of the Bayou, strike one of those tall dead trees, and down would come a shower of dead limbs rattling upon the decks and breaking innumerable holes through the roof; and not unfrequently the whole tree would totter and reel for a moment and then toppling over, fall with a tremendous crash among the smaller trees, and splashing in the water throw a "wet sheet" over the deck and quite up to the cabin. In several instances these trees have fallen across boats, making sad havoc with their cabins. Fortunately this did not happen to the Relief, and in this particular she was highly favored in comparison to several other boats at a subsequent date.

In these dead cypresses the squirrels and other small game found comfortable quarters, and when the trees were struck in the manner I have described, they would come out of their holes and jump for the branches of the tree nearest them. There were hundreds of flying squirrels among them, and these beautiful "little varmints" always endeavored to alight on the boat; and I know I am not exaggerating when I say that before we had run five miles we had more than a dozen of these little visitors on board.

The first two miles of this bayou had no current in those days, and all steamboatmen will agree with me, that a gentle current would have been an assistance in "handling" the boat.

Now, let the reader imagine us starting for a day's run through this "crack in the woods" with all these difficulties to contend with, and he will not wonder that many of us (possibly Mr. Bently) "thought d—n it," with a mental reservation. Job never run a steamboat in Black Bayou; if he had, his complaints would have been louder and longer than Holy writ tells us of.

But let us go along and look for the bee tree. We were fully four hours making these three miles, for at the "Devil's Elbow"[2] we met a very strong current, and the Bayou too crooked for pen to describe; but we made the "pint of dry land" at last, and armed with axes, and provided with buckets, we followed Bale to the bee tree, many of us novices doubting his ability to find it, and expecting to return to the boat without honey, but well humbugged. But Bale found his tree, and while the axmen were cutting away at the old monarch of the forest, he amused us by his marvelous bee-hunting yarns. I wish I had room here to reproduce some of them, but I must forego the "sweet pleasure" for the present, only telling that "six months ago" he found this bee tree.

A full hour was consumed in felling the tree, and when it struck the ground it flew into innumerable fragments. We soon found the part where the honey was deposited, but before Bale would allow us to cut into it, he insisted upon estimating the quantity of honey we would find, and he modestly placed the amount, after examining "the hole" minutely, at "a bushel or more."

Then we went for it, and truly enough we carried from that tree to the boat four buckets full of beautiful clear wild honey in the comb, and I need not say that it served to sweeten our sorrows for many a long day before we got through the bayous and into the river. But I will not anticipate, but must tell you one singular fact connected with this first bee tree I ever saw. The honey was deposited in a large cavity, high up in the tree, the entrance to which was through a hole not more than two by four inches. In this cavity and clinging to the wood, was the body of a reptile of the lizzard species, fully ten inches long and about one inch in size in the largest part of its body. This lizzard was completely embedded and embalmed in the honey; and when, after we had filled two buckets and we came across this mummy, we felt a little dubious about taking the balance, or carrying to the boat that which we had already. When Bale saw us hesitate, he cried out, "Oh damn the scorpion; take the honey; it's all good;" and to reassure us, he took a piece of the comb as near as possible to the carcass of the scorpion, and began eating it, saying to us, "Ef you expect to live in this country you musn't mind the like of that." So we took him at his word and took the honey; but some of the squeamish ones when eating of it would drop it if reminded of the "scorpion."

I asked Bale to give his theory of how the "scorpion" happened to be caught in that fix, and his answer was: "Wal, you see them varmints is mighty fond of sweet, and that damn thief smelt the honey and went up there when the bees was a workin, and they jest doubled teams on him and stung him to death, and thar he stayed till now."

From the bee tree the current grew stronger as we pushed on up the bayou, and not until near dark did we accomplish the balance of the six miles, which brought us to Erwin's Bluff on our left, Caddo Prairie on our right, and a bridge across the bayou "dead ahead." This bridge had been built during the last summer, and was an entirely "new thing" to all of us. On the bridge stood a number of white men and as many negroes as could look over the railing on the side next to the approaching boat. Captain Ross recognized many familiar faces among the crowd, who greeted him with a hearty and loud welcome, and the negroes' eyes glistened with delight at seeing the little steamer coming among them to break the monotony of their secluded life on the beautiful plantation, which being the first we had landed alongside of since we left Red River, was to us like a garden in the midst of a vast wilderness.

We made fast to one of the posts of the bridge; and the "white folks" came on board, when there was a warm shaking of hands on the part of those who had met before, and an introduction of those who were strangers.

Colonel Erwin, seeing a little uneasiness expressed in Captain Ross' countenance when he looked out upon the bridge and ventured to ask "How about that, Colonel?" (pointing his finger toward the "nuisance"), readily assured him that it was "all right," and had been built with a view to letting the Relief and Hunter pass when necessary. So no further allusion was made to it. Then followed a general congratulation, and Bale came in for his share of the praise for bringing the Relief up the bayou at a lower stage of water than any boat had ventured on ever before; and this being his first attempt at piloting,[3] he was the proudest man among us.

I wish the Picayune man could have been there to witness the welcome to these "birds of passage" who had come so far, hoping to earn money "with which to enrich their western homes;" for he would then have seen how the true Southern gentleman always treats the "stranger" and the OUTSIDER.

Notes

1. The Figure 5 features were obtained from Charles Fuller's 1855 *Map of Red River with its Bayous and Lakes in the Vicinity of the Raft*; R. Phillip Baker's 1841 *Map of the Valley of Red River*; the U.S. General Land Office survey plats for T21N R14W, T21N R15W, T22N R14W, T22N R15W, T23N R14W, and T23N R15W; the U.S. General Land Office land records for James Erwin, James Wadsworth, John Herndon, and Robert Hamilton; and information in Withenbury's letters.

2. A prominent bend in the bayou fronting James Wadsworth's plantation.

3. Bails was allowed a hand at the wheel.

12 ✦ At Erwin's Bluff

The *Relief* was at Erwin's Bluff, waiting for a rise to proceed upstream through Sewell's Canal. In the latter part of the letter, an exploratory party in a skiff and on land sets out to see what the conditions are above.

⁂

As I left the Relief tied up below the bridge at Caddo Prairie, and as the bridge question is that which most agitates and interests steamboatmen in these parts to-day, I will venture to explain a little about the bridge across Black Bayou, connecting Erwin's Bluff and the Erwin plantation, which was a part of the Caddo Prairie in the days of which I write, but which is a lake now, during all the months of the year when this route from Shreveport to upper Red River is navigable.[1]

This bridge was simply a plantation convenience, and was built to facilitate the negroes, mules, and the overseer crossing from "the quarters," which were on the bluff, to the prairie cotton-field on the opposite or eastern side of the Bayou. The field contained about seven hundred acres, and there were no buildings on that side of the bayou except the gin-house, a few "cotton pens," and stables for the mules, while on the bluff was Colonel Erwin's house, the kitchen and the negro quarters. No more beautiful or convenient arrangement of hill and prairie could be imagined or desired than was here found, and Colonel Erwin was often heard to say that if he had been appointed to arrange matters to his own liking, he could not have bettered his Caddo Prairie Plantation, as it was in 1840–41.

The crossing of the bayou had heretofore been done by means of a "ferry flat;" but as a sudden rise in Black Bayou, which any heavy rain would produce, (as it took its rise in the hills in the immediate vicinity,) or a runaway negro, was liable to displace "the flat" and put the whole plantation to inconvenience, Colonel Erwin decided to build the bridge; but as the bayou had been made and declared a navigable stream by the Government, and several steamboats had already passed through it, he wisely bethought himself to build the bridge so that it should answer all plantation and neighborhood purposes and still be no obstruction to steamboat navigation. (How unlike some of the men and corporations of our day, who have selfish purposes to serve.)

Colonel Erwin did not know the breadth of the Relief or Hunter, but in order to be certain of placing the trestles of his bridge wide enough apart to allow them to pass without difficulty, he made a journey up Red Bayou to the "Jim Gamble Trees," and there he measured the distance between the ends of the remaining logs on either bank, where Captains Crooks and Ross had cut them, and built the bridge of just as wide a span as were these logs, not dreaming that a larger boat would ever attempt to pass this way. The bridge was so constructed that the floor and timbers could be taken up and replaced by the crew of the passing boat, in which labor the whole force of the plantation were ready to assist if necessary. This explanation was made by Colonel Erwin to Captain Ross as soon as it could be done after exchanging congratulations and "drinks," on the evening of our arrival at the bridge; and as it was a "sure thing" that we could not go more than a mile above the bridge without a considerable rise in the bayou, which must come from the Red River, it was deemed best to remain below the bridge for a while, and wait for a movement of waters.

Captain Ross at once decided to remain at this point and see what was in store for him in the way of water to get through Sewell's Canal, which tapped Black Bayou but a few hundred yards above the bridge, and Red Bayou to the river above the raft; and Colonel Erwin, and the neighbors generally, pledged him every assistance in their power whenever he should deem it prudent to undertake further progress.

I have now brought my readers with me from New Orleans, which city we left on the 2d day of December, and I find by reference to my friend's log-book that the day's occurrences, which I am trying to describe without becoming too tiresome, date December 16, 1841. And now, after having disposed of our visitors who came to bid us welcome, and retired to their homes at a seasonable hour in order to give us an opportunity to rest from the fatigues and exciting labors of the day just closing, it seems to me a fitting time to look back at the labors and risks of these fifteen days, and more particularly at the uncertainty attending the experiment of reaching Port Caddo at so low a stage of water, and that, too, over a route where not one of the boat's officers or crew had ever been before, and with no one but the rude bee hunter, who had only "paddled his own canoe" over these waters and through these woods, to guide us and point the way where a steamboat should go.

It is true that the Relief was not the first steamboat to Port Caddo, but so far as I was informed at the time of her arrival there, but one boat had preceded her to that point. That boat was the Echo, Captain Little, a New Englander. I think she made two trips. The next boat I heard of as having visited these waters was the Manchester, Captain Vandegrift, the father of Captain George A.

Vandegrift of the towboat Tom Rees. The Manchester, however, did not go to Port Caddo; she only went as far as Swanson's and Rives' landings,[2] and Captain Vandegrift left the lake in disgust, as did Captain Little. And so, in view of the little that had been done before to mark out the way for her, and of the fact that we had really no pilot, I shall always look upon the Relief's trip as purely experimental, and can never accord to Captain Ross and his officers less praise for the undertaking and its accomplishment than belongs of right to explorers and pioneers generally.

[Three paragraphs not used.]

Early on the morning of December 17, we were visited by the cook and house servants of Colonel Erwin, who had given them orders the night before to bring us a supply of butter, eggs, buttermilk and a saddle of venison, and to assure us that we were now in a land of plenty and need not want for anything which the plantation, the forest or the bayou could furnish. We received this earnest of good will from these faithful servants with real thankfulness, and we rewarded them for their part in the gift in a manner that made them show their teeth and smack their lips as they went bowing themselves ashore; and as they pursued their winding pathway up the bluff and back to their cabins, they looked back over their shoulders and their smiling faces plainly told us they would come again.

I need not say, perhaps, that our first meal at Erwin's Bluff was the best we had enjoyed for many days, and we felt truly thankful that in the midst of all our hard labor and disappointment, "the lines had fallen to us in such pleasant places."

Before our breakfast was fairly over, Albertus Erwin, a young man of nineteen, came to say to us that himself, his servants, his dogs and guns, were at our service whenever we felt disposed to "take a hunt;" and following close at his heels was a pack of deer hounds, whose eagerness for the chase could hardly be repressed, and their united, deep-toned baying caused the hills to echo to their music, till we all became filled with a desire to "hie to the hills away."

But "business first" was Captain Ross' order, and we at once set about examining into the condition of the bayous above us, and deferred our sports till another day. The yawl was manned with an exploring party, and a party of stragglers on foot accompanied them along the bank; but I will reserve the results of the expedition for another time. OUTSIDER.

Notes

1. The upward growth of the Red River raft caused water to be diverted to the western floodplain higher up when there was sufficient water for navigation, which inundated Caddo Prairie.

2. Harriet Potter in her "The History of Harriet A. Ames During the Early Days of Texas" indicates that the first steamboat on Caddo Lake went to a place that was soon to be known as Rives' Landing.

13 ✦ At the Falls

The exploratory party went up to look at the conditions on Sewell's Canal and at the falls, which extended from the head of Sewell's Canal for a mile up Red Bayou and therefore was more appropriately called a rapids. The falls were caused by the fact that the water level in Red Bayou was higher than in Black Bayou. Sewell's Canal and the im-

provements to Red Bayou mentioned in the letter were part of Lt. Washington Seawell's 1829 project. Most of the letter is devoted to a description of incidents that occurred after the exploratory party returned to the *Relief* at Erwin's Bluff. The letter ends with a decision by Capt. Ross to go by skiff up Red Bayou and down Red River to the head of the raft, expecting to return in two days.

⁂

Our exploring expedition, which was organized on the first morning after our arrival at Erwin's Bluff, extended its researches to the head of "Stumpy Falls," in Red Bayou, which falls were located in that part of the bayou where the canal connects it with Black Bayou. Here I must explain how this fall of about six feet—caused by the level of Red Bayou being so much above Black Bayou—has moved from Sewell's Canal, where I located it, where Captain Crooks, the season before, built his slack-water dams to enable him to take the Hunter through.

The canal was cut, following a little slough, through soft prairie soil, where there were no roots or stumps of trees, and as the current was very swift, the bottom of the canal in time washed out to the level of Black Bayou, and the same difference of level in the two bayous thus connected still remained, and it manifested itself at the point where Red Bayou was tapped by the canal and extended for nearly a mile in a perfectly "straight reach" up the bayou.

This part of Red Bayou in its natural condition was but a mere narrow slough and full of the largest kind of cypress trees. These trees had been cut very close to the bottom of the slough, and everything done that could be except pulling up these immense stumps, to render the bayou in that particular part as good as it was in its general character; and until the canal washed out to the level of Black Bayou, the "Stumpy Falls" were not a very formidable obstruction to keel boat navigation. This information I got from Mr. Bale, who had helped "hook" the first keel-boats through this route to Upper Red River; and Captain Crooks once told me that his last dam in the canal, which was just one boat's length below the upper end of it, backed the water nearly up to the head of "the reach" where "Stumpy Falls" for years after had delayed us all so many days and weeks, and caused us so much vexatious hard labor.

Before we came in sight of the falls, we heard distinctly the rumbling of the water as it came rushing over, among and around these stumps, and our first look at this dreaded place satisfied us that any attempt to take the Relief over would be labor lost; and after making a minute examination of this race track of the rushing waters, we returned to the Relief to consult upon the "next best thing" to do. Here we met the Erwins and several neighbors, who had learned of the boat's arrival, and here we listened to the prognostications of the weather-wise sages, white and black, all of which were kindly intended to console us and cause us to feel resigned to our fate, and to wait patiently for a favorable change in the condition of the bayous. Bale sat in silence listening to all that was said, and when called upon for his opinion, he shrugged his shoulders, winked one eye and changing his pipe to the other corner of his mouth, replied in a slow but emphatic manner, "I tell you, Cap'n, it's might onsartin."

Captain Ross decided to "wait a few days, anyhow," and so every one betook himself to planning how best to enjoy himself and contribute most to make the time pass pleasantly to all hands; and as the whole neighborhood freely pledged themselves to do everything in their power to make our stay among them pleasant, it would seem like folly for any one of us to indulge for a single moment in gloomy forebodings. Mr. Bale suggested the propriety of our paying him off, as he could be no further use to us in any event, and his presence would only add to our expenses. Captain Ross objected to his leaving us, but ordered the clerk to pay him his wages; but the question was, how much? His contract was to show us the way from Shreveport to Port Caddo and back through Clear Lake to the mouth of Black Bayou, for ten dollars, and he thought that as he had come six miles further, and given us his bee tree, he ought to have two dollars more. There was no dispute about the reasonableness of his demand, and Captain Ross added an amendment to his proposition, and that was that Bale should remain with us a "week or ten days," and if he should decide to give up the trip to Shreveport, then Bale should be entitled to receive six dollars more, making eighteen dollars for the "round trip," (think of that you $500 pilots,) and so Bale stayed with us, much to our amusement, as I will show as I proceed.

For me to attempt to give the particulars of each day's occurrences, while we remained at Caddo Prairie, would be tedious; so I will abbreviate as much as possible, only giving a few of the principal incidents, which I hope may possess enough of interest that my narrative will not sound "like a tale thrice told." I will here anticipate just enough to say that not until the 1st day of January, 1842, at dark, did we finish our toilsome trip through Red Bayou, and rest in Red River above the Raft, making us just thirty days out from New Orleans, and forty-eight days from Cincinnati; not very rapid steamboating.

Our position below the bridge was a peculiarly favorable one, as the floor was of just the height of our boiler-deck,[1] and consequently all the crossing of negroes, teams, overseer and neighbors from the bluff to the prairie was to us, sitting at our leisure on the boat, like a moving panorama, and not unfrequently did we find rare amusement in detaining the passing negroes for a bit of a break down upon the planks of the bridge. A plug of tobacco thrown into the crowd would cause a scramble, and not unfrequently a rough-and-tumble fight, that would have been a rich treat to an audience who had paid for "reserved seats" at one of Billy Emerson's best entertainments.[2]

Sunday was the best day for this pastime, for then the darkies, old and young, were "all out in their best," and being free from the restraint of the overseer, they devoted themselves entirely to the business of entertaining us, and picking up the little tokens of approbation which we scattered among them. The foot races of the young negroes across the bridge were not the least amusing of their pranks, for they made the best possible time for the prizes offered.

There were on this Erwin plantation one hundred and twenty-seven negroes, and on Sunday there were frequent accessions to the number from the Hamilton, the Herndon and the Wadsworth plantations, all of which were located within a few miles, and the presence of the "steamboat in the Bayou" attracted every one of the negroes who could possibly get permission to leave home or venture to run away.

Albertus Erwin, determined to do everything possible to entertain us, arranged for a "camp-out hunt," and selecting a few of his trusty negroes, sent them out about five miles toward the headwaters of Black Bayou, to a choice hunting-ground, and there had the tent erected, and we all went out from time to time by detachments from the boat, and enjoyed this unexpected pleasure to such an extent that for the time being we quite forgot the vexatious circumstance which kept us here. This "scribbler" can not forget the scene which presented itself as he approached the camp,[3] about 10 o'clock one morning. Just outside the tent and near the bayou was a rousing, crackling fire, and around it could be seen Captain Ross with a long switch-cane in his right hand, holding the "hind eend" of a squirrel to the hot coals, while with his left he was trying to screen his face from the blazing heat; Captain Hildreth watching and turning a deer's head which he had impaled upon a stake before the fire; Bale roasting a venison steak upon the hot coals, and cursing the "damn infernal smoke" that came in his eyes at every whiff of the wind; Philley sitting on a log at the bank of the bayou cleaning a string of fine fish which he and Mr. Bently had caught; and Mr. Bently making preparation for the morning meal; "all working harmoniously together for the common good."

After the first general salutation, Captain Ross looking out from under the palm of his left hand, and still holding with his right, the "latter eend" of his squirrel to the fire, asked "how's the water in the bayou?" And as the answer came, "falling," he turned his begrimed face around to his squirrel, and said like a true philosopher, "Dod durn it, let 'er rip."

I need not tell old hunters, that this camp breakfast was relished and partaken of without a dissenting voice or a squeamish stomach, and many times before the season was over we would have been but too thankful for an opportunity to exchange the best the boat could furnish for another like it, for we were not always in a "land flowing with milk and honey."

After three days in camp, all returned to the boat fully satisfied with our entertainment, but very impatient to be on our "winding way" up the bayou; but as the water was still falling, there was but little room for hope.

Captain Ross being very impatient, determined to take a trip to the head of the raft in a skiff; he took two deck-hands, Philley, and Mr. Bently, and on the 20th started, expecting to return in two days. The route lay through Red Bayou to the river, fifteen miles, thence down the river twenty-five miles. A pretty good two days' work, which we tried to dissuade him from; but he took his stock of provisions and left us at daylight, determined to accomplish the whole distance before dark. Philley and Bently returned to the boat on the evening of the 22d, and reported Captain Ross gone from the raft to Shreveport on the steamer "Southwestern";[4] so until we hear from him again we will consider ourselves deserted by our captain, and will call him an OUTSIDER.

Notes

1. The first of the elevated decks.
2. A popular minstrel singer and dancer, as indicated by Edward Rice's *Monarchs of Minstrelsy*.
3. According to Withenbury's description, the hunting camp was at the lower end of Black Bayou Swamp to the northwest, from which Black Bayou originates.
4. Captain Ross walked the portage and took the *Southwestern* to Shreveport, which had been operating from New Orleans to the foot of the raft and stopped at Shreveport in both directions.

14 ✦ Back to Shreveport

The *Relief* was at Erwin's Bluff without its captain. A party, including Withenbury, set out by skiff to Shreveport, taking the way they came, to consult with Capt. Ross about turning the *Relief* back because of the continuing low water. Arriving at Shreveport, they found that Ross had left by way of the river. The party took the same route aboard

the *Caddo* with the skiff on board, transported the skiff by wagon at the portage, and proceeded up the river about 12 miles to Coushatta Bluffs.

⁂

As the Relief and crew were left without a Captain, it must not be wondered at if it should appear, upon examining the record of the few remaining days before Christmas, that we indulged our inclinations to frolic, and I don't see how I am to get over this particular time without telling a few "tales out of school."

"Uncle Joe's" nephew, Oliver Ross, was duly installed as barkeeper before we left Cincinnati, a position he never would have been placed in by his uncle had he supposed the lad would ever "take a liking to liquor;" but long before the time I am writing of "his weakness overcame him," and all of us who were disposed to keep a sober crew on the Relief began to take steps for his reformation. His indulgence in "drink of the strong persuasion" brought about a serious fisticuff between him and the Steward (who was a half-breed Indian) one night, and it became necessary for Mr. Bently and myself to interfere in order to save Oliver's eyes, for the Indian was getting the best of the fight, he being decidedly the "sober Indian" on that occasion.

After all was quiet on the bayou, Mr. Bently proposed that we form a Temperance Society on the boat, and accordingly a pledge was drawn up in these words: "We whose names are hereunto signed do pledge ourselves, each to the other, as gentlemen, that we will not drink any ardent or distilled spirits on board the steamer Relief from and after this date, December 16, 1841." Here followed the names of Mr. Bently and the clerk of the boat, and at last "Oliver Ross, barkeeper."

Well, as I said before, Christmas was drawing near, and the inclination to fall in with usages of the country we were in, grew upon the barkeeper, as he was frequently called upon for quantities of whisky by nearly all the "white folks" and every negro who could raise the wherewith to purchase it for Christmas egg-nog; and as he saw the preparations for a frolic going on everywhere, he could not withstand the temptation, nor could he wait for Christmas to come. But how to get over his pledge was the question; and I never was more thoroughly convinced that "a man's wits are sharpened by his appetite," than when I learned how Oliver got drunk on egg-nog without violating his pledge. A negro had brought in a large cedar churn full of buttermilk to the boat that morning, and had left the churn with the steward; Oliver found this churn and poured his whisky into it, and mixed a quantity of honey from Bale's bee tree, and started for the "quarters," ostensibly to carry the churn home; but, with an extra pint of whisky he bribed an old negro to furnish him eggs and milk, and in no time he had a churn full of "splendid nog;" and not being of a selfish turn, he invited his friends out to the shade of a tree on shore, to join him, and there they drank and frolicked until there was "no distinction of race, color or former condition;" and when Oliver (and some of the others) got sober enough to answer to the accusation of having "broken the pledge," he pointed to the words, "On board the steamer Relief," and we were forced to acknowledge that while his thirst for "nog" had caused him to forestall Christmas, his wits had saved him from losing his claim to the title of "gentleman."

On the 24th, as the bayou would not rise, Captain Hildreth who, in the absence of "Uncle Joe," was Captain *pro tem*, directed that an expedition should start from the Relief in a skiff to Shreveport, via Black Bayou and the lakes. Acccordingly, a party was made up for the trip, consisting of Bale, Mr. Bently, Morrison, (our engineer,) Jim Berryhill, (our Indian steward,) and one deck hand, and this "scribbler;" and, with our lunch provided and on board, we cast off from the Relief at the break of day for our voyage of fifty-five miles. Our mission was to find Captain Ross and consult with him in regard to giving up the trip for the present, and returning to the lower river with the Relief. We had a very blustering passage across the lakes, and but for the exercise of rowing the skiff, we would have suffered severely from the cold, as the weather had changed very suddenly from its springlike temperature of the last few days to the severity of winter. We arrived safely at Shreveport a little before dark, and there we learned, to our disappointment, that Captain Ross had left the day before for the Relief, over the same route which brought him to Shreveport.

We put up for the night at the Planter's Inn, kept by Uncle Mike Davis, whom everybody who visited Shreveport in those days will remember as a hospitable host, who never turned away strangers, outsiders or birds of passage, money or no money.

At Shreveport, we found the steamer Caddo, the first of that name. She was on her way from New Orleans to the foot of the Raft, in command of Captain Johnson R. Davis, a native of the Emerald Isle, but a citizen of Pittsburg, Pennsylvania. Captain Davis, in consideration of this being Christmas Eve, gave a party on board the Caddo to the citizens of Shreveport and Caddo Parish. I can not dwell here to decant upon Captain Davis' well deserved popularity on Red River at this time, and, in fact, until his death, but will just call to my aid the testimony of our esteemed fellow citizen, Elias Ehler, Esq., who was carpenter on the Caddo, to prove my assertion that the fact of Captain Davis hailing from Pittsburg was no discount upon his popularity with the people of Red River, for they with one accord agreed, "A man's a man for a' that." How differently would the New Orleans Picayune fix the standard of a man's popularity in these enlightened days.

Captain Davis, as soon as he learned of the arrival of our little party, invited us to join in the festivities of Christmas Eve on his boat. Mr. Bently and myself accepted, and while partaking of this generous steamboatman's hospitality we made several new acquaintances which I will guarantee neither of us have forgotten to this day; nor can we forget the "grand old time" we had till Christmas Eve had faded into Christmas day, and even into the Sabbath of December 26, 1841, when the Caddo started for her destination at the foot of the Raft.

Having failed to meet Captain Ross, we accepted Captain Davis' invitation to go to the Raft on the Caddo, from which point we could return to the Relief much easier than by the route we had come via the lakes. We hauled our skiff on board the Caddo, and on arriving at the Raft we hired it hauled "around the Raft" (three miles) by one of the teamsters of "Fogleville." We got our skiff launched into the river above the Raft on Monday, just before dark, and having learned from George Alban, at the "Dead-fall," that Captain Ross had left there the day previous in a "dug-out," bound for the Relief, with the avowed determination of turning her back from Caddo Prairie as soon as he could get there, we started on our forty miles skiff-ride—twenty-five of which was up stream—in the dark. Twelve miles above the "Dead-fall" we came to the Coushatta Bluffs,[1] and here we saw the smoldering remains of a fire on the bank, and as the night was very dark and cold, we could not resist the warm invitation these flickering embers seemed to hold out to us. On landing we were greeted by the barking of dogs, which although intended by them no doubt as a warning (a-la-Picayune) to outsiders to keep away, we heeded them not, but advanced towards the fire. We stumbled over four sleeping negroes, who, on awakening, were sorely alarmed at our untimely intrusion. These "boys" were soon made easy in their minds when they were told that we were steamboatmen and on our way in a skiff to Red Bayou. They had come from a neighboring plantation with mule teams and two loads of cotton, which they had deposited on the bluff for shipment, and were sleeping while their mules were feeding preparatory for an early morning start for home. They immediately replenished the fire with a quantity of pine knots, and we all sat around it, and soon began to feel that in these faithful negroes we had found warm friends; and even their dogs seemed to be inspired with feelings of friendliness for us, "interlopers" as we were, and approached us, wagging their tails in the unmistakable manner which says to the stranger, in their mute language, "be not afraid," and quietly laid down at our feet.

We easily surmised that the negroes had something to eat with them; and no sooner did we make known that we had had nothing to eat since morning, than they brought forth their simple corn dodgers[2] and bacon and bade us partake. After we had eaten heartily, or rather while we were eating, the boys set about making us some beds; and with the bundles of fodder which they were saving to feed their teams at noon of the following day, they made us real comfortable beds; and after we had remunerated them for the trouble we had caused, and Mr. Bale[3] and the deck hands had divided their tobacco among them, we all lay down to rest, and in a few moments had chatted ourselves to the land of dreams.

I trust there may be some of my readers who, from their own experience, can bring home to themselves the picture I have so faintly drawn of this night's camping among the negroes, dogs and mules of Coushatta Bluffs, and realize the genuine hospitality which was voluntarily tendered to these wanderers in the wilderness. If none of my fellow steamboatmen have had a like experience, then I must ask the soldiers who served in the Southern swamps, in the late war, to draw upon their memories, and I know they can fill up the picture; and many a poor "dark skin" will be remembered as having, like the "Good Samaritan," poured oil upon his wounds while lingering and suffering by the wayside, and in his truly humane heart blessed God that he had been enabled to lighten the sorrows and add to the comforts of at least one OUTSIDER.

Notes

1. At the downstream end of the third large bluff above Shreveport.
2. A small cake of cornmeal that has been baked or fried hard.
3. This is the last mention of Bails as a participant in the trip of the *Relief*, although he obviously went back to the *Relief* with the party. He had left the *Relief* by Letter 20.

15 ✦ To Red River

Withenbury does not describe how Ross or the party of which Withenbury was a member got back to Erwin's Bluff; but this letter finds Black Bayou rising and the *Relief* setting off for Red River. Most of the letter is devoted to a description of Caddo Prairie planters and ends with the *Relief* reaching Red River.

⁂

On the morning of December 28, 1841, new life was infused into all hands by the cheering words, "the Bayou is rising," and from mouth to mouth these words flew until everybody was alive to the importance of making a start. Accordingly, we commenced taking down the bridge, and Colonel Erwin, true to his promise, sent us all the help we needed. The presence of his negro carpenter was very essential, and he was on hand early. We found him an ingenious and practical mechanic, and although not a professional "Hydraulic Engineer," he had evinced a good degree of common sense in the planning and construction of this bridge, which common sense, some whom I wot[1] of about these parts, of the "hydraulic" persuasion, I fear are sadly deficient in.[2]

Before our dinner was announced, the bridge was taken down and the boat pulled above it and made fast, and immediately after dinner all hands went to work and in about three hours the bridge was in place again "as good as new;" and then as we began to get up steam, for the first time in fifteen days, every moment was suggestive of a parting scene, and by the time the engine's "ready bell" had begun its merry jingling, the neighbors all, and some of the boat's company, were in a "mellow mood," and Captain Ross thought it was a little uncertain where the hand-shaking commenced or where was the place to leave it off. (Captain Ross never signed the pledge).

By dint of hard work on the part of everybody, we got through Sewell's canal a little before dark, notwithstanding we had to contend an hour or so with the remains of two of Captain Crooks' dams, which he had built the previous season; and we lay at the foot of Stumpy Falls until morning. Here several of the neighbors visited us to take a parting drink and help us to while away a few leisure hours before lying down to be lulled to sleep by the music of the tumbling waters.

And now, as my "scribblings" at Erwin's Bluff and Caddo Prairie are about drawing to a close, I must take a parting look at the habitués of that particular locality, and review in as charitable manner as possible their manner of living, their peculiar tastes and their social relations to each other.

So far I have made mention of only two persons among the "white folks"—Colonel Leander Erwin and his son Albertus—and now I must mention the fact that the Erwins were from Kentucky, and reported themselves related to that illustrious statesman, Henry Clay. The Caddo Prairie plantation belonged to James Erwin, Esq., a brother of Leander. He owned, also, a large plantation on the Mississippi River, but bought the Caddo Prairie place because of its fertility and its seclusion, or rather isolation, from the outer world.[3] It was a good place on which to reform unruly negroes, for, as will have been discovered from my description of its surroundings, a negro could not run very far away, if so disposed.

Under the old slave regime, the laws of Louisiana required the presence of at least two white persons to every sixty blacks; but, as I have before stated, there were on the Erwin plantation 127 negroes and only two white men,[4] and much of the time only one, the young man Albertus. There was another law in force at that time, also, which in Colonel Erwin's case was just as little heeded; that law forbade the placing in the hands of a negro firearms of any sort. Yet several of the trusty old negroes were allowed to roam over the fields and forests with guns upon their shoulders and pistols in their belts;[5] and while no one could point to a single instance where one of these favored negroes had proved treacherous to his confiding master, or had committed the slightest depredation upon the neighbors' rights, the whole community of that region were determined that the existing laws (concerning the government of slaves) should be more strictly enforced on the Erwin plantation, and for that purpose the neighboring planters had jointly entered a complaint to the "police jury"[6] of Caddo Parish, against the Erwins, but I never heard the result.

One remarkable and noticeable feature in the community I am speaking of, was the total absence of the white woman. Not one for miles around. Colonel Leander Erwin was a widower, and his son an unmarried minor. Colonel James Wadsworth,[7] who lived on his Hill plantation, some three miles south of Erwin's, had been a widower, but at the time of my writing he had an Indian wife—so called. His son James, about eighteen years old, was a chip of the old block. Father and son came frequently to the boat, and generally returned home together in the most dilapidated condition. On one occasion Colonel Wadsworth brought one of his little half-breed Indian boys on horseback behind him. He was a bright little fellow, and seemed very fond of his "Pa," who returned fully all the child's evidence of affection. By the Colonel's invitation, I visited his house, and there I found a meek, quiet, tidy Indian woman, with her four children mingling and playing with the pure white branch of the family as harmoniously as a band of real brothers. I partook of a dinner there, and I must say that I went away favorably impressed with this faithful Indian woman's management of a white man's household.

Above Erwin's, on Red Bayou, lived one John Herndon,[8] quite an old man, I thought in those days, and yet when I met him some fifteen years afterward, he seemed to have grown but very little older. He was a man of many noble qualities of heart and an intellect once brilliant, with a mind well cultivated, and a memory well stored with useful knowledge; but alas!, that "leveler" had reduced him almost to an imbecile. I passed pleasantly the beginning of many social evenings with him, but he never ended them soberly. One night he started home alone, and having to cross the bayou on a log, he fell into the water and barely escaped drowning; and after crawling out on the bank, he well nigh perished with the cold before his faithful old African concubine heard his moans and came to his assistance and drew him into the house. Colonel Herndon was a widower also. He furnished me the recital of the night's adventure I have just given, and thought it was a good joke.

A few miles above Herndon's, and on the opposite side of the bayou, were two plantations owned by "old Bob Hamilton,"[9] a Scotchman by birth, very wealthy and notoriously the hardest master of his negroes and the "meanest white man" among men in the whole country. His negroes suffered for the want of the commonest comforts of life. Their cabins were not fit to stable mules in, and their food not fit for swine or dogs to eat, and they were tasked to the last possible point of endurance. Colonel Bob Hamilton, to the credit of the fair sex be it said, was not a widower; he was a bachelor, and deservedly so. He owned two large plantations on Upper Red River, one at Little Prairie,[10] and one at Pecan Point, where he kept hundreds of negroes in the most squalid misery. Had Mrs. Stowe found old Bob Hamilton when she was writing "Uncle Tom's Cabin," she would never have looked further for a character to illustrate the worst features of slavery and slave owners, for by him was the poor old slave driven and tortured without the least mercy, and in him was the white man debased until nothing but his blood-stained dollars guaranteed him a place in human society. Every steamboatman who had the misfortune to deal with him will remember him as making the heaviest bales of cotton and insisting upon lower rates of freight than were given to his neighbors, and more than one season have his cotton bales laid rotting upon the bank rather than pay the customary freight.

How that man got rich was a mystery to everybody. But he died leaving an immense estate. Colonel Hamilton did not spend much of his time at his Caddo Prairie plantations, nor did he have any regular abiding-place at either of his river places. His time was mostly spent in traveling from place to place, and visiting each one just often enough to keep the negroes and overseers in awe of him, while he "sponged" good bread and meat on his journeyings.

It is needless for me to comment upon the state of society as we found it at Caddo Prairie, if, indeed, that word society can be made to apply to such a community as we found there. I often used to think that the presence among those people of one real good, pure-minded and enlightened Christian white woman would have been like the little leaven of the New Testament, which was hidden in the three measures of meal until the whole was leavened. But she was not there.

On the morning of December 30 we had steam on the Relief at daylight, and commenced the task of getting over the falls, and not until the shades of night were closing around us did we find the work accomplished. We were now out of fuel, but we managed to work along in the dark about a hundred yards to an old cabin which we had been in sight of all day, and, after having demolished it and reduced to a shape suitable for fuel, we brought it on board, and then all hands turned in to rest and prepare for the coming day's toll. Not a moment of the daylight of this last day of 1841 was wasted, for every man of us was tired of this imprisonment and hopeful of getting into the river to-night. We got along very well until we reached Stump Dam, where the narrow bayou commences and the wheels must be stripped. This done, and we were soon at work pulling the boat along slowly by lines around the shaft. We worked along in this way about a mile, and then we found the banks so high from the water's surface that we were obliged to dig them away with shovels. Night overtook us, in spite of our best efforts, about one and a half miles from the river, and there we laid down to rest once more with many misgivings as to the hoped-for success of the next day's work, as we found here the bayou falling rapidly.

On the morning of January 1, 1842, we were at work before daylight, as the bayou was falling so fast as to render it a little uncertain about getting out, as the banks must be cut away for at least another mile and we were well nigh out of wood again.

This will ever be one of the most memorable days of my whole steamboating life, for never did a boat's crew work with a better will, or with more unanimity, than did the whole force of the Relief on this New Year's day. Some with axes cutting wood, some with shovels digging down the banks, some at the fire doors, and others at the lines; and so we worked along until we came, about 3 o'clock P.M., where the bayou was wide enough to admit of the working of the larboard[11] wheel; and then while the carpenter and his helpers were filling the wheel, the rest of the crew were busy picking up wood and bringing it on board; nobody stopped to eat; with one wheel at work we made a little better headway; but not until quite dark did we come where we could see the hole in the woods and the wide Red River before us; and then we shouted until we could shout no more; and as we paddled over to the other side of the river with our one wheel, to a wood pile,[12] each man of us gave expression to his joy once more in such unmistakable tones that the rocking pines of the forest roared, "Welcome, welcome to the OUTSIDER."

Notes

1. Know (archaic).
2. Withenbury is referring to the conflict between bridges and steamboats on midwestern rivers.

3. The 1890 *Biographical and Historical Memoirs of Northwest Louisiana* says that James Erwin, son-in-law of Henry Clay, was one of the earliest settlers in Caddo Parish (formed 1838) and brought 100 slaves from Kentucky. There was a James Erwin who married Henry Clay's daughter Anne in 1823, with Anne dying in 1835 and James dying in 1851 after moving to New Orleans where he remarried. The characteristics described by Withenbury (Kentucky orientation, extensive landholdings, absentee ownership) are compatible with the profile of James Erwin provided by Kent Brown in "The Colonel and His Lady: Colonel Eugene Erwin and His Wife Josephine" (*Filson Club History Quarterly*, Spring 2001).

4. This means that there was no white overseer and that operational control of the slaves on the plantation was in the hands of a slave (or slaves) called a "driver."

5. Because slaves supplemented their diet by hunting and fishing, gun ownership was fairly common in the South despite laws to the contrary. See Christopher Brown and Philip Morgan, *Arming Slaves*.

6. The governing body of the parish (county).

7. James Wadsworth appears in the 1840 Caddo Parish census with three males in the household. The Indian family members were not enumerated.

8. John Herndon appears in the 1840 Caddo Parish census as aged between 40 and 50 years, with three female free persons of color living in his household and with 81 slaves. Herndon appears in the 1850 Caddo Parish census as a 54-year-old planter born in Virginia with 30-year-old Patsy born in Virginia and nine children. Patsy and 12 children are listed in the 1860 Caddo Parish Free Persons of Color census. The online "Herndon History Page" indicates that Herndon petitioned the Caddo Parish Court in 1840 to emancipate his slave Lou Patsy Charles and all of her children.

9. See Note 8 in Letter 19 for biographical information on Hamilton. Hamilton appears in the 1840 Caddo Parish census with one other male in the household.

10. Besides two plantations in Caddo Parish in Louisiana and one at Pecan Point in Texas, Hamilton owned plantations in Miller County, Arkansas, at Little Prairie, and Lost Prairie immediately upstream. A February 3, 1855, Shreveport *Caddo Gazette* estate sale advertisement for his Caddo Parish properties includes over 14,000 acres and nine slaves. It was preceded by an April 1853 hiring out of 60 to 70 field hands by the estate administrator. A "Hamilton's Farm" appears immediately east of Herndon in Section 8 of the U.S. General Land Office survey. plat for T21N R14W. A home has been designated for Hamilton in Figure 5 on high land owned by him.

11. Left side of the boat facing forward, now replaced by the term port.

12. This was a commercial woodpile, which was the primary source of fuel for steamboats.

16 ✦ To the Raft

Having entered the Red River, the *Relief* proceeded immediately downstream to the raft. Withenbury was reminded by Ross of a bear story connected with another trip to the head of the raft.

⁂

[First part not used.]

I sat down to pen this article after having had a conversation with "Uncle Joe," to-day, on the subject of Red River reminiscences, and he reminded me that I had not yet told his best Red River bear story; and so my readers must bear with me while I try to tell a long story with a few words. "Uncle Joe" has told this story himself a good many times, and never yet had an audience where, if a vote had been taken, the majority would not have been largely against a belief in its truthfulness; and now I want it understood that my version of the affair I am about to relate, if not in his exact words, is intended as a full endorsement of Captain Ross' bear story.

The last account I gave of the Relief was on the night of January 1, 1842, when I left her lying in Red River opposite the mouth of Red Bayou. From this point her first move was down stream twenty-five miles to the head of the Raft, *alias* the "Dead Fall," George Alban's headquarters, (not his "Gut.") At this point we were sometimes delayed many days, waiting for the arrival of boats at the foot of the Raft from New Orleans, for from those boats we got our up freights. On one occasion while waiting there, some of our crew in their rambles discovered the tracks of an immense bear, where he was in the habit of coming down to the river to drink. Several efforts were made, by watching through the entire night, to get a shot at the old fellow, but he was too "keen on the scent" for us, and all our schemes failed.

Finally Captain Ross thought of a plan to capture bruin with whisky; and whether the idea of getting him drunk was original with "Uncle Joe," I will not attempt to decide; but that a part of the appliances for the capture of his bearship were of his sole invention, I will bear full testimony. He took an empty mackerel kit,[1] and after washing it thoroughly, filled it with honey in the comb, and then poured hot whisky over it to the full capacity of the kit; and after mixing it in the most approved manner known in those primitive days, we carried it to the place (a mile, at least) where the bear came to drink, and placed it on a drift pile just at the water's edge. Here the bear always came, and at this precise spot he drank every morning just before the break of day. We ascertained this fact by rubbing out his tracks on the sand-bar, and finding them renewed in the same spot on several succeeding mornings.

We took our positions at a respectful distance from the bear trap, and from midnight to near daylight we kept silent. Every man of us was provided with some sort of weapon, except "Uncle Joe," and he had provided himself with a trace chain and a long rope for a lasso, determined, if the bear took all the toddy and got drunk, to capture him alive and take him to the boat.

Just as day began to break we were rewarded for our long watchfulness by hearing a splashing in the water, and very soon after such an unearthly howling as nothing but a bear (and a drunken one at that) could make. We hastened to the spot, and by this time it was good daylight, and there was our bear "as drunk as a beast." He seemed to realize fully the situation, but was totally unable to help himself, and "Uncle Joe" forbade any man to harm him until he had made an effort to put the chain around his neck. This, with a little help, he soon accomplished; and then we all took hold of the rope with a will, and we soon had our prisoner on a smooth sand-bar, where we all had fair play. We found him too heavy in his dead drunk condition to manage; and while we were laying our plans for getting him to the boat he began to show signs of returning consciousness. So we made our rope fast to a tree and waited for the old fellow to recover sufficiently to show fight. He was not long in getting upon his feet; and when he found he was a prisoner, his antics were such as no pen can describe, nor can any other man do it like "Uncle Joe Ross." The more the effect of the whisky wore off, the more savage became the bear; and we began to fear for the strength of the rope; and so the order was given to shoot him; and quicker than I can tell it, a half dozen or more bullets were buried in his carcass, and every one of us had shot a bear. We had bear meat till we were surfeited with it; and for many a day the capture of a bear weighing 378 pounds, in this original manner, was the biggest yarn we could tell among ourselves or to the wandering, unbelieving OUTSIDER.

Notes

1. A small wooden tub. Mackerel, salmon, herring, and cod were sold in barrels, half barrels, quarter barrels, kits, and half kits, as indicated by many advertisements by grocery merchants in period newspapers.

17 ✦ To Pine Prairie

The *Relief* headed upriver from the raft with the mouth of the Kiamichi River as the ultimate destination, stopping in this letter at White Oak Shoals; Nunnely's Landing in Sevier County (now Little River County), Arkansas; Scott's Landing in Bowie County, Texas; and Pine Prairie in Sevier County. This placed the *Relief* well to the west of Fulton, with no mention of a host of intermediate landings from the raft up. The features mentioned in the upstream and downstream movements of the *Relief* above White Oak Shoals are shown in Figures 6 and 7.

White Oak Shoals was located three miles by land and five miles by water east of the point at which the Texas line strikes the Red River.[1] The term refers to the shoals themselves and to the adjacent landing and settlement in what is now Little River County. With a rock and gravel bottom, the shoals were the first place on the upper river that was suitable for fording.[2] It was used for that purpose long before settlers arrived, including probably by the De Soto expedition.[3] The shoals were the major navigation impediment on the Upper Red River. The landing, which apparently was operated by Jesse McLendon,[4] had been a keelboat landing and was a major steamboat landing, often as far as boats could get in moving upstream. The shoals can be seen today south of the small community of Temple, Arkansas, which is east of Ogden.

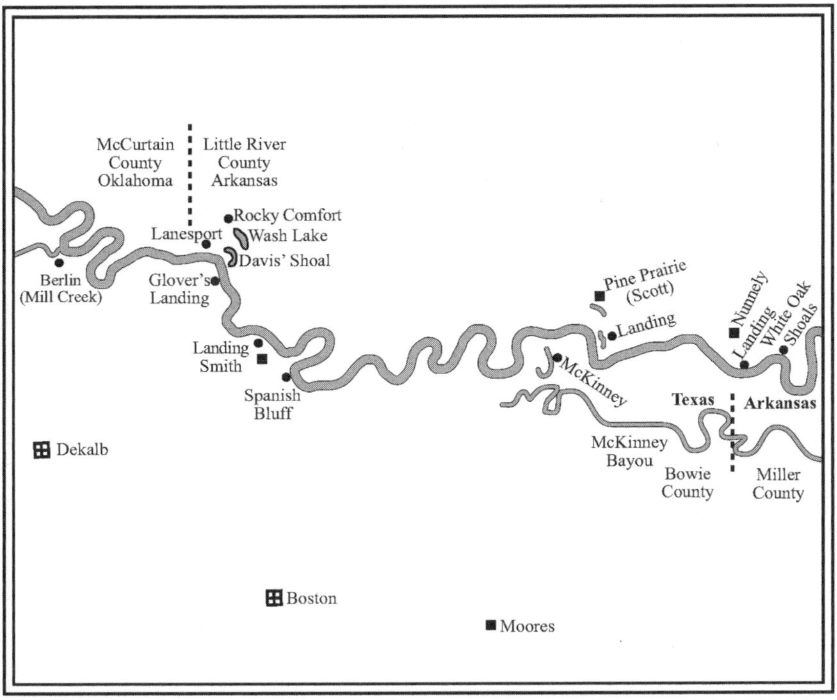

FIGURE 6: ABOVE THE WHITE OAK SHOALS 1

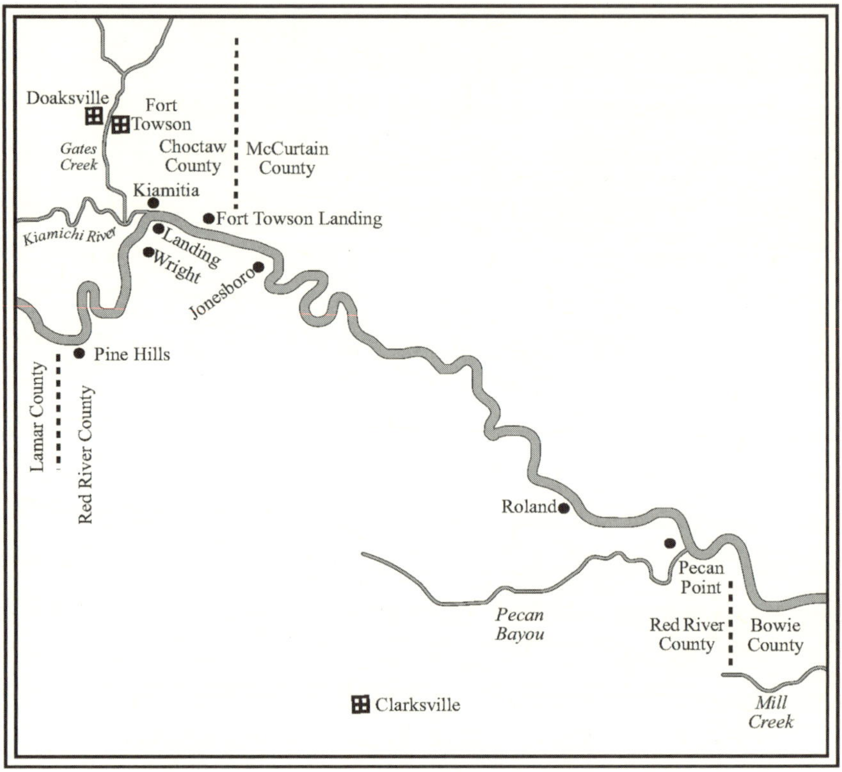

FIGURE 7: ABOVE THE WHITE OAK SHOALS 2

⁂

[First part not used.]

Now, let me return to my old friends, Captains Crooks and Ross, and say a few words concerning the kind of work they were called upon to do in 1842. On the first trip of the Relief, from the Raft to Fort Towson, we found ourselves at the "White Oak Shoals" on the 7th day of January, five days out and only two hundred miles on our way. Here we remained five days waiting for a rise; and true to his instincts Captain Ross, notwithstanding his pockets were being depleted every day, bade us do our best towards passing the time pleasantly, keeping at all times men enough on the boat to see that she was properly cared for, and to entertain the old and new friends who came almost hourly to see and welcome us and to enjoy the novelty of a visit and a dinner, or some little amusement on board a steamboat.

On the second day of our stay at White Oak Shoals, our friends arranged for a grand bear hunt; and when I mention among these friends the names of Andy Armstrong,[5] the Owens Brothers,[6] Captain Grey, Colonel Childress,[7] Tom Scott,[8] and the famous Arkansas bear-hunter, "Old Bill Story,"[9] no one now living who knew those men, or who has since heard of them, will doubt for a moment that we had a good time in the cane brake, on the boat, and at the homes of these hospitable people. The bear hunt itself was a source of great sport at the time, and the details of it, could I enter into them here, would not, I am sure, be the least entertaining of my roving reminiscences. But for the present I must try to confine myself to "business statistics," and trust to the opportunity hereafter of reciting some of the amusing incidents of our Arkansas bear hunt.[10]

After leaving White Oak Shoals, our first landing was at Squire Nunnaly's.[11] We had no special business there, but it would never do to pass the "Old Squire" by without stopping, nor were we in the least inclined to do so, for those who had heard him before desired to hear again the heartfelt, honest greeting of this good man: "God bless you all, gentlemen;" and to those of us who now saw him for the first time, no words could have had a more cheering sound than his welcome extended to us all on meeting us, and his earnest benediction, "Peace and happiness attend you all, gentlemen," as we were leaving his hospitable plantation.

Our next landing was at "Scott's," on the Texas side.[12] Here we were required to take on board two hundred and fifty barrels of corn in the ear, to carry up to another plantation, some forty miles. Next we came to "Pine Prairie,"[13] on the Arkansas side. Here we took a few thousand feet of green pine lumber to carry to "Spanish Bluffs," some forty or fifty miles further up, on the Texas side. These little jobs—the corn and the lumber—were not considered, in those days, as belonging to the regular business of steamboating for pay, and we were expected to do them as one neighbor accommodates another by the loan of his ox team and a nigger to drive, and to expect, in return, the hospitality of the whole people at any plantation or neighborhood where we might chance to be detained, and also all the patronage in the way of legitimate freights up and down, when the time arrived for them. So it will be seen that we had much to do that, in these days, would be called thankless work, but, at the time I am writing of, that kind of work seemed necessary; and, where the spirit of kindness prevailed as it did there, the whole community (if I except a few like old Bob Hamilton,) the effect of one kind act willingly performed on the part of planter or steamboatman was to make the *entente cordiale*[14]—as the Picayune would say—"run smooth and regular through the whole season."

In those days a steamboat's expenses were comparatively very trifling. Pilot's wages above the raft were fifty dollars per month (one man (Cox) got sixty dollars); below the raft, to New Orleans, from seventy-five to one hundred dollars per month.[15] Then pilots could afford to work for reasonable wages, for they had none but legitimate expenses, while now pilots who have been born since 1842 are clamorous for five hundred dollars and upward per month, because of the expense of living, &c. So it can be easily seen how when a little boat is caught out on a long trip the pilot's wages will amount to nearly or quite all the freight earned on the cotton she can carry out. Other expenses of the boats in those early days were correspondingly small also. Deck hands and firemen $15 to $18 per month, mate[16] and carpenter (both duties performed by one man) $35 per month, engineers $50 and $30. Ask Bird Holabird what he got for second engineer's wages on Red River in 1845, and he will tell you $25.

On the Relief, in 1842, we had for cook Ed. Lane,[17] afterward one of the best pilots on the Ohio and Cumberland Rivers. His wages was $20 per month and no "slush," nor did he "carry a second."[18] But as poor Ed. is now dead and gone, I will not tell any more tales about him, but let all his faults lie silent in the grave with his virtues and himself.

I feel that I must now beg pardon for having spun this yarn out to this unreasonable length, without having finished a single trip. But I will promise, in my next, to take the Relief to her upward destination, the mouth of the Kiamitia River, in the Choctaw nation,[19] and back to the Raft, and show that notwithstanding we were thirty-four days out, and our trip a profitless one, pecuniarily considered, we were not without hope of future reward, nor had we the least doubt of the steady increase in our stock of friends, for not a man, woman or child has thus far taunted us with the contemptuous name of OUTSIDER.

Notes

1. The only map representation of the shoals appears to be an 1840 survey plat of T14S R42W. The rendition on which the shoals are marked does not appear in the set available from the U.S. General Land Office but can be seen in the 13-CD set "Original General Land Office Survey Notes and Plats for the State of Arkansas 1815–present" prepared by the Arkansas Commissioner of State Lands.

2. On White Oak Shoals, see the brief comments by Dan Flores in *Jefferson and Southwestern Exploration* in connection with the description of the crossing of the shoals provided by the Freeman and Custis Expedition.

3. Use of the shoals as a ford by the De Soto expedition is covered by T. H. Lewis, "Route of De Soto's Expedition from Taliepacana to Hukasene" in the 1902 *Publications of the Mississippi Historical Society.*

4. McLendon was an early settler in the White Oak Shoals area according to the *Biographical and Historical Memoirs of Southern Arkansas.* U.S. General Land Office land records indicate that he owned property immediately west of the shoals on the river and immediately east of the shoals but not on the river. The list of "Landings from Shreveport, La., to Preston, Texas" in *Gardner's New Orleans Directory for 1866* indicates that McClendon's Landing was equivalent to or in the same place as White Oak Shoals. It is probable given the nature of the impediment and the long waits by boats moving upstream and downstream described by Withenbury that there were landing facilities upstream and downstream of the shoals that provided overland portage.

5. U.S. General Land Office land records indicate that Andrew Armstrong was a large early property owner immediately east of White Oak Shoals. On Armstrong, see Letter 32.

6. U.S. General Land Office land records indicate that George, Samuel, and William Owens were large early property owners in the vicinity of White Oak Shoals. Owens' field, which was owned jointly by George and William, fronts the river at the shoals in the survey plat map.

7. Probably John Childers, who appears in the 1840 Sevier County census.

8. On Tom Scott, see Letter 32.

9. William Story appears in the 1830 Sevier County census, owned property about 40 miles northwest of White Oak Shoals according to U.S. General Land Office land records, and was known as the Davy Crocket of Arkansas according to the *Biographical and Historical Memoirs of Southern Arkansas.*

10. Withenbury doesn't do this.

11. On Nunnely's Landing, see Letter 34.

12. In northeast Bowie County, with the precise location unknown.

13. On Pine Prairie, see Letter 31.

14. A friendly relationship between parties.

15. These numbers should be multiplied by 20 to provide present-day equivalents.

16. The mate was in charge of movement of freight by the deck hands.

17. Corrected to LaRue in next letter (not used).

18. There was no second cook.

19. Withenbury doesn't accomplish this until four letters hence.

18 ✦ To Berlin

The *Relief* dropped off a load at Spanish Bluff in north-central Bowie County, Texas; landed at Lanesport in then Sevier County (now Little River County), Arkansas, just before the Choctaw line (the Indian Territory line, now the Oklahoma line); and proceeded to Berlin in northwest Bowie County. Most of the letter is concerned with the building of the first steamboat in Texas at Berlin.

Berlin was a small community on the south side of Mill Creek at its entrance into the Red River, as shown on Jacob De Cordova's 1867 *Map of the State of Texas* and, more precisely, on the Texas General Land Office's 1841 map of Bowie County. It is first mentioned as a town site in a November 1838 document referenced in *Poor v. Boyce* (in *Reports of Cases Argued and Decided in the Supreme Court of the State of Texas at Tyler Term, 1854*). Town lots were sold in Berlin by at least 1853, as shown in the 1853 Red River County tax rolls. It was established on the basis of a preexisting settlement called Mill Creek, which had been a keelboat landing. As Withenbury suggests in the next letter, the terms Berlin and Mill Creek were equivalent, with the latter being the preferred term for this important landing in newspaper accounts of boat movements. The community was within the headright of John Dyer, but much of the land in the area was owned by William Boyce.

⁂

[First part not used.]

After unloading our lumber at Spanish Bluffs,[1] we made an early start on Saturday morning, January 15, and in about two hours we landed at Lanesport,[2] a little town on the Arkansas side, about a mile below the Choctaw line. Here we found an apparently thrifty community of merchants. They enjoyed a lively trade with the Choctaws,[3] in groceries generally and in whisky particularly, for not withstanding the article was contraband in "the Nation," "Lo, the poor Indian," found it a not very difficult task to smuggle it.

Our next landing, after leaving Lanesport, was at the little Texas town of Berlin,[4] at the mouth of Mill Creek. Here were a few stores scattered, without much order, over a beautiful high prairie, which, stretching away from the river bank for a mile or more, showed us one of the finest cultivated plantations we had yet seen. This entire tract was owned by Dr. Wm. H. Boyce,[5] a Tennessean, and I only wish I had time and space to portray this genial gentleman and his surroundings to my readers; but I must leave Berlin after noting one important fact in its short lived history. Here was being built "the first steamboat ever built in Texas." [6] I made a hurried examination of her as she lay upon the stocks.

I was told by General John H. Dyer,[7] the enterprising projector of steamboat building in Texas, that the Republic had offered a bounty of land and money to a considerable amount for every steamboat which should be built in Texas, and he had conceived the idea of benefiting the country and enriching himself at the same time by this undertaking; and as the Mariner had been providentially (for him) sunk at Pecan Point only a few miles distant the year previous, he had bought her wreck for the engine, and he hoped to be thus enabled to produce a steamboat without much difficulty. [8] General Dyer was a visionary and hopeful man; but before his boat was ready for business he was sadly in need of the forthcoming bounty money promised by the Republic.

The boss ship carpenter was one David Young, who then lived at Lanesport, but who professed to have learned his trade at some one of our ship yards in Fulton.[9] The model of this boat was certainly peculiar, to say the least, but I won't stop to describe it, for my story would not be believed were I to do so.[10] Suffice it to say, that by the perseverance of "David Young under difficulties," and the valuable assistance of Samuel Applegate (then a merchant of Fulton, Arkansas[11]), in putting up the engine, the Texas Planter[12] was launched and finished, at a cost of all that General Dyer was worth, in addition to the bounty received by him from the ungrateful Republic. The country ought to have rewarded him more liberally,[13] for it was but little trouble for the Government to manufacture as much currency as would have fully paid every man who had a hand in the job.

On starting the Texas Planter on her first trip, General Dyer (now promoted to Steamboat Captain) called to his aid the veritable Jim Gamble, who acted as pilot and sub-captain. Jim submitted to the indignity of "sub," as he declared, only for the trip to New Orleans, for he intended to "have another boat for the trade, if there was one to be had." Samuel Applegate, tired of his fruitless efforts to get rich at merchandising in Arkansas, took this opportunity of returning to his old place at the throttle valve, and he never quit steamboating again until the "Confederate authorities" took the John Walsh from him and sunk her in the Yazoo to keep her out of the hands of the Yankees, during the late difficulty[14] in the South. His career was a progressive one, in the Red River and Ouachita trades, from the time he quit the Texas Planter, in 1842. [Part of paragraph not used.] I have been drawn very far out of the channel where the Relief was gliding along toward Fort Towson, and I must close without even "letting go her lines," at Berlin; and I have no apology to make to my readers, and can only urge as an excuse for this greatest of my digressions, my uncontrollable propensity to tell all I know concerning myself and every other OUTSIDER.

Notes

1. On Spanish Bluff, see Letter 29.

2. On Lanesport, see Letter 29.

3. This, and later letters concerning the Texas landings, indicate that much of the trade of the upper landings was with the Choctaw Nation, which occupied the eastern portion of the Indian Territory.

4. A post office was established at the mouth of Mill Creek in 1851, but under the name Mill Creek rather than Berlin (see "Post Offices in New First Congressional District, Texas, 1968").

5. William Boyce is shown in the 1860 census for Red River County as a 57-year-old farmer born in North Carolina with a wife and five children. Although county maps show his headright at a substantial distance downstream of Mill Creek, Texas General Land Office land records indicate that he acquired his brother Jesse's headright in the Mill Creek area by inheritance in 1838 and two other headrights nearby by purchase in the early 1850s. The "United States Census (Slave Schedule), 1850" (available through FamilySearch.org) indicates that he owned 82 slaves.

6. Charles DeMorse in the September 10, 1842, Clarksville *Northern Standard* thought the first steamboat might have been built a few months before by McKinney & Williams for navigation on the Brazos River.

7. According to Texas General Land Office land records, John Dyer came to Texas in 1834 and was granted three parcels of land in the Mill Creek area, the first in 1838 and two in later years as a result of his subsequent marriage and prior service in the Army of the Republic of Texas from May 20, 1836, to November 20, 1836. The Congress of the Republic appointed him Brigadier General of the Texas Militia 4th Brigade in 1837. Headquartered in Clarksville and covering the area from the Sabine River to the Red River, this was one of four voluntary groups formed to combat Indian depredations. In this capacity, he participated in General Thomas Rusk's 1838–1839 Three Forks Expedition. On Dyer's militia activities, see Stephen Moore's *Savage Frontier*. The Dickson genealogy (*Dickson of Ireland and North Carolina*) indicates that Dyer was born

on July 19, 1809, and died on March 25, 1845, which is compatible with his absence from the 1850 census.

8. Steamboat building was not extensive in the South and usually involved hull construction and use of an engine from a wrecked boat because the requisite metal working skills and materials were lacking.

9. The Fulton shipyards were on the east side of Cincinnati near the river, with the first steamboat built in 1816.

10. The boat was described by the Shreveport *Caddo Gazette*, as quoted by the June 15, 1843, Clarksville *Northern Standard*: "A strange looking steam craft touched at our landing on yesterday morning. We do not know her name, as no marks nor brands were perceivable—she was built, we understand, up in Texas, and considering her place of birth, is not to be sneezed at. Though born in the backwoods, she has adopted the fashion peculiar to the white *ladies* of the present day—she carries a very broad *stern*."

11. Sam Applegate had been a steamboat engineer (in charge of the boat's machinery) and was then in a receiving, forwarding, and commission and dry goods and groceries business with Searing Marsh in the firm of Marsh & Applegate in Fulton, with the firm dissolved in September 1841 according to the November 3, 1841, *Washington Telegraph*.

12. The official name of this boat was the *Red River Planter*, which was advertised by Dyer at Berlin in the September 3, 1842, Clarksville *Northern Standard*, saying that she had the capacity to carry 600 bales of cotton.

13. Dyer published a Notice to Creditors in the March 2, 1844, Clarksville *Northern Standard* saying that he would file for bankruptcy at the end of the month.

14. A common name for the Civil War.

19 ✦ To Jonesboro

As this letter began, the *Relief* was still at Berlin, and Withenbury recounted the story of a load of salt that the *Relief* had left at Berlin on her last trip up in 1841. The *Relief* then proceeded to Pecan Point in northeast Red River

County, Texas; Roland in northeast Red River County; and Jonesboro in northwest Red River County.

Pecan Point[1] was located on the north side of the mouth of Pecan Bayou. It had been a keelboat landing and was a steamboat landing of moderate importance, restricted in its capacity for expansion by Roland a short distance upstream. The name referred to the landing and to the adjacent plantation and was derived from a large pecan grove at the mouth of the bayou that pre-existed settlement. Until old Miller County Arkansas was dissolved in 1825, the term was used to refer to settlement on both sides of the river, which began in 1816. The plantation lands were acquired by Jacob Black in 1825 and sold to Robert Hamilton in 1835.

Roland[2] was located in the headright of Roland T. Bryarly. It had been a keelboat landing and (along with Fulton and Wright's Landing) was among the most important landings on the Upper Red River. It was an import and export point for Clarksville (14 miles to the southwest), but also a regional collecting point for cotton and a regional distribution point for up-freights; and half of its trade, as Withenbury indicates, was with the Choctaw Nation. It was located on the inside of a bend that was cut off from the river in 1875 after Withenbury was writing and was replaced by Mound City.

⁂

While the Relief was lying at Mill Creek (Berlin), Captain Ross bethought himself of this favorable opportunity to look up some of his last season's patrons, who, when he last saw them, were slightly in arrears; and as some few of the founders of Berlin who, in the beginning, were supposed to be reliable and "come to stay," were nowhere to be found at this time, "Uncle Joe" wisely took time to make a general settlement, which consumed all that remained of daylight, and we were consequently quartered here for the night; for in those early times there was but little night-work[3] done by steamboats on upper Red River.

It seemed that last year the Relief had on her last trip up about 150 sacks of salt on speculation, [4] fifty of which Capt. Ross had left at Berlin to be disposed of to the people as their needs might require. The party with whom this salt was deposited had "picked up his traps" and left the country, leaving the bulk of about thirty sacks of the aforesaid salt, simply because he could not carry it along, and General Dyer knowing that the salt belonged to the Relief took it into his possession, thus constituting himself her agent for the time, until she should show herself again. "Uncle Joe," when he was taken to General Dyer's warehouse, and his eye fell upon the pile of salt lying in one corner, with but here and there a fragment of the sacks visible, broke out with one of his peculiar ejaculations: "Well, I'll be dod durned if that salt ever was any account, nobody could ever save his bacon with that." General Dyer asked, "Why so?" "Why so?" repeated Uncle Joe, "why don't you see it couldn't even save the sacks it was put up in." The General then explained that the negroes had broken into the warehouse and stolen the sacks to make into Sunday pantaloons, leaving the salt to take care of itself. Capt. Ross' reply to this explanation was, "that Texas, according to my notion, is a poor place for a fellow to store salt on speculation."

The early part of the night was spent in hunting up empty barrels and boxes to hold the dilapidated salt, and in bringing it on board, for it was unanimously decided to try and find a better market for it farther up the river.

At Berlin there was a ferry established between Texas and the Choctaw Nation. Dr. Boyce held the right on the Texas side, and a half-breed Indian named Garland,[5] on the side of the Choctaws. Garland and his sons, together with a trusty old negro belonging to Dr. Boyce, performed the manual labor of "running the flat," which in high water was done by means of a rope across the river, but at the time I am now speaking of, by long poles and oars. This being one of the principal crossing places, great care was necessary to prevent the introduction of whisky into "the Nation," and the privilege of the ferry was granted specially to Garland because he was known to be temperate. The Choctaw laws were very stringent on the subject of whisky; and on all the public roads a mounted police force, called "Light-horse,"[6] whose duty it was to halt all travelers and make a thorough search for the contraband spirits; and if any was found to confiscate it by breaking the vessel containing it, and "spilling the liquor." One of the best evidences of the fidelity of these guardians of the morals of "the Nation," was the frequent finding by the road side of the remains of broken bottles, jugs, kegs and canteens. Occasionally, however, instead of the broken bottles and the fumes of the whisky rising from the ground, one might come across a drunken "Light-horse," with the bottle in his grasp, empty, but unbroken. As a general thing, however, be it said to their credit, these Indian "Light-horsemen" were of a higher grade, when measured by the true moral standard, than are their more enlightened brethren, known in our large towns as the "Police," or what is worse, "Detectives."

As we were detained at Mill Creek all night, some of our crew out of curiosity found their way by means of the ferry into "the Nation;" and from two little occurrences which took place before daylight, I was inclined to the belief that the bottles which accompanied them over the river were not broken until after the whisky had been "spilled" down the throats of the whole party, including the ferry-man and "Light-horse." About midnight a large fire was seen blazing in the neighborhood of Garland's corn-crib, a few whoops and yells were heard, and the fire and noise died away and all was still again; and when sufficient time had elapsed for the "sober Indians" to arrive at the scene of riot, the drunken ones had either made their escape by crawling into the clumps of bushes on the river bank, or fallen asleep upon the ground; and about the time the galloping of the "Light-horse" was heard approaching the ferry, the flat was seen to shove out from the shore and drift quietly down the river. In a moment the "Light-horse" were at the water's edge and lustily crying out in their native tongue, "*Peni, Peni, Minte, Minte, Tushpa*," which translated into English means, "The boat, the boat, come, come, hurry;" but no response from the boat was heard, nor dare those on board the truant flat dip an oar or pole in the water to guide her over the river; for immediately following the demand for the boat to return was heard the sharp crack from the Light-horseman's pistol, and the whizzing of the bullet as it sped on its harmless way over the heads of the fugitives. Finally, all was still again, and the flickering embers of the burned corn-crib died away into the darkness of the night; and not until the bell of the Relief sounded for all hands at the break of day, did we witness the return of a single member of the party who had been foraging for the first time in the Indian Nation. The ferryboat had been allowed to drift with the current about three miles before those on board dared make the least effort to guide her to the Texas shore, and the rest of the night had been spent in wending their way on foot back to the starting point. The old darkey who had charge of the ferry was one of this party; but fearing detection, as soon as the flat touched the shore, he broke for his cabin, prepared to express his wonder and astonishment at the loss of his boat as soon as daylight should reveal the true and unusual state of things at his ferry landing.

The Relief was under way as soon as it was possible to see the heads of snags which filled the bend above Mill Creek; and we had not gone a mile before a voice was heard in the cane brake on the Choctaw side, crying out in plain English, "Ho, the boat! Land and take me in. Ho, the boat!" We soon came to a little opening in the cane brake, and there stood our bar-keeper, Oliver Ross, who, when the stampede occurred in the approach of the "Light-horse," had darted off by himself and was left in "the Nation," while his comrades all made their escape by the ferry flat into Texas. The poor fellow was almost frozen. We took him on board, but it was a long time before he thawed out sufficient to give an intelligible account of how he had spent the night. His joy at having escaped the "Light-horse," of whom he had a great dread, completely cast into the shade all remembrance of the suffering he had endured; and not until the headache came on, and completely prostrated him, would he admit that he had drank any whisky. His Uncle Joe said, "Well, young man, this ought to be a warning to you, as the old woman said when she found her husband hanging by his neck in the barn, dead; and all I wish is, that the Light-horse had got you, for I'll be dod durned if ever I'd come for you."

But I find myself lingering so long about Mill Creek, that I fear I shall be a long time reaching Fort Towson, and so must hurry along.

The navigation of the river at this time was almost impossible, for in addition to its shallowness in all the "crossings," the snags in many of the bends were so numerous and closely planted that we were many times forced to make fast to one of them and then send out men in the yawl with axes and saws to clear away a place wide enough for the little boat to pass. This caused our progress to be very tedious, and my story need not be doubted when I say that in this whole day's run we only reached Pecan Point, some twenty-five miles. Here we spent another night in Texas, and our men were fully employed until near midnight in procuring wood for the next day's run. We were unable to get quite up to the regular landing, as the night was cloudy and very dark; so we "came to" alongside of a shore sand-bar, or rather on the top of it, where the water was not more than two feet deep, and still we were at least thirty yards from dry land. Over this shoal water our men brought the wood in the yawl, they wading alongside. Some of my readers, I have no doubt, will understand about this mode of wooding a steamboat in a new country; but I doubt if any of them, unless they have been in Upper Red River at a very early day, can say, as we could in truth, that every stick of wood so obtained was cut out of the most beautiful, large and perfect red cedar trees. [7] We knowing the value of such timber at home, felt it almost a sacrilege to destroy it in this worthless manner; but it was abundant, easily cut, light for the men to carry, and burned freely, and accordingly we appropriated it.

Pecan Point Plantation was, and still is, one of the choicest places on Red River. At the time of our visit it was owned by "Old Bob Hamilton," [8] but it has since passed into the hands of Colonel Matthew Watson,[9] of Nashville, Tennessee; and it is a real pleasure to listen to that sensible gentleman while he tells of his success in planting there, since the close of the war and the freeing of the slaves.

There is an immense tract of land here that is above all ordinary overflows, and it is of the most fertile character imaginable. Near the river bank, at the landing place where the buildings are located, are a number of Indian mounds,[10] several of them of great extent, and at least fifty feet in height. Colonel Watson, after purchasing the place, erected a new gin-house, and in order to give it peculiar advantages, he caused a large portion of one of these mounds to be removed; and as his overseer was a man of intelligence, he took great pains to preserve every relic which the workmen unearthed, in the hope that some day, through their agency, a clew might be found which would afford some satisfactory explanation of the mystery that still hangs over these works of human hands, the date of whose existence is to the world yet unknown. Had I the time, I could find enough of interest in the early and subsequent history of Pecan Point, to furnish a full chapter, but my lack of space just now admonishes me that I must hurry along.

About noon, January 17, we reached the little town of Roland, in Red River County, Texas. This place took its name from its founder, Roland T. Brierly,[11] and its importance from the fact of its being the shipping and receiving point for one of the richest portions of Texas, including the thriving village of Clarksville, fourteen miles in the interior. I find it very difficult to pass by this particular locality without making special mention of the names of many of the then prominent planters and merchants of Red River Country, as well of the Choctaw nation directly opposite, and giving also a description of the varied products of the land.

I would like to tell the whole of the romance attending the advent and long life of old John Monkhouse[12] at Roland, but as very much of it runs through some dozen or more years of my later experience on Red River, I must content myself with but a passing notice of the old man's existence in Texas after an eventful early life in England, where he was born, of Scotch parentage.

One of the natural productions of the soil in the region round about Roland, on both sides of the river, was Seneca snake-root,[13] and large quantities of it were for many years annually shipped from the little town to New Orleans.[14] A Mr. Davis[15] had erected a press near the river bank, where he pressed it in bales like cotton bales, weighing from 300 to 450 pounds each. The gathering of this snake-root was the principal livelihood of the poorer class of whites on the Texas side, and of the Indians,[16] who had a little settlement of their own about one mile above Roland.

Fully one-half of the trade of the three merchants[17] of Roland was with the Choctaws, some of whom were continually upon the river bank through the day and often till a late hour in the night, crying, "Peni Minte," (bring over the boat.) I need not, perhaps, say that the principal inducement for the Choctaws to gather snake-root was to exchange it for whisky. The "Light-horse" could not prevent them from crossing over to Texas, nor from smuggling "Huki Humi" (whisky) into the nation inside their own skins; consequently, many a "poor Indian" who crossed over to Roland sober, with snake-root on his back, came back to his forest home with "snakes in his hat;" and the demoralizing effect of the trade with Roland, as far as the Indians were concerned, was far out of proportion to its benefits. But Davis and Brierly made money.

We had made but ten miles above Roland when night overtook us, and on this occasion we wooded off Choctaw territory, and had several visitors, among them the "Light-horse." He very promptly informed the bar-keeper that, while lying on the Nation side, the bar must be closed. This officer had visited the boat at Roland, and well knowing that we would not go a great distance before nightfall, he had followed us (in the line of duty, of course);

but he had tasted the quality of Oliver's whisky at Roland, and remembered it too well to allow the taste to get out entirely of his mouth while we were on his beat. It strikes me he was not very unlike his white brethren of the police force in these days.

On the 18th we made an early start, hoping to reach Jonesboro, Texas, before dark; but we spent too much of the day cutting snags out of the way and in pulling over sand-bars, and night found us snugly tied to a snag in the middle of the stream, four miles below the town. Here was no opportunity to wood, or for Oliver to sell whisky, so we amused ourselves as best we could until bed time.

By the hardest kind of work we reached Jonesboro a little after dark on the 19th, having accomplished but four miles that day. This place is six miles below the Fort Towson landing; and as Jonesboro figured conspicuously among Red River towns in those days, I am inclined, before leaving it, to enter more minutely into a description of it than the limits of this chapter will allow. So I must ask the reader's indulgence once more before I finish this perplexing trip of "Uncle Joe's" Relief, and reserve for my next a description of the reception which "Uncle Sam's boys in blue"[18] and the full-blood and "half-breed" Choctaws tendered, on our arrival, to the OUTSIDER.

Notes

1. See the articles on "Pecan Point," "Pecan Point Plantation," and "Pecan Point, Texas" in the *Handbook of Texas Online*. John Sibley in his 1805 "Account of the Red River and Country Adjacent" describes the pre-settlement condition as "a beautiful grove of pecans, intermixed with no other growth" on the left side of the river going upstream. There do not appear to be any map representations of the settlement in Texas, which is compatible with what is known about its dimensions. The Texas General Land Office's 1856 map of Red River County provides a good representation of the configuration of the point and Jacob Black's headright within it.

2. The location of Roland is shown in Jacob De Cordova's 1867 *Map of the State of Texas* and, more precisely, in the Texas General Land Office's 1856 map of Red River County. It is mentioned briefly in the article on "Clarksville" in the

Handbook of Texas Online and in books on Clarksville and Red River County; but the only effort at systematic coverage is provided by Mark Morrow in the online "Roland Thornton Bryarly" (part of the "Find a Grave" series). Morrow includes a document concerning a November 1838 purchase through Bryarly of bacon for supplying troops of the 4th Brigade under General Dyer. Morrow also indicates that Roland was laid out as a town with streets. This is confirmed by the Red River County tax rolls, which indicate that taxes were assessed for town lots in Roland beginning in at least 1846. Mound City is shown in the Texas General Land Office's 1879 map of Red River County.

3. Steamboats tried to operate constantly to maximize profit, and travel and freight movements at night were common.

4. Ross had purchased the salt, intending to sell it at a profit.

5. Samuel Garland was the Choctaw Chief from 1862 to 1864. He was born in Mississippi in 1803 of mixed parentage and came to the Indian Territory in 1833, where he established a plantation home a few miles northeast of present-day Tom, Oklahoma, and operated a store and cotton gin, as well as cultivating extensive Red River bottomlands in cotton with 13 slaves according to the 1860 Choctaw Nation Slave Schedule. Tom is located a few miles northeast of the place at which the ferry crossed. Although there is no direct evidence linking Garland to the ferry, he had the requisite status to be granted operation and the apparent qualification of temperance, being a devout Presbyterian and Mason and considered a man of high character. On Garland, see John Meserve, "Chief George Hudson and Chief Samuel Garland," *Chronicles of Oklahoma*, March 1942; Kenny Franks, *Oklahoma, The Land and Its People*; and the Oklahoma Historical Society's "Notes and Comments: Restoration of the Old Garland Plantation Cemetery," *Chronicles of Oklahoma*, Vol. 36, No. 3, 1958.

6. This mounted police force originated in 1820 in the Choctaw's Mississippi homeland. The Chickasaw had a similar organization. See Carolyn Foreman, "The Light-Horse in the Indian Territory," *Chronicles of Oklahoma*, January 1956.

7. John Sibley in his 1805 "Account of the Red River and Country Adjacent" describes a stand above Little Prairie and below Little River where "the cedar begins on both sides, and is the principal growth on the wide, rich river bottom, for forty miles. In all the world there is scarcely to be found a more beautiful growth of cedar timber; they, like the cedars of Libanus, are large, lofty, and straight."

8. According to an article on Robert Hamilton in the *Handbook of Texas Online*, he was born in Scotland in about 1781, came to the United States in 1807 (Granville County, North Carolina), moved to Texas in 1834, signed the Texas Declaration of Independence (considered the wealthiest person to do so), was appointed in March 1836 (with George Childress) to go to Washington to seek recognition for the new Republic, was appointed chief justice (but apparently not confirmed) of Red River County in 1836, and died in 1845 in New Jersey. Hamilton appears in the 1840 Red River County tax rolls with 66

slaves. A succession notice for Hamilton (with William F. Hamilton as executor) appears in the February 4, 1846, Clarksville *Northern Standard.* A January 8, 1859, Clarksville *Standard* advertisement for the sale of his Texas properties includes the 1,500-acre Pecan Point plantation (640 acres under cultivation), 74 slaves, 7,387 unimproved adjacent acres, and 1,476 acres in Cass County (the latter of which was his headright according to the advertisement and confirmed by Texas General Land Office land records).

9. The January 8, 1859, Clarksville *Standard* advertisement for the sale of Hamilton's Texas properties was signed by Mathew Watson as administrator. The February 22, 1859, Galveston *Civilian and Gazette* reports that the Pecan Point plantation was sold for $106,000, with the land acquired by Mathew Watson. Bowie County and Arkansas planters purchased 30 of the slaves, with the rest purchased by Watson. Watson was assessed on these properties, including 40 slaves, in the 1859 Red River County tax rolls.

10. The mounds were built by a Caddoan Natchitoch group that occupied the site in the late 1600s according to Dan Flores in *Jefferson and Southwestern Exploration.*

11. Texas General Land Office land records indicate that Bryarly came to Texas in 1837. He does not appear in the 1850 or 1860 censuses of Red River County. Mark Morrow in "Roland Thornton Bryarly" indicates that he was born in 1813, never married, and died in 1866. Bryarly began advertising in November 1848 in the Clarksville *Northern Standard* as a dry goods and groceries and receiving and forwarding merchant (which meant that he had a store for the sale of goods and a warehouse for the storage of merchandise that he received and forwarded for others) and began advertising in December 1853 that he sold merchandise on commission for others. Bryarly is listed in the 1841 Red River County tax rolls with 4,140 acres.

12. John Monkhouse's headright was in the Pecan Bayou area southeast of the Bryarly headright. Texas General Land Office land records indicate that Monkhouse came to Texas in 1838. He appears in the Red River County tax rolls in 1842 with five town lots (location not given), in 1844 with sales of merchandise, and in 1846 and 1847 with six lots in Roland. An advertisement in the September 30, 1848, Clarksville *Northern Standard* for the sale of 500 sacks of salt by Monkhouse at Roland indicates that he was a dry goods and groceries merchant. Advertisements by New Orleans commission merchants Taylor & Woodland in the July 5, 1845, *Northern Standard* and by Hamilton, M'Kinder & Co. in the January 7, 1846, issue using Monkhouse at Roland as a reference indicate that he was also in the receiving and forwarding business with an emphasis on cotton. His headstone in the Old Rowland Cemetery indicates that he was born in 1792 and died in 1849. At his death, operation of the facilities passed to his wife, Anne Edwards Monkhouse, as indicated by the 1850 tax rolls and a September 24, 1853, *Northern Standard* advertisement for sale of

unclaimed goods at her warehouse in Roland. Anne Monkhouse (35, born in England) is listed in the 1850 Red River County census with five children and an overseer (for her agricultural operations). Her headstone in the Old Rowland Cemetery indicates that she was born in 1818 and died in 1863.

13. Thought to cure snake bites and with other curative effects. For an early scientific perspective on snakeroot, see Jacob Bigelow's 1817 *American Medical Botany.*

14. The navigation columns in the Shreveport newspapers indicate that snakeroot was an important export commodity from the Upper Red River.

15. John H. Davis had a headright immediately west of Bryarly, with Texas General Land Office records indicating that he came to Texas in 1837. A letter by Edward West, sheriff of Red River County, dated Clarksvillle, July 20, 1841, in volume 2 of the *Texas Treasury Papers* mentions John H. Davis at Roland. A succession notice by William W. Davis in the December 2, 1843, Clarksville *Northern Standard* indicates that John Davis had died. Roland Bryarly published a succession notice for John and William in the May 27, 1846, *Northern Standard* indicating that he was administrator of all of their properties.

16. The Superintendent of Schools continues to report snakeroot gathering as a primary economic activity in the 1899 *Report of the United States Indian Inspector for the Indian Territory.*

17. These were Davis, Bryarly, and Monkhouse.

18. The troops at Fort Towson.

20 ✦ To Fort Towson Landing

Most of this letter is concerned with people and events in the vicinity of Jonesboro; but the beginning of the letter reverts back to the previous night when the *Relief* was tied up four miles below Jonesboro and to an event on the way to Jonesboro. At the end of the letter, the *Relief* dropped off freight at the Fort Towson landing on Red River in the

Indian Territory and had gone a short distance upstream, but failed by a mile and a half to reach its intended destination at the mouth of the Kiamichi River.

Jonesboro[1] was in northwest Red River County about 12 river miles from the mouth of the Kiamichi River. It had been a keelboat landing and was an important steamboat landing until the early 1840s, with a Texas trade and a Fort Towson trade secured by a road that ran directly northwest from Jonesboro to the fort. Settlement began in 1815 and increased substantially in the 1820s. Jonesboro became the county seat of Miller County in 1832 when the county was on the south side of Red River in Texas. George Wright, James Johnston, and William Harrison were among the merchants. The town was incorporated in 1837, but in a state of decline by the early 1840s, exacerbated by the great flood on the Red River in early 1843, which shifted the river a mile to the north. Although the settlement never recovered, Jonesboro continued to be shown on maps and mentioned occasionally in newspaper accounts of boat movements through the early 1870s. The site is presently occupied by the town of Davenport.

Fort Towson[2] was six miles from the Red River on the east side of Gates Creek, which enters the Kiamichi shortly before the Kiamichi enters the Red. Gates Creek and the Kiamichi were not navigable for steamboats. The fort's landing was to the south and slightly east on the Red, about three river miles from the mouth of the Kiamichi and, according to the next letter, had two log warehouses. It had

been a keelboat landing and was among the most important steamboat landings on the Upper Red River until the fort was abandoned in 1851, after which the landing was mentioned occasionally through 1859 in newspaper accounts of boat movements.

⁂

I find that I hurried a little too much in reaching Jonesboro with the Relief at dark on the 19th of January, 1842. It would hardly seem that I hurried very much, however, as we only made four miles in the whole day; but I mean that I hurried with my narrative and left unrecorded one or two little incidents which seem to me now to be necessary to complete the tale of that tiresome day's travel.

As I have already stated, we lay all the preceding night tied to a snag in the middle of the river, and we were thus cut entirely off from any opportunity we might have otherwise had for sports on shore. Sometimes, while lying by of nights, our hunters (and we had three of them among our crew) would spend a portion of the night "fire-hunting"[3] for deer, and we were thus well nigh kept in fresh provisions for the entire trip. Fire-hunting was the favorite mode of capturing deer all through that part of the country, and I may safely say that not a plantation did we stop at where there was a lack of "fire-pans" and guns of all descriptions, and any number of expert huntsmen to show us to the favored spots where the deer were sure to be found, and they were always ready and glad to entertain those of us who preferred this outdoor sport to an evening's amusement on board the boat. Captain Jonathan Hildreth, who on this memorable trip was our principal pilot, was also our chief hunter, and I have many times thought that his presence among us after Mr. Bale left[4] should be regarded in the light of a "special providence," for without him and his old "Derringer" rifle[5] we must have made a good many meals without meat.

On the next day's run before reaching Jonesboro, Ed. LaRue, the cook, gave us notice that the fresh meat was so nigh exhausted that the deck crew alone could have meat for dinner. Just as he announced this unwelcome state of affairs a single wild goose was seen to alight in the river, directly ahead of the boat, and so far away as not to seem in the least alarmed, and with his head turned up stream he quietly pushed on in advance of us. Captain Hildreth was at the wheel, but he sent for his partner, Philley, to relieve him while he went for his rifle. "Uncle Joe" gave the word to the engineer to run her very slow so that the escapement of steam from the engine could scarcely be heard, and in this cautious manner we conducted this "wild goose chase," until a sudden bend in the river hid the bird entirely from our view. Taking advantage of this, Captain Ross ordered the engineer to "give her a few licks ahead strong, and then stop her," (no engine bells were rung,) and by this maneuver we gained some fifty yards on our game; and by the time we came in sight of him again, Captain Hildreth was ready, standing, with his rifle in hand, on the extreme forward part of the hurricane roof,[6] and although the distance was unreasonably great, quicker than I can write it, the "click of the lock" was heard, the goose essayed to raise its wings, but the effort was spasmodic and fruitless, and in an instant his head fell and we knew that we were "all right on the goose," and he was our meat. No one who in those days knew Captain Hildreth (and there were a great many who did now living in this city) will doubt me when I say that the little fellow strutted with more than his usual air of self conceit for a full day after this achievement. And we gladly accorded him full credit for the extraordinary good shot by which he captured one "bird of passage," and the whole boat's company were assured of a good dinner, which at this time was as truly a "God-send" to us as was the manna to the starving Children of Israel in the wilderness.

Before I forget another of Captain Hildreth's exploits, I must mention that on the same day, when about a mile below Jonesboro, we saw in the distance a large white bird moving slowly along the margin of a sand-bar. Captain Hildreth got his rifle in readiness once more, and, with wonderful assurance, (such as he knew right well how to assume,) he took his position between the chimneys, and asked Captain Ross to "have her run slow, and sneak up on him a little." But "Uncle Joe" was not inclined to waste any time, and turning around to Hildreth he said: "Look here, now, old fellow, you'd better save that bullet and your credit, too, for durn my hide if I don't think the shot that killed that goose was a clear accident, and you can't do it again if you shoot a week." This was too much for our proud little Nimrod, and, raising his faithful old Derringer to his shoulder, he took a long, deliberate aim, saying, "I'll show you whether it was an accident or not;" and, as he finished his hasty speech, the crack of the gun was heard, and the poor wounded swan vainly attempted to rise and make his escape. "Uncle Joe" exclaimed: "Well, dang my buttons, if that don't beat me," and he at once ordered the yawl to be brought forward and manned for pursuit of the wounded bird, and the chase lasted a full half hour before he was brought on board; and then, much to the chagrin of Captain Hildreth, it was discovered that the bird had been crippled before, or we would never have got near enough with a steamboat to shoot or capture him. I find, by referring to my log book, written at the time of this occurrence, that "this swan measured eight feet from tip-to-tip," and it was not unusual to see large flocks of them hovering over the river.[7] At this day I would be almost tempted to dispute the correctness of this statement, had it come from any other source; but I know that in those days I was a truthful young man, and what is more, I can prove it to-day by "Uncle Joe." On the following day we attempted to dine off the swan, but notwithstanding the cook had done his best to render it palatable, we found the meat too dry and tough, and so finished our dinner on baked catfish, which dish was our "stand-by" when other supplies failed.

The arrival of the Relief at Jonesboro at that extremely low stage of the river astonished everybody; and notwithstanding the fact that our slow and steady progress up the river had long since been heralded by travelers passing through the country, the citizens would not believe it possible for any steamboat to navigate the river at that stage of water. As we neared the shore a shout went up from the people gathered there, which told us in unmistakable terms that a hearty welcome awaited us. Among the crowd there were some half-dozen Choctaws; and they, catching the spirit of the enthusiastic welcoming by the whites, readily joined them, crying out in their native tongue, "Peni-Luac-Chitto, Bobeshela Chikama feana," (big steamboat, very good friend.)

Jonesboro was admirably situated for an important Texas town or city, and I have no doubt the original settlers built thereabout wonderful castles in the air, and planned much of future greatness for this "last town," in what was then supposed to be the northwestern corner of Arkansas.

Here I must explain that before the "line was run"[8] between Texas and the United States, Arkansas was supposed to extend across Red River, up to a point considerably above Jonesboro. In fact, nearly a whole county, called in those days Miller County, was located on the western bank of the river, and for many years was under the jurisdiction of Arkansas, and Jonesboro was considered the favored spot in Miller County; but the line was established starting from the Sabine River, where the 32° of latitude crosses that stream, and running thence due north it struck Red River about five miles above White Oak Shoals; then the river became the boundary between the two countries, thus leaving to Texas nearly the whole of Miller County, and since that date there has been no such county known in Arkansas,[9] it having been swallowed up by the Republic of Texas and the Choctaw Nation.

Jonesboro was located upon the border of one of those beautiful and fertile prairies which are among the chief characteristics of Northeastern Texas, and owing to the peculiar shape of the river it was but a very few miles further from Clarksville than was the little town of Roland, spoken of in a former number; hence it enjoyed a fair share of the trade of the vicinity of Clarksville, and at the same time held almost a monopoly above that point.

Several Texas towns which are of considerable importance at this time, were then but just springing into existence. Among them I will mention Paris, in Lamar County, which at the time I am writing of was known all over the country as "Pin Hook;" and the man who would then have dared to predict that when Jonesboro had ceased to exist as a town, Pin Hook would have become a "thriving, bustling little inland city," numbering her inhabitants by thousands, would have been unanimously voted a lunatic. Such, however, is the fact to-day, and Jonesboro, despite all its local advantages, has passed away,[10] and on my last visit there my old friend Caldwell[11] was raising cotton on the very ground where, as late as 1844–5, stood the busy little Texas city.

Jonesboro, in those days, had a large trade with the Choctaws and also with the soldiers at Fort Towson, (six miles distant by land,) for they would contrive some means of getting into Texas for whisky, no matter how rigid the discipline or how severe the punishment at the Fort for breaking the regulations. Whisky, as

I have before stated, being prohibited in "the Nation," was a very tempting bait; and with but five or six miles to tramp and a river to cross, neither the soldier nor the Indian could be restrained from making the effort to gratify his appetite; and were I to enumerate all the various schemes for smuggling which were resorted to I should find it necessary to devote an entire chapter to the details. There was no law in the Nation forbidding the Indians from crossing into Texas, nor punishment for returning home drunk; but with the soldier it was quite different, and I am perfectly safe in saying that during the existence of Fort Towson, there was hardly a day that one or more of the soldiers were not in the stocks for this disobedience of orders.

Prominent among the people here was "Colonel Jim Johnston";[12] in fact, he was sole proprietor of the town site, as well as the adjoining expansive prairie, many acres of which he had under most excellent cultivation.[13] He was reputed to be immensely wealthy in Texas lands,[14] and he did not fail in a single instance in his dealings with his neighbors to assume all the importance due to a man of such unquestionable antecedents and large acquisitions of nominal wealth. Colonel Johnston was a man of much intelligence, (had been a lawyer I think,) but so very reticent that his light failed to shine out very astonishingly among his immediate associates; nevertheless he was a just man, (severely so,) and while he was exacting in his rule over Jonesboro, he was prompt to do all that he promised in leasing lots, stores and houses to others engaged in trade in his little city. He monopolized the ferry to the Nation, and thereby commanded most of the Indian trade, which consisted mostly in an exchange of deer skins and snake-root for whisky.

We spent the evening at Jonesboro socially and pleasantly; and at a late hour, after having recounted the incidents of our tedious trip to an eager listening crowd, and listened in turn to a recital of all the most important events which had taken place hereabouts within the last year, we retired to rest preparatory to the difficult task of reaching the "Public Landing" (Fort Towson,) and the mouth of the Kiamitia on the morrow—in all, twelve miles.

One of the incidents most particularly alluded to by our entertainers at Jonesboro was the sinking of the steamboat New York,[15] about a half a mile above the town; and although this accident had happened some two years ago, there was so much of interest attaching to its details that an opportunity was never lost by those fond of the marvelous to refer to, and enlarge upon it, special reasons for which will appear as I repeat the story as told to us on the night in question.

The New York was one among the first steamboats to ascend the river to this point after the Raft was opened by Captain Shreve in 1839.[16] She was from Pittsburg, and loaded in part with Government supplies for Fort Towson, and partly on private account. Having reached Jonesboro with much difficulty, and failed, after repeated attempts, to get over the next "crossing," she dropped back to the town on the Texas side, where there was good water, and a better opportunity for social enjoyment and legitimate trading than on the "Nation side," or among the snags in the middle of the river. While she was thus quietly lying at the bank waiting for a rise, an old keelboat pilot chanced to hear of her detention, and visiting the Captain, he convinced him that there would be no difficulty in his boat reaching the "Public Landing," and he finally persuaded him to start her out and make another trial under this new pilot's guidance. The start was made against the protest of the people of Jonesboro, and all sorts of disasters were predicted; for they were loth to part with so agreeable an adjunct to their place as they had found in the New York and her crew; and when on a bright morning she steamed away from her comfortable moorings, the whole populace stood upon the bank waving their adieus, and watching with doubts and fears her slow progress. Not a half an hour had passed when she suddenly stopped, swung around, and careened over, and the cry "She's sunk! she's sunk!" went through the crowd like a flash; and true enough she did sink, and there she lies to this day. The next move was to save the cargo, and every ferry, flat, and Indian canoe from far and near, was soon brought into requisition, for the news of the sinking of a steamboat spread like wildfire, and a thousand stories were soon current as to what the cargo consisted of, and of course good liquor was believed to be the principal item.

In a very few days after the accident, there came a sudden rise in the river and drove the wreckers away; and when the waters subsided again, the New York was so buried in the shifting sands as to be nearly out of sight. Notwithstanding this interruption, the search for the treasure was renewed and continued long after the wreck had been abandoned by the Captain and crew; and it was said that many barrels marked "Vinegar A. C. S."[17] were found well filled with good cognac brandy, designed, of course, for "hospital uses." And it was rumored, also, that years after sundry packages were brought to light marked "Goodwin, Sutler, Ft. T., C. N.,"[18] which, when carefully examined and "contents noted," were found to contain spirits, much improved by long imprisonment in the sands of Red River. Friend Goodwin, the sutler,[19] who was a genial spirit himself, would never consent to have his name connected with these "spirits from the vasty deep" until he had been favored with a special communication from them; and it was said that in no single instance did he fail to "recognize" them as his friends while on the earth.

It was not long till it was believed that the "N. Y." contained a fabulous amount of whisky and other good things, the search for which was kept up for years; and nearly everybody had a few gallons of choice liquors from the sunken "N. Y.," which was kept, of course, for medicine; and I have no doubt that hundreds of barrels have since been sold in the country as the identical "whisky sunk on the 'N. Y.'"

We found much difficulty in passing over the bar where the "N. Y." was sunk and still to be seen, and we only arrived at Fort Towson landing after those who had been anxiously waiting for us had nearly all left for the Fort, which was six miles from the river.

We hastily put out the little freight we had for the Fort, leaving it in charge of a soldier, who was on duty at the warehouse, and then hurried along, hoping to reach the end of our trip before dark; but we were disappointed once more, and forced to lie up a mile and a half below Kiamitia; and here I must apologize to my readers for having drawn out this story of a single trip of the Relief to such an unwarrantable length that I am afraid they have long since tired of these rambling reminiscences of an OUTSIDER.

Notes

1. See the article on "Jonesborough" (the spelling generally used in the earliest documents) in the *Handbook of Texas Online*. Jonesboro's location is shown on Sidney Morse and Samuel Breese's 1844 *Map of Texas* and, more precisely, within the Alexander S. Johnston headright in the Pine Creek area on the Texas General Land Office's 1856 map of Red River County, which includes a delineation of the changed course of the river. Town lots were sold in Jonesboro, as shown in the 1840 Red River County tax rolls.

2. On Fort Towson, see Letter 26.

3. Fire hunting was done at night by foot, on horseback, or in boats and involved use of a cage (fire-pan) of burning pine knots at the end of a pole that transfixed deer and illuminated their eyes for an easy kill. See Jennie Holliman, *American Sports, 1785–1835*.

4. Withenbury does not say when Bails left the *Relief*.

5. A rifle produced by the Derringer Rifle & Pistol Works in Philadelphia.

6. Hildreth was in front of the pilothouse on the roof of the area devoted to cabin passengers.

7. John Sibley in his 1805 "Account of the Red River and Country Adjacent" mentions Swan Lake (about 35 miles west of Jonesboro), so called "from the great number of swans that frequent it."

8. In 1841.

9. Present-day Miller County was created in 1874 after Withenbury was writing.

10. A historical account of Red River County in the August 25, 1882, Clarksville *Standard* says that although Jonesboro was incorporated in 1837, no corporate authorities were ever elected and that Jonesboro was "abandoned as a business point in 1841 and thoroughly in ruins in 1842, most of the houses being removed, and the citizens of the town scattered through the Pine creek precinct adjacent, and through the prairies in Red River and Lamar."

11. James C. Caldwell, who appears in the 1859 Red River County tax rolls with 200 acres in the William Mays headright. Caldwell is shown in the 1850 Red River County census as a 39-year-old farmer born in Kentucky with a wife and four children.

12. An article on "James H. Johnston" in the *Handbook of Texas Online* says that he was a planter and merchant born about 1807 in North Carolina who probably came to Red River County before the Texas Revolution and was elected delegate to the Convention of 1836 but did not attend because there was a misunderstanding about the number of delegates. He sold provisions to the Texas army from 1838 to 1841, represented Red River County in the lower house of the Eighth Congress in 1843 and 1844, and died at his home in Clarksville on January 15, 1847. James H. Johnston advertised as a receiving and forwarding merchant at Jonesborough in the April 30, 1840, Shreveport *Caddo Free Press*, as president of the Pine Creek Female Institute in the September 3, 1842, Clarksville *Northern Standard*, and as proprietor of the Star Hotel in Clarksville in the November 14, 1846, *Northern Standard*. The Star Hotel advertised in the March 6, 1847, *Northern Standard* that it was under new ownership and that it had been recently operated by the late Col. James H. Johnston. The June 10, 1848, *Northern Standard* contains a notice by William S. Todd, administrator of the succession of James H. Johnston, that he had been appointed in the May term of the court in 1848.

13. Jonesboro was located in the Alexander S. Johnston headright. The William Mays headright was immediately to the west. According to Texas General Land Office land records, James H. Johnston acquired the Mays headright through purchase in June 1838. The Alexander S. Johnston headright was apparently acquired through inheritance, with the acquired land resurveyed. The survey conducted in conjunction with the Mays transfer uses the adjoining survey for James H. Johnston as a reference, and Mays describes his land as "adjoining the land of James H. Johnston, and lying above the town of Jonesborough on Red River." The land in these two headrights totaled about 8,000 acres. Johnston

advertised his Jonesboro land consisting of 8,196 acres (450 acres improved) for sale for $8,000 in the June 26, 1844, Clarksville *Northern Standard*, noting that it had only been partially flooded once in the previous 20 years. This offer had been preceded by a January 15, 1840, *Arkansas Gazette* advertisement for the sale of his plantation near Jonesboro and a September 10, 1842, *Northern Standard* advertisement for the sale of three tracts of land on the Red River in the Jonesboro Prairie that included 300 acres of cleared land.

14. The August 2, 1851, Clarksville *Northern Standard* contains an "Administrator's Sale" advertisement concerning the succession of James H. Johnston that includes 4,996 acres in Cass and Titus counties.

15. This was probably the *New York* that advertised for Coats Bluff in the January 8, 1838, *New Orleans Commercial Bulletin*. William Lytle's *Merchant Steam Vessels of the United States, 1807–1868* lists a *New York* that was a 105-ton sidewheeler built in Cincinnati in 1835.

16. Shreve removed a reformed raft in February 1839, and navigation was reported open in March.

17. Assistant Commissary of Subsistence, who was responsible for ordering rations that were used in the post mess hall and hospital. See the section on "Quartermaster—Commissary Department" in the description of Fort Scott, Kansas, on the National Park Service website.

18. Choctaw Nation.

19. A non-military provider of goods for military personnel. George Gooding (not Goodwin) was the sutler at Ft. Towson for 19 years. Withenbury will have more to say about Gooding in Letter 26.

21 ✦ To Kiamitia

The *Relief* had gone the additional mile and a half and reached the mouth of the Kiamichi River, although a part of the letter is devoted to an incident downstream. There was a landing that served the needs of Doaksville that was separate from the Fort Towson landing. This landing, which

was called Kiamitia, had been a keelboat landing and was three river miles above the Fort Towson Landing and one mile downstream of Wright's Landing.[1] A very early map of Fort Towson by the Engineers Office of the Department of Arkansas[2] shows a road from a landing on the Red River on the east side of the Kiamichi River and running east of Gates Creek to Fort Towson and then to Doaksville and, on the west side of the Kiamichi River, a road from another point (marked "Folsom's") on the Red River running immediately across the Kiamichi River and west of Gates Creek directly to Doaksville (Figure 8). The landing on the east side of the Kiamichi River was the Doaksville landing and was called Kiamitia, which (as Withenbury indicates) included a warehouse. The one on the west side was a ferry landing that connected with Wright's Landing on the south side of the river. The numerous references to Kiamitia in the newspaper steamboat records appear to refer before the Civil War to the landing with the warehouse on the east side of the Kiamichi River and to Wright's Landing (which was also called Kiamitia or Kiomatia) and after the Civil War (when Doaksville declined) primarily to Wright's Landing.

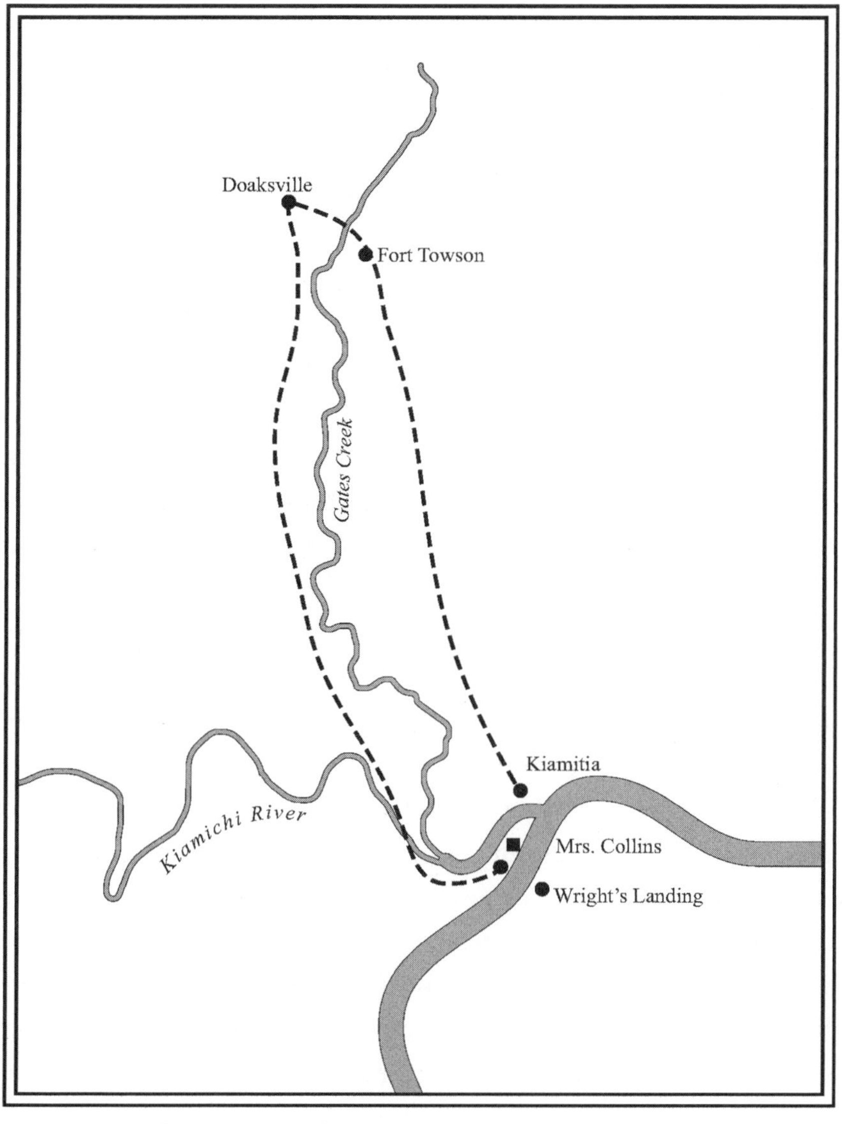

FIGURE 8: ROADS TO DOAKSVILLE

⁂

By referring to my chapter on the 8th inst., I find that I left the Relief tied up to the Choctaw side, one and a half miles below the mouth of the Kiamitia River, and it is needless to add, in the wilderness, for after leaving Fort Towson landing, where there were no buildings except two log warehouses, there was no sign of a human habitation on that side of the river until we arrived at Kiamitia, and there only a warehouse on the lower side[3] of that beautiful little stream, and the residence of the widow Collins and a ferryman's shanty on the opposite bank. This widow Collins was what was usually denominated a "half breed," and the fact of her being joint owner in the ferry from that point to Wright's Landing, Texas, must account for her being located there at the date I am writing of.[4] But I see that I am getting a little ahead of the Relief, so I will leave the widow for a while and return and assist "Uncle Joe" out of his dilemma, for daylight on January 20, 1842, found his little boat hard aground, (the river having fallen very suddenly,) out of wood, and the Captain sick with the ague. Surely nothing more was needed to render our situation deplorable, but, notwithstanding all our trials, there were light hearts and ready hands among us, and soon the woods resounded with the hurried strokes of the axe, and in less than an hour we had, as we supposed, a sufficient supply of wood on board to take us this last remaining mile and a half. By the time the fuel was on board our breakfast was ready, for old LaRue had made short work of preparing it, remarking to us as we were about to partake of his hasty meal, that "there would not be much time lost, for a short horse is soon curried." But we did not mind "short rations," now that we were so near the end of our tedious trip. (I ought to say voyage, for that sounds a little longer than trip.)

By referring to my last it will be remembered that we were only 10 ½ miles above Jonesboro, the whole of the preceding day having been spent in coming that short distance, and we were just beginning to realize the folly of calculating our progress ahead for any particular time. So after an hour or so spent in working the boat off the sand-bar where she had grounded during the night, we shoved out with no feeling of certainty as to how far we would go before night should again overtake us.

On the Texas bank nearly opposite where we spent the night lived a planter named Gideon Mimms, familiarly known all over that section of the country as "Uncle Gid."[5] The old man had a great curiosity to visit the boat during the night, and he made frequent appeals to have the yawl sent over for him; but Captain Ross was two unwell to attempt to entertain him, for he knew him the year before, and had not forgotten that he and his companion, Joe Scurlock,[6] usually became very boisterous when on board a steamboat, and "mixed with whisky." Very early in the morning "Uncle Gid" was seen standing on the bank and beckoning for the yawl, and our steward—Jim Berryhill—who, it will be remembered, was half Indian, thinking he might be able to find some chickens or eggs at the plantation, took our skiff and by himself pulled to the Texas shore, where "Uncle Gid" was standing.

The old man told Jim if he would loan him the skiff to go over to the boat, he would guarantee him all the eggs and chickens he wanted, by going up to "the quarters," and what was more, he would have his negroes bring a further supply up to "Kiamish" after the boat had reached that point; and he would bring the skiff back by the time he could "go to the quarters and back." So the bargain was struck, and "Uncle Gid" took his seat in the skiff, placed the oars in the row-locks, and Jim gave him a good push out into the current. The old man had never rowed a skiff in his life; but in a "dugout," with one paddle, no white man, and but rarely an Indian, could beat him. His maiden effort at rowing a skiff proved a sad failure, for at about the third stroke with the oars they both slipped out of the open row-locks, and "Uncle Gid," who was laying out all his strength, fell backward into the bottom of the skiff, and as he fell he let go both oars, which, long before he could recover himself, were quite out of his reach and quietly floating away, leaving him utterly helpless and rapidly floating down the river about midway between the Relief and the Texas shore. The old fellow's shouts soon brought the whole boat's crew in sight, and their united hooting and yelling quite drowned "Uncle Gid's" loud appeals for help, and not until Captain Ross appeared among them could they be quieted. Just then "Uncle Gid," in his rage, stood erect in his skiff, and, with his clenched fists, pronounced a terrible judgment on those who were making merry over his misfortune. But for a moment only was his six feet three inches seen in a perpendicular attitude, for by a little variation from the center the skiff rolled to one side, and "Uncle Gid" again lay sprawling his full length. Captain Ross, seeing the predicament the old Texan was in, sent a man in the yawl to his relief, and as soon as the skiff oars could be picked up we had the old man safely on board, and with a hearty shaking of hands with those whom he had known the previous year, and a couple of drinks of Oliver's best, he was sufficiently mollified to mix with the crew without endangering their safety, but when he first got aboard he was so enraged that he was, according to his own declaration, "ready to fight every d__n son of _____" that had hooted at him, and that he was physically able to make his words good not one of us doubted. He declined going back to the shore in anything short of the yawl, manned with two good oarsmen and Philley to steer, and so we disposed of the old man according to his dictation, receiving his repeated promise to come and see us at "Kiamish." But before he was well out of hearing, said "Uncle Joe," *sotto voce*,[7] "Dod durn his old drunken hide, I wouldn't a' cared if he'd fell in the river and drowned before anybody had seen or heard him." But, "Uncle Gid Mimms" was a "cotton planter and had his rights," the limit of which it was a little difficult to define when whisky was about.

But I find I am devoting too much space to individuals, so I will dismiss "old man Mimms" with the simple remark, that with all his rough exterior and uncouth habits, he had a good heart, and like thousands of others of whom he was a fair average type, he was honorable in all his dealings, and firm in his friendship as well as in his hate, and up to the day of his death he never looked upon his disaster in the skiff as a "good joke."

A whole day was spent in fruitless efforts to reach the Kiamitia River, and night found us tied up at the mouth of Gates' Creek, about three hundred yards below[8] our long looked for goal. We were now just as near our destination as Moses of old ever got to the "promised land,"—we were in sight of it,—and as the "fates" seemed against us, we submitted with the best possible grace, and flattered ourselves that we were not much behind that foundling of the bulrushes on the score of meek deportment under trying circumstances.

On the following morning after replenishing our woodpile from a fence around an old Indian field, we raised steam and by the aid of a line[9] we managed to pull the Relief to the "Kiamitia Landing," where there was a spacious warehouse for the use of the merchants at Doaksville, a little village about five miles in the interior of the Choctaw Nation, and two miles distant from Fort Towson. Here we knew we were to remain until "Bogue Homa" (Red River) would rise, and we were quite content at having accomplished what no steamboat up to that date had ever done, and that was to reach that point at so low a stage of water, and Captain Ross wisely determined not to risk the downward passage under the same difficulties.

Here and at rest, I find the many incidents of interest crowding upon my memory until confusion seems to reign there supreme, and I am at a loss to decide what to chronicle first, and what to strive and forget until a better opportunity offers for a recital of what to me in those "young days" was full of novelty, and I trust not wholly devoid of instruction.

So far I have not mentioned two passengers which we took on board at Fulton. They have both, I think, relatives still living, although themselves both long since dead. Captain John Sylvester and Charley Dunn had each a small remnant of groceries, for which they found a dull sale at Fulton where they had been located a couple of months before our arrival, and the Relief's trip up the river being their first opportunity to reach a better market for their remaining stocks they were not slow to avail themselves of "Uncle Joe's" characteristic liberality to "take them and their stuff along at their own price." Arkansas at this time was a poor place for mercantile adventurers (to which class our two friends belonged) for the reason that the whole State was deluged with a paper currency issued by the "State Bank" and also the "Real Estate Bank of Arkansas." The latter institution at the time I am writing of was known as the "Real Mistake Bank," and so nearly worthless had the money (?) become that dealers in merchandise found it necessary to so discriminate between its nominal value and gold and silver as to almost entirely exclude the paper from circulation. I well remember the first thing that arrested my attention at Fulton was some barrels of flour lying at Marsh & Applegate's door. (Captain Sam. Applegate.) These flour barrels were marked in large letters on each head, "$35.00 Ark.—$6.50 good stuff." I need enter into no further details to show why Captain Sylvester and Charley Dunn were anxious to leave Arkansas with the balance of their stocks of goods and the little "good stuff" they had pocketed while waiting for an opportunity to get away.

At Doaksville and Fort Towson our two merchants found ready sale for much of their stock. Charley Dunn being the most completely tired out of the two, "closed out" to the firm of Berthelet, Heald & Co., at Doaksville, at a positive loss, in order to leave the country on the Relief. But Captain Sylvester stored his goods in the Choctaw warehouse, and made a journey overland to Fort Washita, in the Chickasaw Nation, some seventy-five miles northwest from Fort Towson. Here he made sale of all his remaining stock, to be delivered by wagons at the Fort, and full of the anticipation of handsome profits, he set about—as he afterward told me—making his arrangements for teams; but before he had taken his goods from the warehouse, there came up to the landing an entire stranger in Red River, with a little steamboat called the Trader. Captain Truesdale was ambitious to go further up Red River than anybody had yet gone with a steamboat, and he offered to carry Sylvester's goods to Fort Washita, which is on the False Washita River, some eighteen miles from its confluence with Red River, for less than the wagons would haul them, and if he failed to reach the Fort, would land the goods at any intermediate point and charge him nothing; and so a bargain was made and the goods put on board the Trader, and she being a very light craft, she managed by the aid of a little rise of water—which had also enabled the Relief to start downstream—to work her way up to the False Washita, and entered that stream, proudly claiming the well-earned distinction of being the first steamboat to disturb its clear waters.

I must here be allowed to make a slight digression in order to describe in part this pioneer steamboat in the far distant Upper Red River and its tributary—the False Washita. Before proceeding, however, I will state that the attempt to reach Fort Washita, with Captain Sylvester's venture, proved not only a failure, but a decided disaster to all concerned. Somewhere between the Fort and the mouth of the river, Captain Truesdale encountered an obstruction in the way of rapids, almost amounting to falls, and his little Trader was unable to stem the current, so he resorted to the old keelboat mode of "warping over,"[10] and when just upon the reef, (I will use the Captain's own words,) "the d____d beast took a swing on the line, came broadside to the current, her stern hanging on the rocks, and quicker than h_ll can scorch a feather she capsized, and overboard went the boiler and cargo, and the first I saw of Sylvester he was standing up to his middle in the water, and beckoning to me to come over to his side." Here ended the trip of the Trader, and the speculation of John Sylvester—(whose brother "Jim," now living at St. Louis, will certainly remember, should his eye fall upon these lines.) When Captain Sylvester met "Uncle Joe," after his mishap, he plead his present inability to pay his freight bill to Kiamitia, but promised to "make it all right in time." But Captain Ross in the characteristic goodness of his heart answered him, "It's all right now, old fellow; you don't owe me nary red cent."

Now for Captain Truesdale and the Trader, and I must close for this time. The old man had lived for many years near the Cherokee Nation, on the Neosho River—a tributary of the Arkansas. There he owned and ran a sawmill, but failing to accumulate money fast enough, he conceived the idea of converting his sawmill into a steamboat. In carrying out his schemes he was opportunely aided by the advent of a small keelboat in the Neosho River. He purchased the boat, broke up his sawmill, and by using the engine and boiler, with his own mechanical skill, he succeeded (to use his own words) "in spoiling a good sawmill, and making a d____d poor steamboat," which he called the Neosho, but he afterward changed her name to Trader, because his old neighbors would insult him by calling her wherever he went "No show." Captain Truesdale, hearing that the Government was opening the Red River Raft, sought the Upper Red River as the most promising field for his future exploits. He worked months in reaching the point where he hoped to mend his broken fortunes, and where the disaster I have related convinced both him and Captain Sylvester that

> The best laid schemes o' mice and men
> Gang aft a-gley

Captain Truesdale spent many days in fishing up his engine and boiler, which he eventually sold to parties near Fort Washita, and then returned to his home on the Neosho, and I never heard of his steamboating any more. Captain Sylvester, sticking to the theater of his ill luck, became afterwards quite a prominent steamboat Captain on Red River, but failing to realize a fortune, and meeting with several disasters, he retired from the Red River in disgust, and ever after until the day of his death he remained an OUTSIDER.

Notes

1. See the list of "Landings from Shreveport, La. to Preston, Texas" in *Gardner's New Orleans Directory for 1866.*

2. A (somewhat blurred) image of this map can be seen in the pictures accompanying the Doaksville page on the Exploring Oklahoma History website. The date is indecipherable, but the map was created after Paris, Texas, came into existence in 1845.

3. Downstream on the Red River.

4. Identity unknown. Ferries were licensed to prominent families in the Indian Territory, and dual licensing was required when ferries operated across political boundaries, as was the case here. Henry Jackson's 1869 *Indian Territory* shows a Folsom's Ferry at this point. An article on "Ferries and Fords" in the *Encyclopedia of Oklahoma History and Culture* indicates that David Folsom was from a prominent family and operated a ferry, but without dates or location; however, Folsom was associated with Doaksville and died in 1847, so it is reasonable to assume that this ferry was initially operated by him and later by

members of his family. Two of his sons—Dr. Henry Folsom and Simpson (Sim) Folsom—were long-term residents of the area. Jordan D. Folsom, a descendant of Henry's slaves, was interviewed in 1938 as part of the "Indian-Pioneer Papers" oral history project (which can be found in the University of Oklahoma Libraries Western History Collections) and indicates that prior to the Civil War Sim Folsom had a home at the mouth of the Kiamichi and that immediately across the Red River there was a place where whiskey was sold to Indians and negroes. Sim Folsom was born in 1828 and was obviously not occupying the house in 1842; but this appears to have always been Folsom property. In any case, the widow Collins would not have been the ferry operator. The missionary William Goode in *Outposts of Zion* reports that he took this ferry from the Indian Territory in 1844 and that it was operated by an Irishman—the apparent occupant of the ferryman's shanty.

5. According to Texas General Land Office land records, Gideon Mims came to Texas in 1836 as a single man, was granted land in what is now Marion County, and acquired the James Wimberly headright on Red River across from the mouth of the Kiamichi River in 1839. Mims appears in the Red River County tax rolls from 1838 through 1851, with 2,235 acres and 48 slaves in 1851 and the Mims estate listed in 1853. An advertisement in the January 28, 1843, Clarksville *Northern Standard* addressed "To the Ladies of the New England States" announced the formation of a society called "The Matrimonial Club" composed of candidates for matrimony and invited ladies interested in joining to send their names to Pine Creek or Jonesboro. The advertisement was signed by 18 men, including Mims as president. According to Sam Mims in "Leaves from the Mims Family Tree," Gideon's will of October 1850 was probated in Red River County in February 1852 and emancipated 10 of his slaves with money allocated to secure housing for them in a free state.

6. Apparently William Scurlock (there are no records for a Joseph Scurlock), who came to Texas in 1837 according to Texas General Land Office land records, obtained a headright on Pine Creek southwest of Mims' property, and signed the advertisement addressed to the ladies of New England. According to an article on "William Scurlock" in the *Handbook of Texas Online*, he served in the mounted rangers in 1839, as postmaster at Jonesborough from 1839–1840, and as representative of Red River County in the Fourth Congress, then married in 1847 and left Texas in 1848.

7. In an undertone, so as not to be overheard.

8. Gates Creek is presently a tributary to the Kiamichi River, entering the Kiamichi shortly before the Kiamichi enters the Red River. At the time about which Withenbury was writing, Gates Creek was apparently a tributary of the Red River, entering the river about 900 feet below the mouth of the Kiamichi River, which is compatible with the topography of the area.

9. The boat was pulled forward by a line attached to the capstan on the boat and trees on shore.

10. Warping involved the use of the capstan with a line attached to a tree to pull a boat over an impediment.

22 ✦ At Doaksville

The *Relief* was at the mouth of the Kiamichi River on the Indian Territory side, and Withenbury made an overland trip to Doaksville, which was one mile northwest of Fort Towson across Gates Creek. Withenbury apparently took the road beginning at the ferry landing on the west side of the Kiamichi because he does not mention passing through Fort Towson.

Doaksville[1] was the capital of the Choctaw Nation from 1850–1863. The trader Josiah Doak located at the confluence of Doaksville Creek (a few miles downstream of the Kiamichi River) and the Red River in 1821 and, with a few additional settlers, moved to the site on Gates Creek when Ft. Towson was created in 1824. It was the center of a great deal of activity because of its proximity to Ft. Towson and because it was one of the places where the Indians collected their annuities. Treaties were signed at Doaksville in 1837 forming the Chickasaw District within the Choctaw Nation and in 1854 establishing the Chickasaw Nation as a

separate entity, and it was the place at which the Choctaw Convention met to draft its constitution in 1860. The town fell into decline with the abandonment of Ft. Towson in 1851 and the move of the capital in 1863.

In the 1842 *Annual Report of the Commissioner of Indian Affairs*, William Armstrong, the Acting Superintendent for the Western Territory, reports that there were five stores[2] in Doaksville, three of which were owned in part by Choctaws and two of which were owned exclusively by citizens of the United States, along with a resident physician, blacksmith shop, wagonmaker, wheelwright, church, temperance society, and tavern (which meant hotel at that time). Armstrong characterizes Doaksville as "one of the most orderly and quiet towns you will find in the west" and states that in his many lengthy visits he had never seen ardent spirits or a drunken Indian. The missionary William Goode visited Doaksville in 1844 and reported in *Outposts of Zion* that it was surrounded by Choctaw and Chickasaw cotton plantations worked by slaves. These observations provide the context for what Withenbury saw in 1842.

⁂

[First part not used.]

But I must proceed now with my little Relief and "Uncle Joe," whom I left at the mouth of Kiamitia, January 21, 1842.

The recollection of the great diversity of character which presented itself to me after leaving the lower portion of Upper Red

River, together with the novelty of the river scenery and the increasing difficulties of navigation, I find has so absorbed me that I have made but very slow progress with the Relief; but now that I have recorded the fact of her safe arrival at Kiamitia, and that in consequence of the low stage of the water we were brought to an indefinite standstill, I will try my descriptive powers upon the beautiful country around about Fort Towson, conscious, however, that I shall fall very far short of doing justice to my subject; for the pen of a hardworking steamboatman, who has spent more than the quarter of a century in battling with the rugged elements in striving to "steer clear" of the freaks of adverse fortune, must necessarily, when three score years are well-nigh passed, be found a little blunted.

Trusting, however, in the charity of my readers, I will proceed to give my first impressions of the Choctaw Nation, and also to mark some of the changes which have come over it since 1842. Before proceeding, however, I must say a few more words concerning the two gentlemen merchants, Captain Sylvester and Charley Dunn, whom I introduced in my last chapter. This much is due them, as they had both been previously engaged in steamboating on Red River. Captain Sylvester made a few trips to Shreveport with the steamboat "Swiss Boy" as early as the winter of 1839–40, but abandoned the business after finding it both unpleasant and unprofitable; but he resumed it again after the disaster I have mentioned, connecting himself with Captain Joe Claibourne, in the steamboats "Yazoo City," "Houma," "Yazoo Planter" and "Vermillion." Mr. Dunn made a season or two as second clerk on the steamboat "Caddo" with his brother John, who was first clerk, and brother of Captain Dunn, who built the "Caddo" at Pittsburg and commanded her in Red River in 1843. I can not leave these two friends (Sylvester and Dunn) without a passing tribute to their memory;

for in them I found more of the characteristics of the true gentleman than were usually met with among the adventurers on the frontier in those early days, each of them possessing traits of character which seemed to unfit them for the rough life they were every day encountering. They were, to use the words of my old friend Captain "Billy" Stewart, of steamboat fame, "too amiable;" and while they would adorn any station in life, the profession of steamboating, at that day, did not much adorn them.

On the morning of January 22, 1842, after the Relief's cargo was all on shore, I started in company with several others for Doaksville, on foot. I proposed to take along a gun, but I soon learned that by the Choctaw laws, no white man was allowed to carry a gun within their borders.

This rule, I afterward learned, was often relaxed where the white man was sufficiently known to be vouched for by some reliable Indian; but the Choctaws as a people were jealous of their rights and distrustful of the pale faces, probably not without good cause. My walk to Doaksville promised to be monotonous and tiresome in consequence of this restriction; but I have often since thought that it was most fortunate, for I was thus left with ample opportunity to take in all the beauties of the forest scenery—the grand and lofty rustic, gothic arches thrown across the winding Indian roadway by the far reaching branches of the sturdy oaks, and the dark-green pine tops towering far above them all, and casting their net-work of light and shade among the fallen cones and faded leaves at my feet, might all have been lost to me, while hunting the *funi*, *chocfa* and *faket*, (squirrel, rabbit and wild turkey) had the carrying of a gun been permitted, and I could not now recall to mind the pleasing picture which was at first sight so indelibly photographed upon my memory, and which "haunts me still." Immediately upon the margin of the two rivers the forest was quite dense, and it had been necessary to cut out many large trees in making the road. But upon the higher ground, after leaving the river, the appearance of the country changed materially, and the timber became so scattering that the road was made by winding among the trees, and the natural beauty of the forest was undisturbed for the whole remaining distance. There were no settlements between the river and Doaksville, on this road, and consequently nothing to draw the attention from a quiet contemplation of the beauty and stillness of nature. Occasionally the road emerged from among the oaks and pines into little patches of prairie, which gave to the whole the appearance of a grand park which had been cleared and planted ages ago, and afterwards been deserted by the hands and left to care for itself, unheeded by any human friend save the poor untutored child of nature, who, by the decree of his white brother, now claimed it as his own inheritance in exchange for the hunting-grounds of his forefathers, east of the Mississippi.

The early grass and tiny spring flowers had just begun to peep above sombrous brown carpet spread over the ground by the frosts of winter, and the birds were flitting about among the branches of the trees, eager to pluck the first tender buds; and with their warblings they were welcoming the warm rays of the bright golden sun, and so fully did I realize the welcome contrast between this heart-warming January day in the Sunny South and the rigorous wintry scenes in my own Northern home, that I felt an impulse to join with the little songsters, singing,

> The springtime of year is coming, coming,
> And all the world is gay, love,
> The blithe busy bee is humming, humming,
> And the wintry months are May, love,
> The wintry months are May.

Catching but a hurried glance of the enchanting scenery, I made haste to the little Indian village, as a part of my mission was to send a doctor to "Uncle Joe," who was shaking with the "ager"[3] when I left him. The village makes its appearance a half mile or so before we enter it, and along the margin of the road were a number of very pretty dwellings, for here at their ease lived the Colberts,[4] the Folsomes[5] and Colonel R. M. Jones[6] (Choctaw families), and their white associates in business,[7] the Berthelets,[8] Alsbrooks,[9] Doaks, Timms,[10] and Drs. Look and McDonough. The latter had married Miss Visey Colbert, a wealthy and educated woman of the Choctaw tribe, while Dr. Look remained from choice a bachelor so long as he lived in "the Nation;" but many years later he removed to Clarksville, Texas, where he married one of his own race, and where he may be living still.

As I shall have something more to say of Dr. McDonough and his wife, hereafter,[11] I will dismiss them for the present and hurry back to the Relief. I soon found Dr. Look,[12] and when he learned that I had come to the village on foot, he sent for an extra pony that I might return to the boat in company with him; and while my pony was being got ready I took a stroll through the principal street, and I can't deny that I took also many a "sly glance" at the pretty half-breed and full blood Indian maidens who came riding into the village. Here was an interesting picture—the rude, untutored children of the forest, full of curiosity, coming to look upon their fairer sisters of the mixed blood and their still fairer ones of the pure white, (for there were a number of them there,) and yet shrinking with the timidity of the fawn from the gaze of any and everyone not strictly of their own Indian blood—and mingling in the same pursuits, some shopping and others visiting—possibly gossiping—with those half-breeds who had been blest with the advantages afforded by association with the more highly cultivated classes, that had come into their midst as companions and, I may properly say, safeguards for their adventurous fathers, husbands, or brothers, who, hoping to increase their worldly store, had left their homes in "the States" and settled in "the Nation."

I was cut short in my musings upon the strange mixture of society which I found at Doaksville; and as the Doctor and my pony were now ready for the ride to the boat, I left my companions to return at their leisure, glad to have pleasant company myself and a pony to ride.

I found Dr. Look a very intelligent gentleman, and thoroughly conversant with all matters pertaining to the Choctaws, both of a public and private character, and consequently, I found the distance much shorter than it had seemed on my morning walk. From him I learned that there were a number of educational establishments in the vicinity, and that most of the half-breeds, whom I had seen of both sexes, had been tolerably well educated; and, as a general thing, the females were the easiest drawn away from the rude Indian traits of character, and consequently were the most enlightened. Quite a number of the pure Indians also attended these schools, and made good progress in their studies, and in many cases evinced a proficiency that would have reflected much credit upon the white race.

A great many of the mixed bloods had been sent to "the States" to school, and there was a number of graduates, some in business, some teaching in the Choctaw schools, and some living at their leisure, the same as white folks. Among the wealthier and cultivated class I must mention Miss Frances Jones[13] (now Mrs. Love, residing in Philadelphia). She was the daughter of Colonel Robert M. Jones, a very shrewd business man, an extensive cotton planter and large slave owner, a merchant at Doaksville, of the firm of Berthelet, Heald & Co., and for many years afterward a merchant at New Orleans, of the firm of Phelps & Jones. Miss Frances, while she was not "spoiled with beauty," was comely enough to be regarded with more than ordinary admiration by strangers, and her accomplishments were of a stamp to enable her to shine among her sisters of the pure white blood anywhere.

My steamboat readers will doubtless remember the Red River steamboat "Frances Jones," named in honor of that young lady, and also at a later date, the "R. M. Jones," built by Captain John Ankrim, of Marietta, Ohio. Both these boats were good Red River boats in their day.[14]

I would like to dwell longer upon the interesting reminiscences of Doaksville and the friends, both business and social, that I made and cultivated there for many subsequent years, but I find myself tempted to trespass too much upon the space allowed me and I fear upon the patience of my readers, and am forced to change abruptly the current of my recollections from pleasant scenes to the rough realities of business.

In a little over an hour my easy ambling Indian pony brought me to the river bank, and Captain Ross soon found that in returning to the Relief so promptly with the Doctor I had rendered him an essential service, and by this time poor Charley Dunn was shaking with the ague also, so the Doctor found a plenty to occupy him until quite late in the evening, and we were all glad to have his company, as we found him both intelligent and communicative.

The consignees of our little freight were also on the spot ready to receive the small accession to their stocks of goods, and the bustle and excitement attending the delivery of goods to the Indian wagoners was really interesting, although at times a little perplexing. One redeeming feature, however, of our business transactions with the people in "the Nation" was their readiness to pay their bills. They came to the boat with their saddle-bags filled with specie, and were anxious to settle "fairly and squarely," a shining example to many of their white brethren "in the States" even at this day.

Among our visitors were many idlers, and we had ample opportunity to see the Indian character in its various phases, rude and civilized, drunk and sober. Our barkeeper was compelled by the Indian laws to "shut up shop" while we lay at the Choctaw shore, but here as well as at every other important point on the Choctaw side, there was in plain sight a store on the opposite shore where whisky could be purchased in any quantity from a "jigger" to a jugfull, and all the poor Indian had to do was to appear on the bank, show a coon or a deer skin, and cry out in his native tongue, "*Peni-Minta*," and Ashbrook[15] (a relative of the great cattle dealer Ashbrook,[16] at Covington, Kentucky,) would come limping down to his ferry flat, and soon convey his victim beyond the reach of the wholesome Choctaw laws, where he could sell him whisky with impunity, for he was an OUTSIDER.

Notes

1. See the articles on Doaksville in the *Encyclopedia of Oklahoma History and Culture* and in the Oklahoma Historical Society's "Museums and Sites" section. Numerous photographs are available through CivilWarAlbum.com's "Doaksville, Indian Territory (Oklahoma)."

2. Four of these can be documented. A letter dated July 1, 1842, in the 1845 *Report of the Secretary of War Communicating Information in Relation to Transfers of Chickasaw and Choctaw Orphan and Incompetent Funds* (Vol. 9, No. 160 in *Public Documents Printed by Order of Senate of the United States, Second Session of the Twenty-Eighth Congress*, December 2, 1844) indicates that Berthelet, Heald & Co., D. & S. Folsom, and Doak & Tims were the primary mercantile establishments in Doaksville at that time, with David Folsom identified as the principal of D. & S. Folsom elsewhere in the document. These three companies along with Shrack & Nail appear in the list of commodities seized in March 1843 from the steamboat *Fort Towson* by the Customs official James Bourland at Bryarly's Landing, as reported in the "Red River Case, and Disarming Texan Forces" (Vol. 1, No. 1 in the same series).

3. Ague, a usually malarial fever characterized by regularly recurring chills.

4. The mixed-blood Chickasaw Colberts were a large family group in the Indian Territory, as can be seen in K. M. Armstrong's genealogy page "Descendants of James Logan Colbert" (on the "Chickasaw Historical Research Page"). Many of the Chickasaw located initially in the Choctaw Nation near Doaksville rather than moving immediately to the Chickasaw District to the west. The most important of these was the Chickasaw Chief George Colbert, who established a large farming operation near Fort Towson according to an article on him in the *Encyclopedia of Oklahoma History and Culture*. However, George Colbert died in 1839. His son Pitman (Samuel B.) offers a possibility for the Colbert family encountered by Withenbury. Pitman was born about 1797, married Sarah McGillivray, with whom he had four children, and died in Doaksville in 1853. The Vicy Colbert mentioned in this letter was Pitman's sister. Emma Christian in "Memories of My Childhood Days in the Choctaw Nation" (*Chronicles of Oklahoma*, June 1931) says that she was born three and a half miles west of Doaksville in the 1860s and that Pitman Colbert had operated a large plantation one mile west of Doaksville.

5. David Folsom was a mixed-blood Choctaw born in 1791 who had been a district chief in Mississippi before he came to the Indian Territory in 1832. He married Rhoda Nail in 1810, with whom he had 10 children, and after her death in 1839, Jane Hall, with whom he had four children (see the Folsom Family Association's genealogy page "Descendants of Israel Folsom"). Joseph Thoburn and Muriel Wright in *Oklahoma, A History of the State and Its People* indicate that David Folsom was among the large Chickasaw and Choctaw plantation owners, a group that included Robert Jones, Sampson Folsom, Pitman Colbert, Jackson Kemp, Joel Nail, and Benjamin, Henry, and Sloan Love. That the David Folsom plantation lands were contiguous to the road to Doaksville is known from the 1938 Jordan D. Folsom interview in the "Indian-Pioneer Papers" (University of Oklahoma Libraries Western History Collections). The junior partner in D. & S. Folsom was probably David's nephew Sampson Folsom (1820–1872), who is characterized as a merchant in "Descendants of Israel Folsom." William Goode indicates that he met with David Folsom when he visited Doaksville in 1844 and stayed at Folsom's public house (i.e., hotel). Folsom died in 1847 and is buried in the Old Doaksville section of the Fort Towson Cemetery.

6. Robert M. Jones (1808–1873), a mixed-blood Choctaw leader, was the wealthiest person in the Indian Territory and is listed in the 1860 Choctaw Nation Slave Schedule with four plantations (Walnut Prairie, Shawneetown, Kiamitia County, and Lake West) and 224 slaves. In a letter dated December 12, 1841, in the 1845 *Report of the Secretary of War Communicating Information in Relation to Transfers of Chickasaw and Choctaw Orphan and Incompetent Funds* (Vol. 9, No. 160 in *Public Documents Printed by Order of Senate of the United States, Second Session of the Twenty-Eighth Congress*, December 2, 1844), William

Armstrong, the Acting Superintendent for the Western Territory, states that he has known Jones since Jones came to the Choctaw Nation in 1832. Withenbury is referencing a location for Jones prior to the erection of the famous Rose Hill, which was located seven miles southeast of present-day Hugo, Oklahoma. Jones was married to Susan Colbert (1810–1860) at the time, with a son, George (1840–1845), and a daughter on the way (Frances, who was born in April 1842). See the article on "Robert M. Jones" in the *Encyclopedia of Oklahoma History and Culture*; W. B. Morrison's "The Tragedy of Rose Hill" (transcribed from the March 11, 1928, *Daily Oklahoman*); and (for the Jones-Colbert relationship) the genealogy page "Descendants of James Logan Colbert."

7. By including the doctors, Withenbury indicates that he is not necessarily referring to business partnerships. William Goode in *Outposts of Zion* states that he met with William Armstrong and John Heald at Scullyville (extreme northeast corner of the Indian Territory) in 1843, with Heald described as a member of the firm of Berthelet, Heald & Co., composed of Heald, the Canadian Berthelet, and the half-breed Choctaw Robert Jones. Goode describes the firm as the licensed traders of the Choctaw Nation, with establishments at different places, who "supplied the natives with goods of good quality and at fair rates, scorning to deceive or take advantage of their ignorance; a great contrast with the character of most Indian traders." Heald was at that time living in Scullyville. Muriel Wright in "John Hobart Heald" (*Chronicles of Oklahoma*, September 1924) indicates that he did not locate in Doaksville until 1846 and that he left in 1851 for New Orleans, where he established a commission business, handling cotton sent to him by Robert Jones from Doaksville. With the departure of Heald, this firm became Berthelet & Jones, advertising in the October 15, 1851, *Choctaw Intelligencer* as dry goods and groceries merchants. The August 10, 1853, *Washington Telegraph* reports the destruction on July 17 of the storehouses in Doaksville of Berthelet, Jones & Co. and Garland & Co.

8. James Morrison in "Notes from the Northern Standard" (*Chronicles of Oklahoma*, summer 1948) provides documented information from a Berthelet relative indicating that Berthelet operated a store in Doaksville in 1836 under the name J. R. Berthelet & Co., that he and his wife Eliza lived in a house that was built with the help of soldiers at Fort Towson, and that he established a partnership in 1836 with Robert Jones, who was operating a store in Skullyville under the name R. M. Jones & Co. William Goode indicates that he met with Berthelet in Doaksville in 1844 at the recommendation of John Heald. Berthelet was postmaster at Doaksville in 1847 (J. Y. Bryce, "First Post Offices in What is Now State of Oklahoma," *Chronicles of Oklahoma*, June 1926).

9. L. D. Alsobrook published the *Choctaw Intelligencer* in Doaksville during its short life from 1850 to 1852. This was the third newspaper published in the Indian Territory and was preceded in Doaksville by the *Choctaw Telegraph*, whose publisher was D. G. Ball and whose editor was Daniel Folsom, a nephew

of David Folsom. On these early newspapers, see James Morrison, "News for the Choctaws," *Chronicles of Oklahoma*, Summer 1949. For an indication of Alsobrook's mercantile activities in 1848 and 1849, see the 1850 *Report of the Second Auditor of the Treasury, with Copies of Accounts of Disbursements for the Benefit of the Indians* (Sen Ex. Doc. 41, 1st Cong. 1st Sess.).

10. John Morris in *Ghost Towns of Oklahoma* cites an 1843 document in the Indian Archives of the Oklahoma Historical Society by Alvin Goode (another missionary), which says that "The trading establishment of Josiah Doak and Vinson Brown Timms, an Irishman, had the contract to supply the Indians their rations, figured at 13c a ration. A motley crowd always assembled at Doaksville on annuity days to receive them." The latter was Vinson Tims, who, along with Joseph Berthelet, represented the Choctaw Nation in a raft removal convention in Clarksville, as recorded in the December 22, 1847, *Washington Telegraph*. James Brown Tims in a 1937 interview included in the "Indian Pioneer Papers" says that his grandfather's store was located in front of the rock jail in Doaksville.

11. See Letter 25.

12. Enos Look, a 45-year-old married physician from New York, appears in the 1860 Red River County census. His obituary in the October 21, 1881, Clarksville *Standard* says that he was Post Surgeon at Fort Towson in 1842, moved to Clarksville in 1843, was twice married, and died in 1881 at the age of 78. He began advertising in January 1844 in the Clarksville *Northern Standard*, with the advertisement indicating that he was a graduate of the Cincinnati Medical College.

13. Frances was born in 1842 and married Samuel Love in 1859.

14. The firm of Berthelet & Jones later owned the *R. M. Jones*, and Jones himself owned the *Ariel* and *Victoria* in the 1850s. The *Frances Jones* was owned by others.

15. As will be indicated in the next letter, Ashbrook was partner with Travis Wright in the store at Wright's Landing. Henry Ashbrook appears in the 1840–1842 Red River County tax rolls.

16. William Ashbrook was co-owner of major stockyards in Covington, Kentucky, according to a "Covington Biographies" profile of him at the Kenton County Public Library website.

23 ✦ Wright's Landing

Most of this letter is concerned with Travis Wright[1] and Wright's Landing in northwest Red River County, Texas, across from the mouth of the Kiamichi River. The first half provides a discussion of the earliest routes around the raft far downstream (Figure 9) as a prelude to the description of Wright's flatboat and keelboat activities. Wright's Landing had been a keelboat landing and was one of the three (along with Fulton and Roland) most important steamboat landings on the Upper Red River. Withenbury indicates in this letter that it was the upper limit of commercially feasible navigation and served Paris, Bonham, and Sherman and the whole of Lamar and Fannin counties.

Claiborne Wright brought his family, including his sons George and Travis, from Tennessee to Pecan Point by keelboat in 1816. George had the headright in which the landing with its mercantile facilities was located, as well as Kiomatia Plantation,[2] where Travis also lived. Travis opened a store at Jonesboro around 1830 and another in Clarksville. In 1838, he married Mary Eliza Johnston at Jonesboro, and in 1839 acquired the Kiomatia property from his brother. He moved to Paris, Texas, in 1850, where he was president of the Memphis, El Paso & Pacific Railroad and participated in the formation of the Paris Exchange Bank. Withenbury indicates that he continued to operate the plantation and landing until his death at Kiomatia in 1875 at the age of 68.[3]

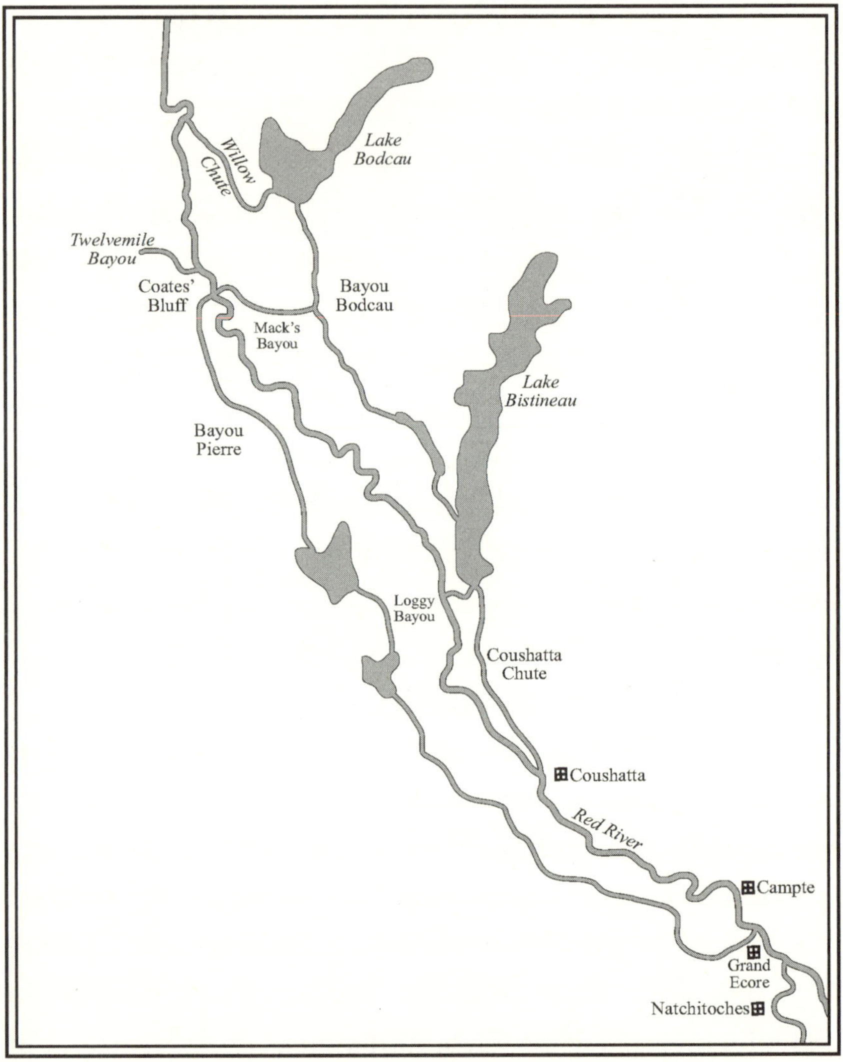

FIGURE 9: EASTERN KEELBOAT ROUTES

⁂

Fort Towson was established years before the waters of Upper Red River could be made available by steamboats for the transportation of supplies. This was owing to the existence of the "great raft," which at the time Captain Shreve attacked it with his "Eradicator," extended from near the mouth of Loggy Bayou 120 miles below Shreveport, to the Hurricane Bluffs, sixty miles above that point, thus rendering Red River for 180 miles entirely useless for all purposes of navigation. When Fort Towson was first organized, the ordinary head of navigation on Red River was at Natchitoches; but occasionally a venturesome steamboatman would go as far as Campte, twenty-eight miles by the river, but by land via Grand Ecore, only ten miles. At times, also, boats of a small class ventured as far as "Couchatta Chute," some forty-five miles still further up; but none of those points afforded any facility for reaching Fort Towson, except by overland route. Accordingly a military road was constructed from Campte to Fort Towson, and the troops and supplies for the fort were for a long time sent over that route in wagons and on foot. There was a time, however, when keelboats could navigate the Upper Red River, and make the passage around the raft by entering the mouth of Willow Chute, which is about forty miles above Shreveport, and which was then above the head of the raft, and following its crooked course into Lake Bisteneau, thence across the lake to the head of Loggy Bayou, and down that dangerous little stream to the river, below the raft, from which point there was comparatively but little difficulty in reaching steamboat navigation and effecting an exchange of freights with steamers from New Orleans.

By reference to the map of Louisiana it will be seen that the route which I have just in part described lies entirely on the northeastern side of Red River, and there was no possible way of getting around the raft on the other side, for notwithstanding there was a chain of water communication on the west side of the river, commencing at Bayou Pierre, two miles above Grand Ecore, and extending by an intricate network of lakes and bayous to within a few miles of Coats' Bluff, (now Shreveport,) at that point the river washed the base of the hills, and thus the chain of communication was broken.

The uninterrupted growth of the Red River Raft in time closed the mouth of Willow Chute, and so that keelboat route was lost forever; and then came the necessity for a new passage around the raft, and it was found by leaving Red River on the western side four miles above Shreveport, at Twelve mile Bayou; thence through Sodo Lake and Clear Lake, and up Black Bayou to Caddo prairie, where "Sewell's canal" was cut and a connection formed with Red Bayou, and thence out to the river twenty-five miles above the point the raft had reached in 1839, and sixty-five miles above the mouth of Willow Chute, the whole of which route I have described minutely in former chapters.

After this last route was opened and before Captain Shreve had reached Coats' Bluff with his snagboats, the Upper Red River keel-boatmen could reach the river after passing through the lake at the mouth of Twelve-mile Bayou, and then work their way along some six miles down to the mouth of Mack's Bayou, which debouches from Red River on the eastern side and leads into Lake Bistineau via Red Chute, and finally to the Red River again via Loggy Bayou.

I doubt if there are many of my readers who can understandingly follow me through the various routes which I have just attempted to describe, but they must not doubt me, when I state as a matter of fact in the history of the navigation of Red River, that these intricate channels have all been successfully used, and each in its turn has served as the only means of water communication between Upper and Lower Red River. And when we look back to the days when the patient keelboatman started out for the long voyage from Red River at Kiamitia to Red River below Loggy Bayou, and contrast those days and their trials with the present time, when magnificent floating palaces can plow the Red River waters almost uninterruptedly from the Mississippi to the mouth of Kiamitia—a distance of nearly twelve hundred miles—we ought not to be too sparing of our praises of the men who from time to time have borne a part in the labors and trials incident to this slow, and at times almost hopeless process of development of a river, a country and a commerce of which we are all proud to-day, and in the benefits of which we are all anxious to share.

In some of my former articles I have brought into particular prominence many of the men who were foremost in the ranks of explorers and pioneers of these doubtful ways. But they were almost without an exception steamboatmen. And I must be pardoned now for going back to the times of the keel and flat-boatmen;[4] and while lingering about Kiamitia and Fort Towson, waiting for a rise, introducing to my readers one of the old stock, Captain Travis G. Wright, who I am quite certain is the only living representative of those very early navigators of Red River. Captain Wright, at an early day, many years anterior to the time I have been chronicling, became the owner of the land directly opposite the mouth of the Kiamitia River. He was joint owner with the Indians in the ferry, and also in "the store" with Ashbrook at the time of my visit in 1842. A short distance above the point, [5] and just back from the river, he owned and cultivated a large cotton plantation. He kept also a warehouse for his own convenience and that of the surrounding country, and Wright's Landing is to this day the principal shipping and receiving point for the towns of Paris, Bonham, and Sherman; in fact I may say for the whole of Lamar and Fannin Counties. Occasionally, however, the high stage of water permits steamboats to go to Pine Hills,[6] twenty-five miles further up, but as a general thing, freight contracts are made to Wright's Landing, and no farther. Several steamboats have ascended the river since the days of Captain Truesdale with the Trader to Preston, Texas, but I have never heard of a profitable trip being made to that point, nor of the same boat going so far the second time.

But I started out to speak of Captain Wright, the keelboatman, and I find myself drifting away from him. I think I am correct in stating that he was a Tennesseean; but it matters not where he came from; it is sufficient to know that he emigrated to Texas when quite a young man, and although the life of a keel and flatboatman, which he led for many seasons, would seem to class him among the "rolling stones" of humanity, I am, with his host of other admirers and friends, happy to be able to say he has "gathered much moss," and now enjoys a competency of this world's goods as the well deserved reward of his untiring labor and honorable dealings.

In the business of keelboating and flatboating he was the contemporary of Captain Dick Finn, a man of much notoriety, of whom I may speak more particularly as the Relief approaches on her downward trip and his old homestead and plantation at Lost Prairie. [7]

Captain Jim Gamble was also one of Captain Wright's fellow workers in those early times; [8] but as I have given him an overhauling already I will let him pass now with the simple remark that he made his principal mark afterward as a steamboatman, and in cutting the heavy timber across Red Bayou to keep out honorable competition—verily there are some of his sort living yet. Captain Wright's labors on the river began before the great raft had closed up the mouth of Willow Chute, and he made a number of trips by that route through Lake Bisteneau and Loggy Bayou, carrying his own and his neighbors cotton a distance of at least seven hundred miles through a perfect labyrinth of rivers, lakes and bayous, and with but little else than a wilderness on either shore. After Willow Chute "growed up and har'd over," as old Jack Bradley, another of his contemporaries, used to say, Captain Wright was among the first to try the new route through Red and Black Bayous and the lakes to Shreveport, and then down Mack's Bayou through Lake Bistineau. [9] And among his associates in those days were, in addition to the old ones, Captain Abram Block, of Washington, Arkansas, and several of the planters who were cultivating the rich, alluvial lands below Fulton, and also about this time our quondam friend the teamster, Mayer, of the "dead fall," explorer, keelboatman, steamboat Captain, pilot, and, finally, the man who cut a "gut" at which he took toll for all cotton and merchandise which has passed around the raft for the last two years, and, if I mistake not, who still sits gathering tribute from the people for the privilege of floating the products of Upper Red River through his last "gut" into Kelly's Bayou, and thence to the river below. George Alban, I think, is the only man now living who can date his keelboat experience back to the days when Captain Wright, toward the close of his river career, was still devoting a part of each year to that calling. Truly, "we are all passing away."

As soon as the way was open for steamboats to enter Upper Red River, Captain Wright abandoned the idea of floating his own cotton out on flatboats, and he was by this time too much engrossed in planting and profitable mercantile pursuits to think of following the hazardous business for others. But he was a provident man, and always guarded against the chances of being shut out from a market by any such contingency as low water—too low for steamboats—and for several years after the time when I first met him he always kept a good sized flatboat all framed and ready to be put together and housed until all probabilities of the failure of steamboats reaching his landing had passed away. In addition to the above characteristic, Captain Wright was always a sober man—a rare quality among river men in those parts—and so it will not be wondered at when I say that he has been prospered in all of his undertakings. The Red River steamboatmen, without a single exception that I ever heard of, regarded "Travis Wright" as their friend; indeed, he was a "model man."

The country around Wright's Landing had proven itself well adapted to wheat raising, and Captain Wright and his brother George were foremost in urging its culture, and they were the first to make a shipment of wheat from that part of Texas to New Orleans. I think it was in 1857 that they put up one hundred sacks of choice wheat, and it was the finest I ever saw, for a sample of Texas product, and shipped it by the steamboat Reub White. She carried it safely to Erwin's Bluff on Black Bayou; and at that point the Captain (W. W. Withenbury) deeming it advisable to send the "Reub" back up the river for another load, put his load of cotton and the one hundred sacks of wheat off, and went to Shreveport in a skiff, where he engaged the steamer Swamp Fox to go to Erwin's Bluff and take his load for New Orleans. This trip of the Swamp Fox was, indeed, a memorable trip, as she was the largest steamboat[10] that ever attempted to go up Black Bayou; and when she came to a place where she was six feet too wide to pass between the cypress trees, Captain Kimball looked back at the pilot-house where Captain W. W. W. was stationed with the pilot, and cried, "Stop her, Withenbury; stop her, you are getting my Fox into a swamp where she will never get out;" and from this dilemma Poor "Billy" Kimball began to look for a place of escape by backing out. But not so Captain Withenbury; he had been through Black Bayou before with boats too wide, and he knew just how to cut his way through, and in about two hours the troublesome trees—four of them—were lying prostrate in the Bayou, and the

"Swamp Fox"—much to the delight of Captain Kimball—on her winding way to Erwin's Bluff. The whole six miles of Black Bayou cost them six hours of patient and persevering labor; but before night overtook the Swamp Fox she was lying at Erwin's Bluff with her head down stream, ready for an early start on the following morning. The whole of the Reub White's cargo, consisting of 790 bales of cotton and 100 sacks wheat, was put on board by midnight, and the Swamp Fox safely landed at Shreveport the next day before dark; a proud achievement for Captain Withenbury, he having accomplished what everybody said at Shreveport could not be done—he had taken the Swamp Fox through Black Bayou and returned her safely to Shreveport; and here I will add that no other boat of her size has as yet ever been there.

The Swamp Fox finished her load and started for New Orleans, but ill luck attended her, and she sunk above Campte, and there was lost Capt. Travis Wright's first shipment of wheat from Upper Red River, and there in front of Carroll's plantation lies to this day the remains of the Swamp Fox, one of the best Red River steamboats ever built.

Now, I find myself fast encroaching upon my limits, and I have not said the one-half I feel inclined to say of Capt. T. G. Wright. Nor have I spoken of Fort Towson, as it was in those days; so I must crave the indulgence of my readers once more, while I promise not to leave that locality without a more extended notice of that important military post.

Captain Wright has been honored within the last two years by having an Upper Red River steamboat (the Travis Wright) bear his name to his own door; and however much he may have considered himself flattered by the kindly intended compliments of "Tommy" Reeder, I am certain that if his judgment had been consulted the "Travis Wright" would have been a better boat—she could not have been named for a better man. But she went up in a cloud of smoke the other day, and ended her career, with probably more profit to her owners than if she had lived to battle another season against low water, "bad luck" and the meddlesome OUTSIDER.

Notes

1. See the article on "Wright, Travis George" by Skipper Steely in the *Handbook of Texas Online* and Steely's coverage of the larger Wright family in *Six Months from Tennessee.*

2. There do not appear to be any map representations of the landing, but its location is not problematic. The Texas General Land Office's 1856 map of Red River County indicates that the ferry at Wright's Landing had been replaced by Ragsdale's Ferry a short distance downstream. The plantation home was also named Kiomatia and was located on a Caddoan mound (for the location, see the section on "Kiomatia" in T. Lindsay Baker's *More Ghost Towns of Texas*). The Kiomatia shown on maps such as A. J. Johnson's 1860 *Texas* was a small settlement that developed south of the plantation home.

3. Paris is in Lamar County west of Red River County, but only 30 miles from the Wright plantation home. Wright is listed in the 1850 Red River County census but not in the 1860 census, which is compatible with the move to Paris. However, he continued to pay taxes as a resident of Red River County on the plantation properties throughout his life. George Travis Wright, his grandson, was interviewed in 1937 as part of the "Indian-Pioneer Papers" oral history project (University of Oklahoma Libraries Western History Collections) and confirms the continuous operation of the plantation and occupancy of the plantation house by the family, but not the operation of the landing. Wright is designated a citizen of Red River County in a legal notice in the April 3, 1852, Clarksville *Northern Standard*, and the December 31, 1880, Clarksville *Standard* says that Wright had been a Red River County subscriber through 1867. The September 14, 1875, *Daily Shreveport Times* reports Wright's death through the Paris *North Texan*, which says that Wright came to Texas in 1816 and lived in the Red River area for 59 years.

4. Flatboats were elongated boxes that were propelled by the current and therefore could only be used for downstream movements. Keelboats were more ship-shaped, had keels, and were propelled by poling and therefore could be used for upstream and downstream movements. Flatboats brought cotton from the Upper Red River to Shreveport during low-water periods for decades after steamboats became the primary mode of transport.

5. Upstream of the point on which the Kiamitia warehouse was located, where the river drops sharply to the south.

6. Pine Hills was in the northwest corner of Red River County and had been a keelboat landing. As Withenbury says, steamboats occasionally went to Pine Hills. The first advertisement in relation to Pine Hills is for the groceries and dry goods store of J. P. Reilly in the August 16, 1845, Clarksville *Northern Standard*.

7. Withenbury doesn't do this. The 1850 Lafayette County census indicates that Finn was aged 47 and married with four children. The October 30, 1844, *Washington Telegraph* reports that Finn had acquired the Cross Keys Tavern in Fulton, which he was operating with his wife, and the April 5, 1854, issue reports the killing of Finn in Washington. With respect to Finn's character, see *McDaniel v. Crosby* in the January 1858 Term of the Arkansas Supreme Court, in which the Supreme Court affirmed findings in lower courts (including a jury trial) that Finn had coerced a will.

8. Gamble was a keelboatman and flatboatman because he operated a plantation on Red River east of Wright.

9. Willow Chute was closed in 1828, and the route on the west side of the river through Sewell's Canal was not completed until 1831. Prior to 1831, Wright appears to have been primarily involved in the transport of cotton downstream by flatboat. In a letter in the December 16, 1828, *Arkansas Gazette*, Richard Finn says that he was paid $600–$800 by merchants and farmers to explore an alternative route on the west side of the river. The February 5, 1881, *New Orleans Daily Democrat* reports that around 1831 Wright and Finn went to Natchitoches where they purchased keelboats for the movement of freight upriver, utilizing a portion of what became the western route on the return trip.

10. The *Swamp Fox* was 162 feet long by 30 feet wide.

24 ✦ Home Amusements

The *Relief* was still on the Choctaw shore at Kiamitia, and the crew was looking for amusement, which was found in a cock fight on a Red River sandbar and a trip to Gates Creek to gather Bois d'Arc wood (also called Osage Orange because of its fruit and its association with the Osage Indians). Bois

d'Arc is native to the Upper Red River area and took its name from the fact that it was highly favored by the Indians for bow making (thus, bow-wood). The wood is yellow-orange, dense, extremely strong, flexible, and takes a high polish. The root bark and sapwood produce a yellow-brown dye.[1]

⁂

[First part not used.]

In my last chapter I neglected entirely to speak of the Relief or "Uncle Joe;" and to make suitable amends, I suppose I ought to devote a whole column to them; but I have so often heretofore set them aside without ceremony in order to catch a flitting thought of some incidental personage or locality, and give it preference, that I will impose once more upon good nature, and only say that the Relief lay still at Kiamitia, while "Uncle Joe" kept shaking with the "ager;" but he consoled himself with these words: "It's a good time to shake when a fellow's nothing else to do."

On the third day of our stay at this last landing place, our crew began to look about for home amusements, as we were all pretty well tired of tramping about the woods, and the novelty of observing Indian life had begun to grow monotonous. Ed. LaRue fancied that among the chickens in his coop there were some who showed signs of game; and no sooner did he begin to talk about pitting "Choctaw against Texas" (for he had supplied himself from both countries) than our second engineer Morrison began to rummage among his "traps" for gaffs; for he had been a pupil of Henry Dawes, one of the most scientific cock-fighters in the South. Dawes was a steamboat engineer,[2] and for many years he was Captain John Smoker's best man on Red River. He was a skillful mechanic, and no man knew better than Henry Dawes how to "heel," trim or weight a chicken for a fight; and Morrison had studied the art so thoroughly, while with Dawes, that he attained such perfection by the time I am writing of that there was but little to choose between master and pupil. Now as good luck would have it, the falling river had brought to the light a smooth circular sand-bar, some seventy-five feet in diameter, and entirely disconnected from either shore; in fact, it was a little island, and on this island it was soon decided that we should have a treat, in the way of the sublime and intellectual sport nowhere to be found outside of the cock-pit. Morrison and LaRue were the self-constituted managers, and they took care to select, each according to his own taste and judgment, the best birds, which, when they were heeled and trimmed, and placed on the sand-bar face to face, seemed each to consider himself in the presence of a perfect stranger, notwithstanding the fact that but an hour before they had both been friendly inmates of the same coop. They were now so completely metamorphosed that they were as ready to enter the gladiatorial contest as though they had never seen a "dung hill." About the time we were being ferried over to the island, "Uncle Joe" crawled out of his berth, and wanted to know "What in the name of the seven wonders" all the rumpus was about; and, when told of the sport about to be inaugurated, he simply said, "Let 'er rip, but don't waste them roosters."

By the time the fight was fairly under way, the sand under our feet, which but two days before had been covered with water, became a perfect jelly, and we were obliged to keep changing positions in order to save ourselves from going below. Those of my readers who have been favored with an acquaintance of Red River quicksands, will not fail to appreciate the predicament we were in. But not a man would willingly return to the boat, so long as either chicken could be persuaded to face his foe and strike at him. The quicksand, however, soon forced the umpires to cry out "draw;" and as we made haste to the yawl and skiff as our only "arks of safety," LaRue and Morrison gathered up the few bones and feathers that were left. And thus ended the first and last cock fight ever witnessed in the middle of Red River. At supper that night, we put forever out of sight all that remained of the two unfortunate chickens which had been selected for their supposed game qualities, and so we convinced Captain Ross that "them roosters were not wasted."

On the next day after the chicken fight, a new programme was announced, in which an attempt was to be made to combine somewhat of the useful with our pleasurable pursuits. Captain Hildreth, on one of his rabbit hunts with Ed. LaRue's dog, had discovered along the valley of Gates' Creek a great many Bois d'Arc or Osage orange trees, many of them of great age and immense size; and as they were growing immediately on the bank of the creek, his prolific brain at once conceived the idea of cutting at least a skiff-load of beautiful yellow wood, and carrying it away to his home, where he could furnish his friends with walking canes and such other ornamental articles as their fancies might suggest.

Mr. Philley, our pilot, conceived the idea of having a pilot-wheel made of the wood, and Ed. LaRue, not dreaming in those days that he would ever rise from the cook-house to the pilot-house, was content if he could only procure enough of the solid wood to make handles to all the butcher knives and cleavers in the Relief's kitchen. Morrison's aspirations only extended to water-gauge sticks and a few other little traps about the engine. And as for "Uncle Joe," he'd "be dod durned if he cared for any of it, unless 'twould cure the ager."

The first thing to be done now was to prepare the axes and cross-cut saw and organize a force to proceed on foot to the spot where the favorite trees were standing, and a party also who would undertake to row the skiff up the creek, where it was proposed to load it for the "down trip," all of which could be accomplished long before night, if every man did his duty. The overland expedition was off in a hurry; and when the skiff was ready, this scribbler took his seat in the stern sheets, with the expectation of having an easy time; but we had not proceeded a half mile up the crooked and rapid little stream when the difficulties of navigation increased so that all hands were required to labor in a manner unlooked for at the outset, to propel our little skiff up over the rapids and around the short turns; and long before we came in sight of the choppers we heard their shouts; and occasionally when some great bend of the stream brought us very near them we could hear distinctly the sound of axes through the dense thicket that fringed the margin of the leaping little rivulet; then we would be borne again far away into the stillness of the forest where nothing but the gurgling of the waters as they leaped among the rocks and over the trunks of fallen trees disturbed the silence; and as we rested our "weary oars" and looked down into the depths of the clear sparkling waters we for the moment seemed to well nigh forget that we were not preparing for sport in the mountain brooks of far off New England.

After some four hours of alternate labor and rest we came to the end of our voyage, and our skiff rested in a quiet little pool where the current was so gentle that it was scarcely necessary to make her fast. Our woodsmen had felled two large trees and were ready to load the skiff with several beautiful cuts of about five feet in length and from twelve to eighteen inches in diameter. Their plans for taking them on board were also well digested, and they had cleared away all obstructions between their logs and the water, and were waiting and ready to roll them down the steep declivity into the creek, when it would be but trifling labor to put them on board, and away we would glide without an effort to the Relief with our trophies from the Indian Nation. In order to prevent the logs floating away from us before we could get them into the skiff, she was placed across the creek just below where the logs were to plunge into the water; and at a given signal—Philley suggested "like the launching of a steamboat from the stocks"—they were started, and swiftly they chased each other, and in the twinkling of an eye the mirror-like surface of the deep, clear pool was broken into fragments of thousands of little circles by the plunge after plunge of the Bois d'Arc logs as they successively struck the water and hurried to the bottom among the rocks, where they lie probably to this day, for we never fished them up.

The wise men of our party—Hildreth and Philley—had made no estimate of the density and specific gravity of the green Bois d'Arc, or they would never have dreamed of its floating. Well, there, in plain sight, but at a depth of at least ten feet, lay the labor of our hands, and one of the errors of our heads. Captain Hildreth looked wise, shifted his quid, and exclaimed "Who would have thought of that?" Philley said "That beats h_ll; no pilot-wheel for me." Ed. LaRue gave one "whoop," and comforted himself because he had not knocked the handles off all his knives, and Morrison said "Hickory makes very good gauge sticks, boys, and I don't care; we've had the fun anyhow." We were unanimous in determining to hurry back to the Relief; and while we sped down the swift current some four miles, to the river, we made the woods ring with our merriment for we were each and all striving to prove ourselves philosophers and look upon the "bright side" of our disappointment. When we arrived at the boat we found "Uncle Joe" chatting with Dr. Look, whose visit had cheered the old man up. They both listened to the recital of our day's adventure and experience; and when the story was told the laugh came in, and Captain Ross said he was satisfied now that the fools were not all dead yet. But we had our frolic, and professed to be satisfied with it, which, were it to be repeated the next day, there was not one of the party who would not have relinquished his claim to Bois d'Arc canes, &c., and be content to be called an OUTSIDER.

Notes

1. See the section on Osage Orange in Matt Turner's *Remarkable Plants of Texas*.

2. A brief profile of Sam Applegate in the October 2, 1880, *New Orleans Daily Democrat* says that he was in command of the *Duck River* in 1846, which he had purchased along with the engineer Henry Dawes and Capt. Joe Clark. Morrison was second engineer on the *Relief* and apparently operated as second engineer under first-engineer Dawes on many boats.

25 ✦ Dr. McDonough

The *Relief* was still on the Choctaw shore at Kiamitia, and Withenbury recounts a promised (in Letter 22) story about Dr. McDonough and his wife Visey of the mixed-blood Chickasaw Colberts. Levica "Vicy" Colbert[1] was the daughter of the mixed-blood Chickasaw Chief George Colbert. She was educated, fairly wealthy, and owned property in Mississippi before moving to the Indian Territory in 1838. John McDonna[2] was born in England in 1818 and married Vicy in 1840. Their only child, George, was born in 1842. Vicy died in 1846. McDonna moved to Clarksville in 1848,

where he established a medical practice, became partner in a drugstore, and remarried.

⁂

[First part not used.]

In a former chapter I spoke of Dr. McDonough, who had married into one of the wealthy Indian families, and settled at Doaksville in the Nation, and I had in mind then to relate at least one little incident which transpired while the Relief lay at Kiamitia, and in which the Dr. and his wife were the principal actors; and as they paid us a visit on the day after our cock-fight and Bois d'Arc expedition, I may as well tell my story here.

The Dr., by marrying into the Nation, or more properly speaking the tribe, had become by their laws fully enfranchised as a Choctaw citizen, and by virtue of his profession he held a position far above the rank of ordinary white citizens engaged in other pursuits in the Indian Territory. The liquor laws, as I have before stated, were very stringent, so much so that none was allowed to be sold except upon an order from a physician, and consequently our bar-keeper found a very dull trade while we were tied up to the Choctaw shore.

On two or three occasions parties had come to the boat with Dr. McDonough's prescriptions and got their bottles filled, and Dr. Look hinted to us one day that Dr. McDonough himself probably took most of the medicine which he thus prescribed. So we were not surprised when on the day of his visit, while his wife was in the ladies' cabin, he called for the bar-keeper and wrote an order for a bottle whisky, for a half-breed named Dougherty Colbert—a relative of the Doctor's wife.[3] Very soon after Dougherty had gone ashore, the Doctor followed him, and when he came back we found him more entertaining than usual, in fact very loquacious; and in less than half an hour another Indian came and the Doctor wrote an order for the filling of his half-gallon jug, (all "for medicine" of course.) By this time the Doctor's better half was amusing herself in the pantry, looking over and admiring the various articles which were new to her, and appeared not to notice her husband, who had followed the jug on shore and was busy behind the warehouse filling a couple of bottles out of it, one of which he carefully placed in each end of his saddle-bags, and then brought them back and hung them over the branch of a tree precisely were he had placed them when he and his wife dismounted from their ponies on their arrival.

By the time Mrs. McDonough's curiosity was satisfied, her husband was sitting on the boiler deck[4] pretty mellow. She approached him, and addressing him in the Choctaw dialect, seemed to say more than simply "Let us go home." The Doctor essayed a dignified reply, and undertook to appear very amiable. He rose to his feet, attempted to adjust his equilibrium, and seizing her by the arm he managed, as she was considerably the tallest—and decidedly the most "sober Indian" of the two—to steady himself and walk to the shore and up the steep bank, without any serious *faux pas*. But once ashore and in her own territory, Visey began to overhaul her little husband in rather an authoritative manner, and her words, although all in an unknown tongue (to us on the boat) and her tone plainly told that the Doctor was getting a severe lecture.

We all watched with increasing curiosity the *denouement*, and we were not a little amused to see the Doctor leaning against the tree where the saddle-bags with the "contraband spirits" were hanging just above his head, and striving to defend himself against the evident accusations of his proud, spirited and highly offended Indian wife. The longer he stood there the more silly he looked, and the more helpless he became. He made one bold effort to disengage his saddle-bags from the branch of the tree and signally failed, and the poor little fellow looked imploringly up into the face of his now enraged wife, and she in answer to his fruitless effort took hold of them, and as she felt their increased weight she let one end fall rather heavily against the tree and upon his "devoted head," from which his hat had already fallen; and in some almost unaccountable manner, she managed to bring the other end of the saddle-bags into a like contact with the Doctor's upper regions, nor did she heed his cries for mercy until every drop of the *hucki-huma* (whisky) was spilled in strict accordance with the laws of the Choctaw Nation. While all this was going on, to the infinite amusement of the lookers-on, I felt that I would have given a month's hard labor to have understood fully the Choctaw language just then; for I would gladly have treasured up the words in their fullest meaning that fell hurriedly from the lips of that haughty, dignified and offended Indian wife, while the contents of the two whisky bottles was streaming over the face of her besotted husband. Possibly some of my readers who "have been there" may form a correct idea of the gentle reproof which Visey Colbert visited upon the head of her erring spouse on this occasion.

"Uncle Joe," who had witnessed this performance, held his peace until the storm was over, and then turning to Morrison he said: "Dang my buttons, old fellow, if she ain't better game than ary one of them roosters that fit on the sand-bar the other day;" and Morrison quietly replied, "She's better heel'd."

By the help of some Indians the Dr. was at last seated in his saddle and his feet placed in the stirrups; and his pony seeming to appreciate the situation, carefully trotted along homeward behind the erect form of one of the proudest Indian women of the Choctaw Nation, though now humbled, insulted and silent, because of the beastliness of her liege lord, whom she had chosen from among the superior (?) white race for his brilliancy of intellect and his high attainments.

I met the Doctor years afterward, and he alluded to this occurrence with a sense of shame; but that sentiment was doomed to be short-lived whenever the tempter was near, and, finally, I am told, that while in the midst of his manhood, his bright intellect withered and his body returned to the dust, leaving his widow and a bright little son to bear his name,[5] and risk the inheritance of his vices or his virtues.

Dr. McDonough was of either English or Scotch extraction, a polished gentleman, a brilliant scholar, and professionally an ornament to his profession. His marriage with Miss Colbert was not among the causes which led to his fall from the place among men in which both by native talent, noble instincts and education, he was so well calculated to shine. His wife was a noble and true woman, the pride of her race, of an impetuous temperament, a fair exemplar of woman's rights, but honest and honorable withal; and probably the great mistake of her life, and that which caused her many regrets, was the stepping aside from her own people, and taking to her bosom an OUTSIDER.

Notes

1. See the article on George Colbert in the *Encyclopedia of Oklahoma History and Culture*. Vicy's birth year is unknown, but she is listed in the 1818 Chicasaw Census Roll (prior to removal to the Indian Territory). Vicy's Mississippi background is covered in Dunbar Rowland, *Encyclopedia of Mississippi History*. Mary Ann (Duncan) Dobson in "Duncans in Pontotoc Co. MS Land Records" points out that Vicy acquired her land through the 1834 treaty between the U.S. and the Chickasaw Nation and demonstrates that speculation about a previous marriage is unwarranted. The family relationships and Vicy's marriage to McDonna are delineated in K. M. Armstrong's genealogy page "Descendants of James Logan Colbert" (on the "Chickasaw Historical Research Page"). Vicy appears on the 1839 census of Chickasaws made in the Indian Territory. George

McDonna was born on June 1, 1842, which meant that Vicy was pregnant at the time of this incident.

2. McDonna appears in the 1850 Red River County census as a 32-year-old M.D. born in England with a wife, Mary, aged 24 and born in Alabama, and a son, George, aged eight and born in the Choctaw Nation. Companion advertisements in the June 8, 1850, Clarksville *Northern Standard* indicate that he practiced medicine in Clarksville in 1848 and 1849 and was starting a drugstore with H. Rhine under the name McDonna, Rhine & Bro's. He participated in the formation of the Medical Association of Texas in 1853 according to the Act of Incorporation recorded in Vol. 4 of Gammel's *The Laws of Texas, 1822–1897.* The August 28, 1860, *Galveston Weekly News* indicates that McDonna died in 1860 in Lamar County.

3. Daugherty (Winchester) Colbert came to the Indian Territory in 1837 and was second governor of the Chickasaw Nation, which was formed out of the Choctaw Nation in 1855. He was the son of Levi Colbert (brother of George Colbert) and Vicy's first cousin. See John Meserve, "Governor Daugherty (Winchester) Colbert," *Chronicles of Oklahoma*, December 1940.

4. The deck above the main deck (where the boilers were located). The passenger quarters were located on the boiler deck.

5. Withenbury is apparently referring to McDonna's second wife. Evidence provided in the case of *Davis v. Wells* (*Reports of Cases Argued and Decided in the Supreme Court of the State of Texas, Term of 1872–73*) indicates that Mary was a resident of Paris, Texas, and died between 1864 and 1869 and that she and McDonna had more than one child.

26 ✦ Fort Towson

On the last day at Kiamitia, Withenbury took an overland trip to Fort Towson.[1] The fort was erected in 1824 with logs and was abandoned in 1829, after which settlers burned the structures. It was reestablished with new log structures under the name Camp Phoenix in 1830 in the context of

the removal of the Choctaws to the Indian Territory and was renamed Fort Towson in 1831. The log structures were replaced with plank and stone in 1842. Facilities included a parade ground, officers' quarters, barracks, storerooms, guardhouse, hospital, commissary, bakeshop, carpenter and blacksmith shop, powder magazine, and stables. Troops were withdrawn from the fort in 1851, and it was officially abandoned in 1856, although it continued to be used by the Choctaws. Most of the letter is about George Gooding, who was introduced in Letter 20.

⁂

[First part not used.]

But I find that I have allowed myself to drift a long way from Fort Towson before the water got high enough to allow the Relief to leave her moorings, and so must return and finish my story of our wearisome detention, for on the fifth day we found the color of the water in the river changing to a deep red, and a rise beginning to manifest itself. These rises come very suddenly, at times, and frequently without any premonition in the way of rains, and so when the water becomes suddenly red we know that "old Red is coming," and make our preparations accordingly.

The last day the Relief lay at Kiamitia I spent in a visit to the Fort and Doaksville, which are situated about two miles apart, and a more charming locality, the Fort upon much higher ground than the little Indian village, and the beautiful little Gates' Creek winding and tumbling over its rocky bed between them.

I find myself so completely carried back in my recollection of the scenes of those early times that I am writing of Fort Towson as though it still existed. Such, however, is not the case, for the necessity of maintaining a military post at that point was obviated years ago by the annexation of Texas, and the subsequent establishment of a number of our forts on the still further Western frontier. But at the time I am writing of, Fort Towson was in the zenith of its glory and usefulness; and although it was built of rough materials and was far away in the wilderness, there was a charm about it that those who visited it either on business or pleasure can never forget. Its particular site was the very best that could have been selected while keeping in view the necessity of locating it at a convenient distance from the river, and also near to Doaksville, the principal village in the Choctaw Nation.

Among the officers there I remember General Thomas and Colonel Clark, as two of the most polished, genial gentlemen and hospitable withal, that it has been my fortune to encounter among military men; and then, too, there was a fair sprinkling of young bucks, who, after putting on and showing off the necessary amount of West Point airs to convince strangers of their importance and of the fact also that the country would be lost without them, were a right jovial, social set of fellows, and on the whole it was pleasant to meet them; and the recollection of the good times enjoyed among them forms no small feature of the bright picture which my memory has kept for me until these days of lengthening shadows as I am traveling toward the sunset side of life. Lieutenant Monroe and Major Hammond are two names among the young officers especially remembered; and should they be still living, and this mention of their names ever meet their eyes, I am sure they will not have forgotten the little Relief and Captain Ross, nor this humble writer, who will always look back to the days spent in their good company with special delight.[2]

In speaking of the officers at Fort Towson, I must not fail to mention that important personage, the sutler, for what would a fort be without a sutler? Well, my friend, and everybody's friend, "Goodwin, the sutler," filled his post like a man, and from my first introduction to the fort up to the day of his death, many years after, he continued in that position.[3] He was a man of a generous nature, and so full of human sympathies that no one, from the humblest private to the officer in command, or "the stranger within the gate," was ever turned away empty handed, (or with an empty bottle). Indeed, it used to be said that many a soldier's vinegar jug had been known to leave the sutler's store fairly dancing with joy and ready to burst with the exuberance of the spirits pent up within, and thus was accounted for the noticeable fact of a great many barrels and smaller packages of sutler's stores being marked "vinegar."

But with all his strong points of character, Goodwin was weak; too weak, indeed, to shun the rock on which so many split; and day by day, by yielding to temptations, he slipped backward until at the time of his death he found himself little better than a total wreck. His estimable wife[4] stood by him to the last, always doing her part toward making his home happy, and by her good example rendering the entire social atmosphere about Fort Towson refined and cheerful. But, alas; how sadly do we often see falling to the ground the best efforts of one good woman where there are so many who should be her constant helpers scattering evil seeds broadcast. Mrs. Goodwin found her well directed influence too weak to drive the tempter far away from her husband, but she remained true to him while he lived; and so attached was she by long residence and association, to the beautiful scenery about the

Fort, and so beloved was she by a wide circle of friends both in Texas and among all classes in the nation, that she could not be induced ever to leave the spot where she had spent so many years of her life; and those who visited her after the Fort had been reduced to a garrison of a mere handful of men, found her house the abode of Christian refinement and apparent contentment. And even after the Fort had been scathed by fire and scattered by a tornado, the old lady clung with the home-loving tenacity of childhood to her own little humble cottage which a kind Providence had preserved from the thirst of the devouring element, and from which He had turned the storm aside, even as He "tempers the winds to the shorn lamb." And even when the last vestige of military occupancy was removed and but little left to mark the spot where Fort Towson had stood, save the charred remains and foundation stones of the barracks, and the broken and scattered timbers of the officers' quarters, which had been sent "hither and thither" by the furious tornado which had swept over it, there could be seen the humble home, the pretty little flower garden, the faithful old watch-dog, and the few trusty servants of Mrs. Goodwin, "the sutler's wife;" and on this writer's last visit to the spot, (which was in 1858, if my memory serves me correctly,) he found Mrs. Goodwin still occupying her old quarters, quietly seated in an old-fashioned arm rocking-chair, herself too feeble to walk about the room, and dependent entirely upon the attentions of her daughter, who so long as I continued to hear from them, had been unable to prevail upon the old lady to accompany her to her own home at one of the distant forts, and there spend her declining days surrounded by all the blessings and comforts which filial affection and the pure love of children and grand-children could bestow upon her. She preferred rather to remain near the grave of him whom she had faithfully devoted the best days of her life, and rely upon the tried and well-deserved friendship of those who had known her through so many years of her pure and spotless life. Her two old negro servants and one faithful Choctaw Indian, were ever near her, and charity from every quarter came to the relief of her daily needs, without waiting to hear her speak her wants; and thus was saved from suffering and humiliation one heroic woman, who from a sense of duty was content to live and die an OUTSIDER.

Notes

1. See the articles on Fort Towson in the *Encyclopedia of Oklahoma History and Culture* and in the Oklahoma Historical Society's "Museums & Sites" section. Numerous photographs are available through CivilWarAlbum.com's "Fort Towson Historic Site."

2. Among the officers mentioned, Charles Thomas, Owen Clark, and James Monroe, Jr., are listed for Fort Towson in 1842 in Ancestry.com's "U.S. Returns From Military Posts, 1806–1916" (a cooperative program with the National Archives and Records Administration).

3. The sutler was a non-military provider of goods for military personnel. At posts, they were licensed by the post, generally operating in their own facilities on or immediately off post. On sutlers in general, see David Delo, *Peddlers and Post Traders: The Army Sutler on the Frontier*. George Gooding was born in 1802 and was the sutler at Ft. Towson for 19 years according to his obituary in the October 15, 1851, *Choctaw Intelligencer*. He was the first postmaster at Fort Towson (actually Doaksville) in 1832 (J. Y. Bryce, "First Post Offices in What is Now State of Oklahoma," *Chronicles of Oklahoma*, June 1926) and operated a dry goods and groceries store, advertising as a new Cheap Cash Store in Fort Towson in the June 14, 1845, Clarksville *Northern Standard*. Photographs of Gooding's store and of his gravestone in the Fort Towson cemetery can be seen in the CivilWarAlbum.com's "Fort Towson Historic Site."

4. Esther, who was born in 1806 and died in 1863, appears in the 1860 Federal census of non-Indians in the Indian Territory with Carrie Gooding (23) and Manuel Gussea (19) in the household and in the accompanying slave census with one male slave. Grant Foreman in *The Five Civilized Tribes* indicates that the Choctaw allowed Esther to continue to occupy her house after the troops were withdrawn.

27 ✦ Back to Jonesboro

The long-awaited rise finally came, and the *Relief* left Kiamitia, stopping for the night at Jonesboro, where an incident is recounted concerning a "buzzard dance" conducted by Choctaws who had come across the river. The letter ends with the *Relief* tied up at night in Texas 25 miles below Jonesboro.

⁂

In reading over my last communication I find that I have almost entirely abandoned the business of steamboating, and allowed myself—by the vivid recollection of persons and incidents on shore both here and there—to dwell possibly at too great length upon such matters as can have but little in them of interest to the readers of your river columns. I promise now, by way of making amends for all past digressions, to stick close to my subject, and—starting down stream with the Relief on the last day of January, 1842—confine myself to a narrative of the occurrences particularly incident to her trip.

The red water which made its appearance yesterday began to grow pale again without having increased the depth of the channel very much; but, slight as was the rise, Captain Ross decided to take advantage of it and make his way down to the Raft. Much of the early part of the day was spent in preparations for the start, and the first thing to be done was to cross over to the Texas side and get some wood which Captain Wright's negroes had prepared and hauled to the bank for us while we had been detained at the opposite shore. While we were wooding I took a stroll up[1] to "the store," which was owned jointly by Captain Wright and one Ashbrook, familiarly known as "Peg Leg." (The poor fellow had the misfortune to have one short leg, and it was lengthened out by a sort of stump or "peg," hence his nickname). Ashbrook was a clever and good-natured fellow, but he no more liked the *soubriquet* "Peg Leg" than did a certain Captain Wilson of more recent Red River notoriety that of "Horse Head." Ashbrook's peculiar feet-ure was many times a great disadvantage to him; for whenever he went in his daily or nightly rambles, whether on Texas soil or among the friendly Indians in the Nation, his "peg" told tales on him; it made a "hole in the ground" that was "Ashbrook's mark," and therein he differed from "Horse Head," who was frequently known to go in up to his ears without ever making his mark for any account.

At the store I saw quite an assortment of goods and gew-gaws suited to the trade with plantation negroes, and the Indians who were constantly coming over from the Nation. Whisky, however, was the principal inducement for the poor Indian; that article he could not procure at home, while at the village of Doaksville could be found every other nick-nack or useful article he was in need of or able to pay for. Ashbrook, however, by virtue of his *hucki huma*, got the entire trade of the whisky loving Indians; and there was hardly an hour of the day that drunken Indians could not be seen "lying round loose."

At 2 P.M. we left Wright's Landing, and by the hardest kind of work we reached Jonesboro—twelve miles—at dark; here we were obliged to spend the night, and that night was to us a memorable one, and I must be pardoned for entering a little into the details of our second night spent at this place.

There happened to be congregated here on this occasion some fifteen or twenty Indians and squaws, most of whom had managed to purchase more whisky than they could safely carry into the

Nation; so they wisely concluded to spend the night in Texas, and they were so overjoyed to find that the "peni luac" (steamboat) would also remain here until daylight on the following morning, that they determined to devote themselves to the entertainment of the unexpected strangers. After the excitement consequent upon the arrival of the Relief had subsided, these besotted Indians set about organizing one of their peculiar dances called the "buzzard dance."[2] They selected a spot on the bank of the river in front of the boat where we could have a good view of their grotesque performance without the trouble of going on shore.

In order to get some idea of the mode of arranging and conducting this "buzzard dance," which was a favorite with them when on a bender, the reader must imagine a circular spot of ground of suitable extent to accommodate the number of Indians engaged in the dance, in the center of which they usually place the dead carcass of some animal; but as on this particular occasion the entertainment was to be of a purely impromptu character, and no dead animal was at hand, nor any living one which they could well afford to sacrifice, a large log of wood was substituted and this placed in position; and a large fire made at a point well selected for lighting up the scene, the dance commenced. At the particular spot chosen, the river bank had been at a former high stage of the water "cut" by the swift current, so that a perpendicular precipice had been formed, and from the top of this bank to a projecting strata of half-formed rock below, which had resisted the action of the current, was a distance of at least twenty-five feet. Here the dance commenced, and I will add by way of parenthesis that if there had been "one sober Indian" in the party they would probably have chosen a less dangerous spot.

The Indians begin the dance by joining hands and slowly walking around the carcass, first to the right, then to the left, all with their eyes upon the savory feast before them, (they usually cook the animal and eat it after the frolic,) and as they seem to get a scent of it, their steps are quickened and their appetites sharpened, and in their eagerness to appease their hunger they, in imitation of the buzzard or carrion crow, bring their heads close to the ground, throw out their arms in the semblance of wings, and as nearly as possible for human beings to do it, they put themselves into the precise shape and attitude of a flock of hungry buzzards just pouncing upon a newly found carcass. They draw nearer and nearer by slow degrees, but with wonderfully accelerated motions and considerably increased confusion; there is an apparent hesitating timidity among them, and only occasionally will one more venturesome than the others, approach close enough to strike with his beak the body of the animal, and then with a hurried backward movement indicate his doubts as to whether the animal is quite dead yet. In an instant the circle widens to its fullest extent, and then, as if partially reassured, they all approach it again. These maneuvers are repeated until all seem satisfied that their prey is really dead, or so nearly so as to be helpless and harmless; and then they all "pitch in" pell mell; and, to carry out truthfully the whole character of the turkey buzzard, there is a general scramble for the tit bits of the carrion; and not unfrequently a fight occurs between two or more individuals, and then, in an instant, the crowd scatters as though signs of life had been discovered in the victim, or some danger threatened from the approach of "outsiders."

No doubt some of my readers who have witnessed the awkward and disgusting pranks of a flock of hungry buzzards around a newly-found carcass, may be able to follow my lame description, and by the firelight of Jonesboro fancy themselves looking on with me at the little amusement prepared for us by these untutored children of the forest. But before I proceed with my story, I must caution all sensitive readers against surmising for a moment that the picture I am so faintly drawing is in the least degree intended to represent or delineate the scramble of 1870–71 upon Red River, and which for the time being is history, but as time rolls on, will hereafter become a part of somebody's reminiscences. The carrying trade of the river must not be understood as the carri-on trade among the buzzards; nor must the "legitimate carriers" consider themselves personated by the buzzards, or their delineators (in this particular instance) the Choctaw Indians; for however close the analogy may seem, of a truth no such allusion is intended. I have made this little break in my story of the dance, fearing that some buzzard may feel himself wounded by a random shot, and proclaim to the world hereafter that he is aggrieved.

And now for the *denouement* of the dance. As the excitement among the Indians increased, and each individual seemed to be vieing with his fellows in his efforts to portray the true buzzard, they lost all sense of the danger of tumbling over the precipice on the river side of their central object; and the wild confusion of the scene there being enacted certainly beggars all my powers of description; and the Indians seemed to outdo themselves in their enthusiastic endeavors to please their bewildered audience.

All at once one buzzard, who seemed a little more methodical in his movements than the others, pounced upon the log as though he was battling with an animal in whom life was not yet quite extinct, and he never let go his hold upon it until he had rolled it considerably nearer to the bank than where it had been quietly lying from the commencement of the dance. This struggle seemed to inspire the other Indians with still wilder enthusiasm, and they attacked it *en masse*; and he whom I have called attention to as slightly sober shifted his position to the safe side of the party, and, with a sudden, dextrous movement and almost super human strength, he pushed the whole crowd to the edge of the precipice; and not until four or five of them had gone headlong over the bank did he relax his strength. At that instant a loud, shrill "whoop-oop-oop-whoo-oopee" went up from this mischievous Indian, while the rest of the party seemed stricken with amazement and horror, and scattered in all directions. The squaws, with the timidity peculiar to the sex, ran skulking to an old log cabin that stood near, while some of the most sober of the male Indians ran to the place of disaster as soon as the first shock was over, and looked down to assure themselves whether those who had gone over were dead or alive. Others ran to the water's edge in the vain hope of rescuing their unfortunate comrades, or of affording them some relief, but no one could reach them without going nearly neck deep in the water.

By this time the wailings of the wounded could be distinctly heard, and among the rest the voice of one squaw. "Uncle Joe" caught the plaintive tones of the wounded woman and, although he was at the moment (with the rest of us) convulsed with laughter, it softened his heart, and in his most authoritative tones he called out, "Bring the yawl! Bring the yawl!" and seeing no movement on the part of anyone toward obeying the order, he cried out, "Where are you, Tom?"

At that moment Tom McClanahan, our principal deck-hand, seemingly quite out of breath, answered "here I am, sir." "Well, dod durn it; don't you hear that woman crying for help? Hurry with the yawl," responded the Captain. The yawl was soon along side of the fallen Indians, and such a jabbering of Choctaw as there then was I never listened to before or since. Tom McClanahan understood the language perfectly, and mingled his voice in the chatter with a fluency apparently equal to the nativeborn tongues that were so busy in asking questions and giving explanations as to how the catastrophe had befallen them in the very midst of so much fun and frolic.

It was soon ascertained that nobody was killed nor were any bones broken; they were all too drunk for any such bad luck as that; and just then and before the yawl had brought its cargo to where they could clamber up the bank, Tom's voice was heard to cry out, in response to some questioning Indian above him, "*Picoli*." This was the name of a notorious Indian woman of the party who had gone over the precipice. The word "*Picoli*" signifies ten in Choctaw, and was bestowed on this woman as a nick-name, and therein hangs a tale, which Tom McClanahan explained to us the next day, but which I won't repeat here.

By the time quiet was restored we retired to rest and prepare for the coming day's labors; but before Tom left for his quarters below, he advised Captain Ross to have a close watch kept on the boat for the balance of the night, "for," said he, "them d___d Choctaws will begin to get sober before morning and then they will be suspicious of foul play on the part of somebody on board; but I'll tell you more about that to-morrow; you watch out."

We left Jonesboro at the dawn of day February 1, 1842, and only made twenty-five miles when we were brought to the Texas bank by the darkness. In the forenoon Tom came up on the roof and proposed to relate to a few of us the origin and cause of the disaster to the Indians the night before. Tom had spent some years of his life in the Nation and had chosen him a wife from among the young squaws. He lived for a while happily with her; but he confessed he was a little erratic at times and had given her good cause to distrust him; and she had left him, declaring she would never live with him again. Among the crowd at Jonesboro he met her that night and tried to prevail upon her to return to him and flattered himself that he would have succeeded but for the interference of "Picoli," and so he swore vengeance upon the whole tribe, except his "little wife," but upon "Picoli" in particular; and he chose the opportunity when they were in the midst of the orgies of the "Buzzard Dance" and not dreaming of him, to disguise himself and take his place among them, and at the risk of killing two or three innocent Indians, wreak his vengeance upon "Picoli."

"Twas me," said Tom, "that rolled the log close to the bank, and me that pushed the whole d___d crowd overboard; but I waited till I got 'Picoli' in the right place, for it would have been a d___d poor joke to send others over the bank and leave her safe to poke fun at them. Why, I tell you, Cap'n, she's worse than any ten women in the whole Choctaw tribe. Her name's ten, and she's a hundred at least."

Here ended Tom's narrative, for he was cut short by the boat "getting fast" on a pile of logs, and all hands were called to pull her off. As Tom McClanahan's head disappeared below the roof, Uncle Joe just took time to say: "Well, I'll be blamed if I'd like to be in that fellow's place and stay about these diggings, for if them Choctaw bobeshelas ever find him out they'll make him wish he'd always staid an OUTSIDER."

Notes

1. Upstream.

2. According to Suzanne Crawford and Dennis Kelley in *American Indian Religious Traditions: An Encyclopedia*, there was a Turkey Buzzard Dance that was traditional among the Choctaw, but it was restricted at festivals to members of the Turkey Buzzard Society, which was a mortuary cult.

28 ✦ Back to Berlin

The *Relief* arrived back at Berlin in Bowie County. The first half of the letter provides a followup to the incident in Letter 19 concerning the temporary loss of the ferry flat by William Boyce's ferryman Tom in the altercation with the Choctaw mounted police. The second half is concerned with a toast in relation to the prospective transport of Joseph Leeper's cotton.

⁂

[First part not used.]

As I stated in my story of the buzzard dance, the Relief made only about twenty-five miles on the first day out from Jonesboro, and if called upon to tell where she lay that night I would be forced to say: "I don't know." I can only say that we were tied to the Texas shore where there was not the least trace of civilization; the forest and the canebrake were an unbroken wilderness; and the rapid running river as it twisted its troubled way among the snags and rippled over the sand bars, furnished the only accompaniment to the croaking of the frogs in the adjoining swamps, and the humming of the countless insects which lulled us to sleep far away from our homes and kindred.

We lost none of the precious daylight, but on the morrow pushed our way along as rapidly as possible, only stopping once to wood from a cedar brake, and at 2 P.M. we found ourselves at the little town of Berlin, Texas. Here the anxiety of some friends of

Captain Ross overruled his judgment, and he was prevailed upon to take ninety-nine bales of cotton, notwithstanding the low stage of the river was constantly admonishing him to hurry along in order to escape from Upper Red River on this "little swell," and seek a field of brighter promises for his future labors. I have since thought in this unlooked for interruption to our rapid (?) progress down the river, the hand of destiny was manifestly at work, and although unseen, was wisely guiding our course in the far distant future. With our weak force of men, the work of taking on board the cotton was slow, and long before the last bale was on board we were groping in the dark. So, of course, we were to spend another night at this place, where I described a little adventure as we passed up the river.

No amount of money or promise of other rewards could prevail upon the old negro ferryman to carry one of our crew over the river who might be disposed to renew his acquaintance with the Choctaw neighbors; and the old fellow turned a deaf ear to the oft and loudly repeated cries from the other side of "*Peni Minte, Talla holisso lower faeni, Chactaw, bobeshela Chicama,*" &c., meaning, "Bring over the boat, plenty of money here, and Choctaws are good friends," &c. But no amount of Choctaw pleading could prevail upon old "Tom,"[1] the ferryman, to risk another such a disaster to himself and his "flat" as happened on the night we spent here on our upward-bound trip. The old darkey, years afterward, used to refer to that memorable night and the following day, and when he would come to the closing scene, the pulling of the truant ferry-boat back to her moorings, he seemed to have a vivid remembrance of the stimulant applied to his back by his master, in order to accelerate his movements; and the cringing shrug of his shoulders, as his mind wandered back to the transaction, plainly told how salutary had been the lesson, and how lasting the effect promised to be; for he had borne many stripes for that little deviation from the path of his duty, and many, too, which with more justice might have been laid upon the backs of his white brethren who had beguiled him into the error.

As we were closing our labors for the night, word was brought to us from "Major Leiper," who had a plantation near by,[2] that early in the morning he would come and ship his cotton, one hundred and seventy-nine bales, and he would pay an extra dollar per bale, as an inducement, for he was about quitting the country[3] to return to his native State, Tennessee, and was desirous of taking all his effects along with him.

"Uncle Joe" consulted with his officers as to the propriety of taking more cotton while the river was so low, and after listening to their opinions, which were almost unanimous against loading any deeper, (for we were all anxious to get out of the country;) and, paying due heed to Captain Hildreth's weather-wise prognostications of "another rise before we reach the raft," to which he sagely replied, "That's as sure as falling off a log if we take this 179 bales," he turned to the messenger from Major Leiper and said, "Well, old boy, you may tell your master that I'll take it. Dod durn it, we'll let the tail go with the hide, and take the chances. We may as well die for an old sheep as a lamb. We're in for it anyhow; so let 'er rip." The poor negro stood amazed at the Captain's long sentence in reply to his master's written message, and after he had recovered sufficiently from his bewilderment to speak, he said: "Yes, massa Cap'n; but hadn't you better put dat down in writin? I don't b'leve I could 'member all dat 'bout de tail and de hide and de sheep and de lam. May be so massa mought fotch you some of dem ef he knowed you want 'em; but he never said noffin to me 'cept bout de cotton. We cullud folks has got plenty of hides wid de tails and horns befo on 'em, but we haint got no sheeps, nor lams, but we'se got plenty young shoats, and we'll fotch you some of dem in the mornin' ef you say so."

By the time the negro had finished his speech the whole company was in a roar of laughter, and "Uncle Joe," seeing the joke fairly turned upon him, ordered the clerk to make a written reply to Major Leiper; and, while this was being done, he called the old darkey to him, and said: "Boy, you'll do; what's your name?" "My name Pomp; but dey calls me Juno, caze dere's 'nother Pomp on de place what mar'd a gal on de Warhop place, and he's al'ays runnin off to see his wife, and getting licked when he comes back, and den he's all de time doin a heap of other tricks 'bout de place, an I don't like dat name no more; and so you kin just call me Juno, massa." "There, that'll do," said Uncle Joe; "dang my buttons, if you don't make a longer speech than mine. Here, Oliver, give Pomp (beg your pardon—Juno) a drink, and then, boy, do you make tracks for home, nor don't you fancy you're that other Pomp, and run off to the Warhop place after his wife." "No, massa," said Juno, "I neber does de like o' dat, dem's white folks' tricks;" and then swallowing the half tumbler full of whisky which Oliver handed him, he made a characteristic bow to the company, and commenced another speech, but "Uncle Joe" interrupted him by asking if he could not give us a toast? He said: "Yes, massa; but you know de tose al'ways comes 'fore de licker, and dat's done gone now." So "Uncle Joe" ordered another drink for Juno, and, with the glass in his hand, raised up above his head, old Juno gave us—

> De little bee suck de blossom,
> De big bee eat de honey;
> Nigger man make de cotton,
> White man get de money.

And with a broad and significant grin such as no pen can describe, he bowed himself out of our presence; and as the night was now well nigh run into the small hours, we retired to fall asleep as the remembrance of Juno's pranks should flit away, and the spirits of loved ones at home come in their place to watch over our slumbers.

Morning came, but no Major Leiper, nor any word from him or Juno; and after waiting until the sun was full two hours high, "Uncle Joe" concluded that in all probability the hitherto faithful Juno had been overcome by his double potation and had fallen by the wayside, and, so by a little indiscretion of his own the "tail had gone with the hide," and the Relief went on her way without the cotton. We consoled ourselves for the loss, hoping that it might in the end prove a gain, and if we came back again we would find it here, and if not it would fall to the lot of some venturesome OUTSIDER.

Notes

1. The 1850 Bowie County Slave Census indicates that William Boyce had 82 slaves, but none meeting the description.
2. Joseph Leeper's headright was immediately southeast of the Dyer headright at the mouth of Mill Creek.
3. Leeper does not appear in the 1850 Bowie County census and therefore apparently achieved his objective.

29 ✦ To Spanish Bluff

The *Relief* left Berlin and proceeded downstream to Spanish Bluff, stopping on the way at Lanesport and Smith's Landing. Lanesport was located in the southwest corner of

Little River County, Arkansas, a short distance from the Choctaw Nation line and on the first high land above the floodplain. It was founded by Benjamin Layne, a large early property owner in the area according to U.S. General Land Office land records, and was referred to as Laynesport as well as Lanesport. It had been a keelboat landing and was an important steamboat landing, although it never developed into a town, probably because of the limited nature of its commercial activities cited by Withenbury.

Smith's Landing was the landing for James N. Smith's plantation, with facilities apparently restricted to those described by Withenbury. It had been a keelboat landing and was a steamboat landing of modest importance. Smith's headright was in north-central Bowie County. From Withenbury's description, it is apparent that Smith's house and landing were on the eastern edge of his property, with the house located on bluffs a half-mile south of the landing. Spanish Bluff was located in the Richard Ellis headright in north-central Bowie County, one headright downstream of Smith's headright and was the place at which Spanish forces stopped the upstream movement of the Freeman and Custis expedition in 1806, as recounted by Dan Flores in *Jefferson and Southwestern Exploration*. Spanish Bluff had been a keelboat landing and was an important steamboat landing. Town lots were sold at Spanish Bluff by at least 1853, as shown in the 1853 Red River County tax rolls.

⁂

Since leaving the vicinity of Fort Towson I have made rather slow progress; but my readers must remember that the Relief was a pet of "Uncle Joe's," named in honor of his pet fire company, whose engine-house still stands on George street, [1] between Central avenue and Plum street, with the name, "Relief," carved on a stone tablet and set conspicuously in the front wall; and I never look upon it that a thousand memories of the past do not rise up before me, each one of them as indelibly stamped in "relief" as is the old engine-house on George street.

But, I said the Relief was "Uncle Joe's" pet, and for that reason, if for no other, I would have it understood that over the unfrequented track of Red River we moved with much caution. That was one reason for our slow progress; and another was that Captain Ross would never consent to the loss of a social chat among pleasant people for the sake of a "little matter of business." In fact, there were no very fast men on the boat.

Soon after leaving Berlin, or what is now only known as "Mill Creek," we began to fall in with a class of people at every landing whose friendly acquaintance the crew of the Relief had made during the previous year, and once among them, it was almost impossible to get away. I recollect one day, while we were wooding at Martin Glover's plantation, [2] the wood all in, and only one plank remaining out for the neighbors to go ashore on, Captain Ross was standing about midway on the plank, shaking by the hand some friend who was going ashore, but who was trying to prevail upon the Captain to "lay up and wait for the June rise;" another anxious one reached around the first, and caught hold of one side of "Uncle Joe's" coat-tail, (it was of the "steel-pen" pattern,[3]) and began pulling at him to come on shore; and the old man, in the hope of saving his coat began to yield, and took a step or two toward land, when Captain Hildreth from on board caught the other tail of his coat and began pulling in a contrary direction. The boat in the meantime was swinging out from shore; and before the party could be brought to a full realization of the dilemma they were in, the plank slipped from the boat's guard, and some half a dozen men were in an instant floundering in the mud and water. Once on shore and dripping wet they took a sober (?) look at each other, and there stood "Uncle Joe" with his "best coat split clean up to the collar." Philley says he heard the old man in the midst of all the confusion cry out, "let 'er rip." This little occurrence put a stop to our progress for the remainder of that day. But I am getting a little ahead of the boat with my story. After leaving Mill Creek we made no stop until we reached Lanesport, [4] Arkansas, just at dark. This little town as I have said in a former paper[5] is situated one mile below the Choctaw line, and as a consequence it was a lively little place day and night in the times I am writing of; but it has never increased in importance since; on the contrary, it has steadily retrograded. In 1842, and for a few succeeding years, Colonel Lane,[6] the old patriarch for whom the place was named, was living here, but he has long since passed away, and the place that knew him knows him no more.

Some three miles back of this town was for many years the residence of Colonel Henderson D. Jones.[7] It was, and is still, known upon the map of Arkansas as "Rocky Comfort." I can not understand why it should have been thus named, unless it was because the weary traveler was sure to find under Colonel Jones' roof real solid comfort. [8] Colonel Jones lived a quiet life, keeping a little store, where he traded with both Indians and whites. He kept, also, a house of entertainment, which was managed chiefly by his wife and servants; and many a time has the way-worn wanderer pushed on for a few more weary miles after nightfall had overtaken him, in order to "put up" at Rocky Comfort; for there he knew was always rest and food for man and beast.

The alluvial bottom-land of the river at Lanesport is not more than a quarter of a mile wide; and close to the river is a beautiful circular lake, about six miles in extent, evidently once the bed of the river, but so long ago was it "cut off" from the channel that no traces of its former connection can now be seen. [9] The people call it "Wash Lake," simply from the fact of its water being always soft and clear, and made use of for washing by everybody living near it. The land immediately around Lanesport is of the very finest description, both above and below the town. Colonel R. M. Jones owns one of the best farms that ever was cultivated in the Choctaw Nation, about three miles above;[10] while below live the Hamiters and Hawkinses, known all over Arkansas as among the most thrifty, intelligent and successful planters in the State.[11] They and their descendants live there to this day, and have withstood all the political, social and commercial changes (I might say revolutions) of the last decade, without murmuring or experiencing a tithe of the evils so generally foretold by the wiseacres of 1860.

As we pass along down the river some ten or twelve miles, we come to a settlement on the Texas side where there was gathered together the pleasantest little community of neighbors that one may hope to meet with in a lifetime. I speak now of Smith's Landing, in Bowie County, Texas. There was nothing to mark the spot save a little cotton shed, with an inclosed room about eight by ten in one corner; but a half a mile back, on the high table land, was the ever-to-be-remembered hospitable and comfortable mansion of Judge James N. Smith.[12] And as I write of this spot there seems to be a voice within me saying "Oh, carry me back." But, why go back, when I know "they are gone, all gone?" Judge Smith—or "Jim Smith"—was certainly one of the most genial men I ever met; and his good wife, the mother of a family of girls and boys in those days so promising, was truly a bright and shining light in her family, in the neighborhood, and in fact throughout the whole country. She had a smile for every one, and in the quickest possible time the stranger introduced by her husband or a neighbor was made to feel the genuineness of the words of welcome with which she greeted him. It so happened that Judge Smith's house, on more than one occasion, was transformed into a hospital for unfortunate steamboatmen; and how truly he and his whole household tilled the office of the "good Samaritan" I am sure will not soon be forgotten by "Uncle Joe," nor was it, while he lived, by poor old Captain Noland, of the Bogue Houma and Mariner, nor by Ambrose Arnold, of the Vermillion. Judge Smith was a Tennesseean, and one of the earliest settlers on Upper Red River.

In the same neighborhood lived Judge Richard Ellis,[13] and his son Dandridge Ellis, a lawyer of much promise in his young days; but he, like his brother-in-law, "Jim Smith,"[14] had a "heart too big for his head." He was known from the northern boundary of Texas to New Orleans as a whole-souled, genial fellow, a good counselor, a man of honor in all business transactions, always hospitable at home and frolicsome abroad. The Ellises were Virginians, and when they emigrated to Texas they brought with them a number of slaves of the "real old stock," not a few of whom claimed to have been the servants of General Washington, or descended from his servants. One I remember as claiming to have a little of the real Washington blood in her veins. Little Mary, a beautiful octoroon[15] of about twelve years, was the pet of the two families, and a general favorite in the neighborhood. Her mother, who was cook in Judge Smith's family, claimed to have descended, by some lucky or unlucky mischance, from the George Washington stock. So it need not be wondered at that little Mary, who by another mischance was still whiter than her mother, should fancy that she could feel a slight tingling of the aristocratic "can't tell a lie" blood coursing through her veins.

But I see that I am inclined to linger too long among these good people, and to enter too minutely into the details of their private affairs; and as I shall have occasion to refer to this locality hereafter when speaking of several steamboats which have laid themselves down to sleep, I will push along down the river, only mentioning by the way the flourishing little town of Boston, the county seat of Bowie County, and also its rival and competitor for the trade of the surrounding country, DeKalb. The inhabitants of these two places have continued to increase and multiply, up to the present time, and some of the merchants of 1840 and '42 are still holding on and dispensing the necessaries of life to the hungry people, and gaining a competency, I hope, for themselves as the population increases and the country develops into importance in consequence of their enterprise and continuance in it.

Spanish Bluff, prior to 1842, was located about six miles below Smith's Landing, following the serpentine course of the river; but a change has since come over the topography and geography of that particular section, by which the two points have become much more neighborly, and now they are but little more than a stone's throw—or speaking more in keeping with the vernacular of that country—"a squirrel's jump" apart. This change was brought about partly in the natural way, but more especially by the instrumentality of "Uncle Joe," who, while he was sojourning at Judge Smith's awaiting the arrival of the Relief, on the trip following the one I am now dragging my readers through—sat one day upon the bank of the river striving to convince a few silly fishes that they would better their condition by taking his bait, and trying the experiment of breathing the free air of the Republic of Texas, instead of the vile water of Red River; and being in bad luck, getting no bites but mosquito bites, he fell into a reverie. (The old man has a habit of ruminating even to this day.) Which reverie was suddenly broken by the caving in of a large portion of the river bank near where he sat; by which he came well nigh to falling into the river. In the twinkling of an eye the thought of making a "cut-off" flashed upon his brain, and he immediately stuck the butt of his fishing pole into the soft bank, and set about immortalizing himself by digging a little canal and leading the rising water of the river through the narrow isthmus. He found an old grubbing hoe near at hand, and without waiting for any preliminary survey or report of scientific "hydraulic" engineers, such as we have among us at this day, he went to work, and before another twenty-four hours had passed he had the satisfaction of seeing his labors crowned with success, and nearly the whole volume of the river hurrying through his ditch which a short time before was but a furrow in the sand. Then it was that Smith's cut-off was made,[16] and some hundreds of acres of Texas land were annexed to the United States, before the treaty of annexation was ratified by the two countries.

The cut-off, which should have been called Ross' Cut-off, proved a great benefit to the navigation, for it left out of the channel one of the worst "rack heaps" above White Oak Shoals. "Uncle Joe," in his eagerness to make the cut-off, forgot his fishing tackle, and he is willing to swear to this day that he don't know if he got "ary 'nother bite after he stuck the eend of his pole in the mud."

But I said something of Spanish Bluff,[17] which, in consequence of "Uncle Joe's" cut-off, is now almost synonymous with Smith's Landing—and I must not pass it by without a word or two in remembrance of its natural beauty, breaking as it does for the first time the monotonous level feature of the bottom lands on the Texas side. Right here the river makes a sharp bend on the right (descending), washing with a rapid current the base of this beautiful range of red clay hills which rise to a height of from fifty to one hundred feet. I have called it red clay, but I should have said variegated, for there is every possible shade of red from the palest to the deepest, from the darkest brown to the brightest crimson, all blended in as perfect harmony as are the colors of the rainbow; and the whole surface above is clothed with a forest of beautiful, medium-sized pines, which seem to have been crowded out upon the very brink of the cliffs above us to salute us with their evergreen plumes as we glide along on the swift current below.

About the year 1845, a German[18]—whose name I have unfortunately forgotten—came straggling through the country and stopped at the Spanish Bluff settlement, where he soon made a favorable impression upon the people; and he conceived the idea of a warehouse upon a high point of the Bluff where, by means of a windlass and crane, he proposed to hoist the freight from steamboats some forty or more feet up to his warehouse, and by the same apparatus lower the cotton down.

The planters looked upon his plans as anything but practicable, but allowed the Dutchman to do as he pleased, knowing that no harm could result to anybody but himself, and to him it could be but little more than the loss of his time and labor. So the old fellow worked away through a whole summer diligently, until he could look upon the labor of his head and hands and pronounce it well done. On the first attempt to put into use his plans the utter failure of the whole thing was manifest; and after struggling a year or two to force it into use, the whole was abandoned, and ruin was written upon every part.

During his labors at the base of the bluff in the lowest summer stage of the river, this old German came upon the skeleton of some huge animal buried in the solid clay of the hill where there was fully forty feet of earth above the big bones. He labored many days with much care, and succeeded in exhuming many parts of the skeleton so prefect as to enable scientific men to ascertain the enormous size of the animal; but were I to undertake to give the size of some of those bones and more particularly the teeth, my story would sound too fabulous; so I will leave the reader just where I found myself, wondering when this monster moved upon the earth, and by what disaster or convulsion he had been buried so far beneath its surface. Knowing full well that we must all come to the conclusion that he belonged to the ante-diluvian age, and that when Noah built his ark he made no preparations for passengers of his class, and when the beast applied for a room he was told there was no place in the Association for him, and so he was forced to take his chances and perish with every other unlucky OUTSIDER.

Notes

1. In Cincinnati.

2. Martin Glover's headright was across the river from Lanesport but extended to the south where Glover's landing was located. The described incident is from a later trip by the *Relief*, and, as Withenbury indicates, was out of order in describing the downstream movement of the boat.

3. A coat with a long deeply forked tail similar to the split tip of a steel pen.

4. Laynesport is shown on Sidney Morse and Samuel Breese's 1845 *Arkansas* and continues to be shown on contemporary topographic maps. An article on "Little River County" in the *Encyclopedia of Arkansas History and Culture* says that Laynesport was the first town to be plotted in the county, in 1836 on the basis of land donated by Benjamin Layne. The U.S. General Land Office survey plat for T13S, 32 and 33W shows only a field for Benjamin Hartfield in the area. Laynesport had a post office in 1839 according to backwardbranch.com's "Early Post Offices in Little River County Arkansas."

5. Letter 18.

6. Benjamin Layne appears in the 1850 Sevier County census as a 55-year-old farmer born in Virginia with a wife and two children. A profile of Layne is provided by H. M. McIver in "Water Bound in Arkansas" (*Arkansas Historical Quarterly*, Summer 1955), who says that there was a small settlement of trappers and hunters at Laynesport and that a man named Hartfield had a trading station.

7. U.S. General Land Office land records indicate that Henderson Jones was a large early property owner in the Rocky Comfort area.

8. Rocky Comfort (originally called Willow Springs) is shown as "Rocky Comfort Academy" on Sidney Morse and Samuel Breese's 1845 *Arkansas*. There was an academy at this place that was incorporated in 1840 according to Josiah Shinn's *History of Education in Arkansas*. The Arkansas Historic Preservation Program's "New Rocky Comfort Jail, Foreman, Little River County" says the place was named Rocky Comfort by the Indians because there was a spring in the limestone rock surrounded by willows.

9. Withenbury is referring to present-day Hamilton Lake about a mile northeast of Lanesport.

10. This was Robert Jones' Walnut Prairie plantation.

11. U.S. General Land Office land records indicate that David Hamiter and Benjamin and Henry Hawkins were large early property owners in the Lanesport area. Profiles of Benjamin and Henry Hawkins are provided by H. M. McIver in "Water Bound in Arkansas" (*Arkansas Historical Quarterly*, Summer 1955).

12. Smith is listed in the 1850 Bowie County census as a 48-year-old planter born in Tennessee with children and his mother living in the household. His Texas General Land Office headright certificate indicates that he came to Texas on February 1, 1834, with the headright application approved in March 1838 in Red River County (the predecessor to Bowie, which was created in 1840). The 1875 *Journal of the Constitutional Convention of the Republic of Texas* indicates that he was appointed a trustee of the College of DeKalb in January 1839. Numerous public notices in the Clarksville *Northern Standard* from 1842 to 1849 indicate that he was Chief Justice of Bowie County. He last appears in the Bowie County tax rolls in 1853, with estate taxes in 1854 (Richard Ellis, executor).

13. According to an article on "Richard Ellis" in the *Handbook of Texas Online*, Ellis was born in Virginia in 1781 and moved to Texas in 1834, locating at his Spanish Bluff headright. He was president of the Texas constitutional convention in 1836, a signer of the Texas Declaration of Independence, and senator in the first four congresses of the Republic. His wife, Mary Dandridge, was also from Virginia and a second cousin of Martha Washington and a first cousin of Dolley Madison. She died in 1837 (which is why she does not appear in the account), and he died in 1846.

14. Nathaniel Dandridge Ellis had a headright between his father on the east and James N. Smith on the west. According to the "Richard Ellis Family Tree" prepared by the Star of the Republic Museum, Richard Ellis had two children, Nathaniel Dandridge (1808–1870) and Sarah Ann (1810–1849). The name of Smith's wife does not appear in any readily available documents and was obviously Sarah Ann.

15. A person with one black great-grandparent. In the Slave Schedule connected with the 1850 U.S. Census for Bowie County, N. D. Ellis is listed with 38 slaves and James N. Smith with 37, but none fitting the description.

16. Withenbury is referring to the large bend immediately above Spanish Bluff that has since been reoccupied by the river, as shown on contemporary topographic maps. Ross made the cutoff in a May 1842 voyage by the *Relief*.

17. See the article on "Spanish Bluff" in the *Handbook of Texas Online*. Spanish Bluff is shown on Jacob De Cordova's 1867 *Map of the State of Texas* and continues to appear on contemporary topographic maps.

18. Possibly Frederick Siedikum, Bowie County Surveyor, whose name appears on many documents on file in the Texas General Land Office and who prepared the first map of Bowie County in 1841. The Bowie County tax rolls indicate that Siedikum acquired property in the Ellis headright by at least 1846.

30 ✦ To McKinney's Landing

McKinney's Landing was the landing of Collin McKinney[1] located in his headright in northeast Bowie County in an area that was called Hickman's Prairie. It had been a keelboat landing and was a steamboat landing of modest importance. McKinney was born in New Jersey in 1766, and the family migrated to Kentucky, where McKinney married Annie Moore in 1792, with whom he had four children and, after her death, Elizabeth Coleman in 1805, with whom he had six children. McKinney was the oldest person (70) to sign the Texas Declaration of Independence in 1836 and served in the First, Second, and Fourth congresses of the Republic. He was a prominent member of the Disciples of

Christ and a lay preacher. When Withenbury met him in 1842, he was aged 75. McKinney last appears in the Bowie County tax rolls in 1846, after which he brought his family to Collin County, where he died in 1861 at the age of 95.

⁂

After leaving Spanish Bluff, the first place of which I shall take note is McKinney's Landing, in Bowie County, Texas, and I would not dwell here for anything which occurred on this trip to the profit of the Relief; for, in consequence of the low stage of the water, we were unable to do much freighting business, and our principal reason for stopping at all was to procure fuel and provisions; the former we generally supplied ourselves with at night, on which occasions all our axes were brought into requisition, and the crew went grumbling to the work of wooding from the standing timber. But as there was a wood-pile at McKinney's, and any number of anxious looking individuals standing on the bank watching our approach, Captain Ross ordered the boat landed. And now, before she touches the shore and the rush on board takes place, I must go back a little and tell my readers that we have Judge Smith[2] and his fiddle with us. He is making a pleasure trip as the guest of the boat, and he has been with us long enough already to get both his fiddle and himself in tune. Oh, how I wish all my readers knew the old Judge as well as the crew of the Relief did; for then they could see him wherever his name occurred in these lines, just as "Uncle Joe" and myself can see him before us whenever his name is spoken or thought of, and I would not then find it necessary to attempt to describe this almost indescribable man. But I will not dwell upon his peculiarities here, but content myself with the bare introduction I have given him and hold myself in readiness to speak of him occasionally, as I am chronicling the remaining incidents of this time consuming trip.

When the bell sounded as a signal for landing, everybody came out to look at the place. The clerk left his books, the cook his kitchen, the bar-keeper left his bottles, the chambermaid her washing tub; and Jim Berryhill, our Indian steward, ran up to Captain Ross and said: "Cap'en, do, for God's sake, try and get some beef here, for you know we've not had a bite since we left Shreveport, and old man McKinney is a Kentuckian, and has lived here so long that he has a plenty, and the crew have lived on deer meat and catfish so long there's no end to their grumbling." Captain Ross promised to make the effort, and motioned to Jim to go below, and as he turned his face toward the shore again he muttered, rather audibly, "A dod durned poor crew that can't live on what I do without grumbling, I say."

At this instant, and just as the boat was rounding to, Judge Smith came on the roof from the cabin, with his fiddle in his hand, and in his loudest and most frolicksome voice finishing a favorite song with which he had been entertaining the bar-keeper and Bill Smith, ("sucker-mouthed Bill,") our First Engineer, who happened to be off watch at the time; and no sooner was his face seen and his voice heard by the people on shore, than the exclamation was heard from the lips of every one of them: "There's Jim Smith!" for everybody, far and near, knew Jim Smith, and what was more, they knew that wherever he was with his fiddle, and a little "resin for the bow," which Oliver kept bottled up and ready for use, there was sure to be fun.

The ceremony of hand-shaking which the Judge went through with, and in which he was followed by "Uncle Joe," not missing a single individual, black or white, male or female, young or old, took up at least a half an hour, and not until that was done was any business attended to except to take a few cords of wood on board. Here the anxious steward reminded Captain Ross of the beef again, and to our great joy the good "old man McKinney" agreed to sell us a young beef provided we could capture him. This proposition hit Captain Hildreth on his strong point, and without a moment's hesitation he was ready with his rifle, and Ed. La Rue following him with his knives. The two made short work of selecting a fat two-year old steer from a herd of cattle which had congregated close upon the bank, attracted there by the unusual appearance of a steamboat. At the crack of the rifle one of their number "fell in his tracks," and the balance broke for the thicket just above the landing and were not seen again. Capt. Hildreth came strutting back to the boat with his rifle on his shoulder and face beaming with the amount of self-gratulation which would astonish even one at this late day, when the "conquering hero comes" from the fierce strife of the bloody battle-field with his well earned trophies around him, or the "Big Injun," with a score of white men's scalps at his belt, the results of many moons spent upon the war path. But the little fellow couldn't help it; "'twas born in him" as Judge Smith remarked when he saw Hildreth loading his gun and getting ready for another act of bravery.

Now while we are waiting on the butchers, let me introduce to my readers the good old patriarch Collin McKinney, who emigrated to Texas in 1816,[3] and who had lived upon this very spot from that early day. From the picture which I have attempted to present of Upper Red River and the people whom I found scattered along its fertile valley in the year 1842, it will not be very difficult for an attentive reader to imagine what must have been the state of affairs there when Collin McKinney left his home in Kentucky, and went in search of a new one in the far distant Southwest; and when I take into consideration the fact that, at the very time to which the recollection of these trivial incidents carries me back, he had lived upon that very spot twenty-six years, I am positively lost in wonder when trying to arrive at a good reason for any man with a family wandering so far from civilization as this place must have been when Collin McKinney halted here, too much fatigued with his wearisome journey to pursue it any farther. I have heard from the old man's own lips much of the history of his trials during the years when there was no communication between this country and the world from which he had strayed, and but for the fear of exceeding all reasonable limits, I would enter upon the recital of much that to me was full of exciting interest as related by this old pioneer, and out of which an abler pen than mine might weave a thrilling romance "founded on fact." But I must content myself for this time by merely making note of the fact that long before the river was navigated by even the primitive keelboat, or the country traversed by roads that were anything more than Indian trails or dim bridle-paths, the McKinney family was planted here as it were, solitary and alone; and here the McKinneys flourished and multiplied for several years after the period of my first visit among them, until they could have been counted by scores. Three times did Collin McKinney journey from his new found home to his native Kentucky, but in so doing he never could be prevailed upon to swerve in the least from his early habit of journeying on horseback the whole distance. Old Capt. Ben. Crooks told me that he once offered the old gentleman a free passage upon his first little steamboat, the "Indian," as he was returning from Fort Towson to Pittsburg about the year 1838, but although the old man was all ready to start at the time the passage was offered him, he declined it, and with his saddle-bags filled with a change of clothing and a few day's provisions, he mounted his horse and started upon his lonely overland journey, returning by the same route at the appointed time. He used to say it was no hardship for him to travel alone on horse-back, for "he knew every road, trail or bridle path from the famous 'Trammell's Trace' in Texas to the Bluegrass country in Kaintucky."

One would naturally suppose that a man possessed of the daring spirit of the venturesome pioneer as Collin McKinney must have been, would also have had something of the frontier desperado mixed up in his composition, and that when he started out on his long and solitary journeyings, his weapons of defense—not to say of offense—would have formed no small part of his outfit, but such was not the case; for Collin McKinney was a man of peace, a Christian by profession, and his whole life in Texas was marked in a manner which plainly showed that in dealing fairly and honorably with all men, he knew that he need fear no evil, and no evil ever befell him.

As the country filled up with new adventurers, McKinney's Landing became quite an important point in the way of business, for every body knew that their business would be properly attended to by the old man and his sons. They built a warehouse, and became the shipping and receiving merchants of the whole region about there, and to this day a boat rarely passes McKinney's Landing without having freight to put off or cotton to take on board; and although the old man's business habits and notions were peculiar to himself, (they would be called in these days "old fogyish,") every body allowed him to have pretty much his own way, for they knew he was honest, and would come out all right in the end. I must relate one little anecdote of the old man before I leave him, just to illustrate one strong point in his character:

In the year 1844, Captain Joe Lodwick and one of his younger brothers, in connection with Erastus Smith, an old Red River pilot, known from one end of the river to the other as "Joe Tague," built at this city the steamboat Planter, and under the command of "Joe Tague," with the younger Lodwick in the office, she made several trips above the Raft, on the last of which they had a considerable lot of freight to put off at McKinney's. When they arrived there the river was rising very rapidly, and by one of those unaccountable freaks peculiar to Red River, as well as to the Mississippi and Arkansas, the bank was "cutting," and large portions of what had formerly been the landing had already fallen into the river.[4] The little warehouse had been torn down, and the materials removed to save them, and the spot where it stood was already in the river. Captain Smith was in a great hurry, and against the protestations of the old man McKinney, who happened to be about the only one at the landing at the time, he had the freight piled up above the regular landing and very close to the edge of the bank; and when the clerk went out to get the old man to sign a receipt for its proper delivery to enable him to collect his charges from the shipper at New Orleans, he was met by a mild request that, as he was alone and unable to remove the freight to a safe place, the Captain should send his men out and place it out of danger, when he would receipt for it, and have it put in his gin-house as soon as the negroes should come in from the fields. At this, "Joe Tague" cried out with an air and tone of authority quite out of place when addressing such a man as Collin McKinney, "I say, I say, by G_d, old man, I want you to sign that receipt, and no more fooling; I say, I say—that there freight is marked for McKinney's Landing, and that's where I have put it." I wish now that I could just draw that old man's picture as he stood leaning upon his staff, and give even a faint idea of the tone and peculiar accent with which he replied in these words, (as I heard him a few days afterward repeat the story,) “Keaptun Smuth, I hain’t lived here twenty-seven years without knowin’ whar Muckinney’s Landen is; nor I never had any difficulty with any steamboat Kaptun; but I’ll never sign for them things till you have ’em put whar they won’t fall in the river before my boys comes in from the field to put ’em away, for if you leave ’em thar, they’ll be in the river before you get round the bend thar,” pointing up the river.

“Tague” refused to have the goods—all of which belonged to McKinney’s neighbors—moved from where he had first put them, and called out witnesses to see him count the articles and make a formal delivery of them, and to hear the old man refuse to receipt for them; and thus was as much time consumed as it would have required to remove the freight to a place of safety, but that was “Joe Tague’s” way of doing business. He then repeated: “I say, I say, by G_d, old man, are you going to sign that receipt?” “Not till you move them things further back I ain’t,” said the old man. “Well, I say, I say, by G_d, you can just go to h_ll then,” said “Tague.” “Nor I shan’t do that, nuther,” said Father McKinney, and so the controversy ended. “Tague” tapped his bell, and the Planter started up the river, and as her wheel was passing the freight pile its swells started the loose soil to caving, and before the boat had got three lengths away the whole mass fell into the river. Much of the freight was bagging and rope[5] which floated, but the sacks of salt and the barrels of sugar went quickly to the bottom.

The Planter was quickly stopped and dropped back below the floating goods and the crew ordered into McKinney’s ferry flat to save what they could, which was but a small portion of the whole. This was a bad day’s work for the owners of the Planter, and the occurrence would have been a good lesson to any man who had sense enough to profit by it, but that man was not “Joe Tague.”

The Planter sunk, the following summer, with a load of Government freight, about six miles below Alexandria, and was never raised. "Joe Tague," not content to go back to piloting, induced some planters in Caddo and DeSoto Parishes to assist him in building another boat, and he built the "Col. Edwards," but his career was short on her, as he soon fell out with the owners. He died soon after, and the boat took fire while at Mad. George's wood-yard, eight miles below Alexandria, with a load of cotton and cattle, and was a total loss.

But I have got a long way from McKinney's,[6] and must return just to say that a few years after the incidents I have been narrating, old Collin McKinney, having still a spark of the adventurous spirit left in him, which guided him from Kentucky into the wilderness of Texas, conceived the idea of going still farther from his native land, and planting the McKinney standard more firmly and (as he said to me) "imperishably on the soil of the State of his adoption." He went to what was commonly known as "the three forks" of the Trinity River, and there he planted his standard, as he had promised to do, "imperishably;" and Collin County, with the flourishing town of McKinney, for its seat of justice, bears witness to this day of the fulfillment of all that old Collin McKinney promised to do when he left Kentucky.

He was another of the men whom it has been my good fortune to fall in with during the years of my life, as a drifting and observing steamboatman, who has seemed to be following the path in which by an unseen and overruling power he was destined to move, and as he has scattered good seed wherever his footsteps have marked the way for future generations to follow, I am sure that in holding him up as a shining exemplar I shall never be accused by those who knew Collin McKinney of too much individual laudation when I say that could I have the privilege of writing upon the tombstone of this unpretending pioneer in the wilderness his epitaph should be:

> Mark the perfect man, and behold the upright,
> For the end of that man is peace.

Collin McKinney walked in advance of the great army of human progress, toward the heart of the struggling Republic of Texas, and the good fruits of his labors so abundantly growing in the "Lone Star" State to-day should stimulate to like efforts every other wandering OUTSIDER.

Notes

1. See the articles on "Collin McKinney" and "Christian Church (Disciples of Christ)" in the *Handbook of Texas Online* and the profile of McKinney in J. K. Greer, "Committee on the Texan Declaration of Independence," *Southwestern Historical Quarterly*, July 1927.

2. James N. Smith, introduced in the previous letter.

3. That McKinney came to Texas and established the landing in 1816 is problematic. There is general agreement that the extended McKinney family arrived from Kentucky in 1824, but located first in Arkansas southeast of present-day Texarkana at Elam's Prairie, which is delineated on the 1842 U.S. General Land Office survey plat for T15S, R27W. The *Arkansas Territorial Papers* indicate that McKinney served in minor public offices in Hempstead, Lafayette, and Miller counties from 1825 to 1831, all of which would have been compatible with an Elam's Prairie location because of changes in county boundaries. John Henry Brown's 1892 *History of Texas, 1865 to 1892* provides compelling evidence through an 1874 letter from William McKinney that his father, Collin, had a house at Hickman's Prairie (the location of the landing) in 1826 that was visited by Ben Milam. McKinney's headright certificate in the Texas General Land Office files indicates that he had established continuous residence in Texas from December 4, 1824. It is likely that McKinney had houses at Elam's Prairie and Hickman's Prairie in 1824, particularly because these properties were only about 20 miles apart.

4. The New Orleans *Daily Picayune* reports the arrival of the *Planter* from Fort Towson in 1844 under Capt. Smith on March 31 and under Capt. Lodwick on May 4. In relation to the latter trip, the April 17 Clarksville *Northern Standard* reports the following: "The river is again out of its banks and rising rapidly. Yesterday morning it was within five feet of the high water mark of last year at

Bryarly's. Most of the cotton deposited there for shipment, has been hauled to the hills, and that which remains has been elevated four feet above the earth."

5. For baling cotton.

6. The location of the landing as shown in Figure 6 is chosen because it was the highest point among McKinney's properties along the river and because the survey records for Ashley McKinney's headright (immediately to the west of Collin's) in the Texas General Land Office say that Ashley's headright was about one-half mile west of McKinney's Landing. The landing was on a bend of the river that has since been cut off and is now designated Roseborough Lake. The survey records for Collin's headright in the Texas General Land Office disappeared many years ago. However, the area in which the landing was located was subject to an archeological investigation that was reported on by Kathleen Gilmore in her 1986 *French-Indian Interaction at an 18th Century Frontier Post; The Roseborough Lake Site, Bowie County, Texas*. Gilmore cites an October 1, 1835, Collin McKinney Survey in the McKinney Papers in the Garrett Collection at the University of Texas at Arlington, which says that the northwest corner of the survey began at a point about three-fourths of a mile below McKinney's house. This would mean that the house was located contiguous to the landing.

31 ✦ At Pine Prairie

Pine Prairie was located in southwest Little River County, which in 1842 was part of Sevier County. The name referred to a settlement that is still in existence, a landing to the south, and the prairie on which the settlement was located. Pine Prairie had been a keelboat landing and was an important steamboat landing located on a bend of the river that has since been cut off. The settlement and the landing were located on properties owned by Robert H. Scott,[1]

who appeared in the 1850 Sevier County census (Sevier was created out of Hempstead in 1828) as a 61-year-old planter born in South Carolina. Scott had brought his family to Pine Prairie in 1834 and was county judge from 1836–1840 according to the *Biographical and Historical Memoirs of Southern Arkansas*. Withenbury introduced Robert's son Tom, who was the perpetrator of a practical joke described in the next two letters.

⁂

[First part not used.]

Our arrival at McKinney's Landing, where I left the Relief in my last chapter, in order to follow the old patriarch to the "three forks of Trinity," and where I with so little ceremony buried him among his children, occurred at an early hour in the morning, and we hastened along with rather unusual dispatch for "Uncle Joe," hoping to reach the White Oak Shoals before dark. And now in view of the prosiness of my descriptions of all the previous incidents of this trip, I feel like passing in silence every intermediate point between McKinney's and the raft. [Rest of paragraph not used.]

But as I am passing Pine Prairie, some twenty or so miles below McKinney's, and see standing there upon the bank the venerable form of Judge Scott, the proprietor of that Arkansas plantation, who, with his head uncovered, and with his old slouched white hat in his hand, is waving us a welcome as we approach, and hear his voice as we glide along close to the shore, bidding us God speed, and a quick return, I feel that it is quite impossible to proceed without stopping here in my narrative and introducing to those who have had the patience to follow me, and stick to me, a few of the people along here on the Arkansas side of the river—among them a son of Judge Scott, who, for years, was honored with a seat in the Arkansas Legislature, which body has never, since the organization of the State, failed, even up to the present day, to furnish ample materials for the descriptive powers of better pens than mine.

But I find that I shall not in this chapter have space to properly place before my readers Colonel Tom Scott, of Sevier County, Arkansas, and so I will close this number at Pine Prairie, notwithstanding the Relief did reach, on this day's run, 'Squire Nunnaley's, five miles above the shoals, where we spent the first night after leaving Spanish Bluffs; and as I propose to do Colonel Scott the justice to relate an anecdote of him dating back to the days when he was a legislator, and thereby perpetuate the remembrance of some of his noble traits of character, as well as his marked and amusing eccentricities, to none of which I am sure his living friends, (nor himself, if still living,) will take the least unfriendly exception, I will leave him here, with the promise to show in my next how, long years ago, he fixed for himself a "place in the memory" of this OUTSIDER.

Notes

1. U.S. General Land Office land records indicate that Robert H. Scott acquired extensive acreage in T13S, R29W from 1841 to 1860. Part of this acreage encompassed what is shown on contemporary topographic maps as the "populated place" of Pine Prairie, with a few structures shown north of Scott's Lake. Scott's field is shown at the same place on the U.S. General Land Office survey plat for T13S, R29W, indicating that Scott's home was on the north bank of the lake. The probable location of the landing was about 10 miles to the southeast because this was the only land owned by Scott on the river.

32 ✦ A Practical Joke: Part 1

While at Pine Prairie, Withenbury was reminded of a practical joke that was perpetrated a few years before on an unnamed traveler by Tom Scott (the son of Judge Robert H. Scott), his wife Betty (Elizabeth), and his friend Andy Armstrong. Thomas W. Scott was state senator from Sevier County from 1840–1843 according to the *Biographical and Historical Memoirs of Southern Arkansas.* Andrew Armstrong was a planter in the White Oak Shoals area and served as state senator from 1848–1849 and in the lower house from 1842–1843 according to the *Biographical and Historical Memoirs of Southern Arkansas.* The incident takes place at Tom Scott's Pine Prairie plantation home, which was next door to his father's house, but apparently on his father's property, because Tom Scott was a planter but not an independent property owner.[1]

⁂

Taking up my pen again, after a long interval of silence, I am reminded that in my last I had only reached Pine Prairie, Arkansas, where I introduced, by name only, "Colonel" Tom Scott, one of the early legislators of the then frontier State on the southwestern boundary of this "great and galorious Union of ours."

Some few years prior to the time of which I am writing, there traveled a stranger through the northern portion of Louisiana and Western "Arkansaw," whose special mission was to drum up reliable customers for various commercial establishments in New York; and I suppose that in introducing him I ought to give his name, in order that the great and indispensable army of "commercial travelers" of this day may recognize and do proper homage to this pioneer in a calling then in its infancy, but which, by the indomitable perseverance of the Yankee, has since grown to very respectable proportions. But as I purpose in this chapter to speak of a resident citizen of Arkansas, I will omit the name of the "New York drummer," contenting myself with the bare incidental introduction I have given him, and refer to him as I proceed only where it is necessary to do so in order to illustrate more clearly than I could otherwise do, the eccentricities of my hero "Colonel" Tom Scott. I must state, however, that in addition to the ordinary duties of a "drummer" our traveler had bethought himself of the favorable opportunity thus offered for writing a book, relying entirely upon the varied incidents of his journeyings, and the many different phases of human nature which should present themselves as he went from place to place seeking new acquaintances and fresh customers for his employers.

The first I heard of him he was among a jolly set of fellows at the thriving town of Washington, in Hempstead County, Arkansas; and if my readers only knew as well as "Uncle Joe" and I do, a few of the frolicsome spirits of those early days, they would not need be told in detail of the way this stranger was "taken in and done for" by that grand, old fun-loving Israelite, Abraham Block, his precocious son "Gus," Mat. Moss, the Hempstead County fiddler, Bill Andrews, the "liveliest Yankee" merchant ever known in Arkansas, (unless I except "Dan." Fellows, of Camden,[2]) and "Hal" Cheatham, who kept *the* tavern,[3] (where "Lev." Cooper administered the beverages and chalked down the drinks, in his youthful days, and before he became the infallible Red River

Steamboat Inspector and Dictator for the New Orleans Board of Underwriters.) But it is of no use to go any further with this list of hospitable entertainers, for it seems to me endless, and I find myself led into digressions which possibly are unwarrantable in this connection, and so I leave my readers to judge whether a stranger alighting in the midst of a little isolated community, made up largely of shrewd business men, who were in the habit of making annual pilgrimages to the great centers of trade for fresh supplies of merchandise, and where, also, they were sure to gather up all the new jokes and tricks of the metropolis, which in the leisure intervals between their business hours, they would practice upon each other, provided no stranger or "outsider" came along—I say I will leave my readers to judge whether the aforesaid "outsider" would or would not be well attended to and regularly inducted into all the mysteries that were worth knowing before he would get away from the place.

Well, the commercial traveler, drummer, book-maker, or what not, passed through the gauntlet at Washington, and after having settled up a good many old scores, secured a long list of new customers for his sundry employers, and filled his portfolio with rich and rare items for his forthcoming "Notes of an Arkansas Traveler."[4] He began to prepare for his journey toward Columbus, Paraclifta and Lanesport, in Sevier County, and as the country through which he must travel to reach these points was very sparsely settled, he very prudently consulted with his friends at Washington before starting, as to the routes, and what was quite as important, the best stopping places by the way. And among others, he was advised to make it a point "by all means to stop at Colonel Tom Scott's," and spend a day and night with him, no matter if he did have to deviate a little from his direct route to do so,[5] for a sojourn of a day or so with that genial and intelligent gentleman would be worth to him a whole week spent in almost any other part of Arkansas.

One of his Washington friends volunteered to write for him an open letter of introduction to Colonel Scott, which would entitle him to all the hospitalities which the Colonel and his estimable wife could command, and the very best of everything for man and beast which the house and plantation could afford. And once favorably installed with "Tom Scott," he would be set all right for the balance of his journey northward.

While the introductory epistle was being penned, it occurred to another friend that he had some very important business with Colonel Scott, and "Would the gentleman be kind enough to carry a letter to him?" "Most certainly, with pleasure," was the reply. And so, with quick dispatch, the letter was written and sealed, in the most elaborate manner, to give it the appearance of an important official document.

Now, who it was that wrote this sealed letter is to this day one of the profound secrets of that mysterious set of jolly wags, each of whom loved a good joke too well to let an opportunity for its perpetration pass unimproved. But certain it is that no sooner had Colonel Scott read the letter than he understood that he was to entertain the stranger in a manner such as none but himself could do. The letter of introduction, which of course was the first one presented to him, was read, and the bearer warmly welcomed, and he made to feel at home before the dust was fairly shaken from his garments, and so was ready to take for granted every thing that Colonel Scott said, and to acquiesce in whatever he proposed to do or have done; and, in fact, so well assured was he of his welcome, and that he had at last struck a good place where to spend a week resting himself and his jaded horse, that he was bold to announce his determination to do so, and also to reveal to his affable host what to him was the most important part of his mission "to and through a country so remote from the centers of business and civilization"—the writing of a book, a sort of penciling by the way, which would serve the double purpose of filling up the leisure hours of his travels, thereby relieving a wearisome journey of much of its monotony, and also greatly amuse and edify his friends at home, and possibly at some future day put a few extra dollars into his pocket. Little did he dream that the sealed letter which he had just presented to his new entertainer was written especially to make known to "Tom Scott" that the traveler was writing a book, and that he must be sure and furnish him a few items with which to embellish the same to the taste of his wonder-seeking readers at home. But such was the fact, and Tom Scott, whose wits were always ready, and whose fund of humor was inexhaustible, saw at a glance the part his Hempstead County friends had arranged for him.

For the sake of brevity, I will pass without comment all that occurred from the hour of the arrival of the stranger at Pine Prairie Plantation, until he was called to dinner, where he met the unpretending Arkansas lady, Mrs. Scott, and found in her all the dignity of deportment which his Washington friends had prepared him for by their truthful descriptions of this truly estimable woman.

Dinner over and a stroll over the plantation was enlivened by Colonel Scott's vivid description of all that pertained to the planter's life in Arkansas. The labors were described as moderate, while the pleasures were magnified into real Munchausen[6] proportions, and the profits were made to appear fully up to the capacity of the most avaricious.

The sports such as "fire hunts," bear hunts, and fox chases were amplified in a manner well calculated to astonish, if not enlighten, the denizens of the crowded cities of the North and East, where the Colonel knew they would be carried, provided his visitor should survive the vicissitudes of his journey. And so the afternoon passed quickly and pleasantly.

After returning to the house Colonel Scott was gratified by seeing his visitor retire from his presence and resort to his memorandum book and pencil, and while he was thus engaged the jolly host sat down to chat with his wife (who was as fond of a joke as he was) and prepare her to carry on her part of the entertainment.

The Colonel told me the story years afterwards, and he said the hardest task he ever undertook was to prevail upon Mrs. Scott to "take her part in the play," for she importuned him so earnestly to spare her and "let the poor fellow go" that he was well nigh persuaded to forego the fun in store for himself and neighbors, at the expense of the wonder hunter, the recital of which to his friends at Washington, he knew would be anxiously looked for by them, and he could not bear for a moment the thought of being delinquent when they should meet.

Old Judge Scott (the Colonel's father) and Major Haynie,[7] his comrade and neighbor, joined with the Colonel's wife in her laudable pleadings on behalf of "the stranger," for the days of fun and frolic with them were well nigh past, and they would have spared the bookmaker. But not so Tom Scott. However, he came well nigh relenting under the pleadings of his good wife assisted by his father and Major Haynie, but just in the nick of time there came to his aid the veriest wag in all Western Arkansas, Andy Armstrong, from White Oak Shoals, who happened to be journeying that way and stopped for the night.

As soon as Tom Scott initiated him into the secret, he assisted him to "double teams" on the "old woman" and, having overcome her scruples, they decided to have their fun, cost what it might.

Andy Armstrong was introduced as a prominent planter in the county, and Colonel Scott left the two new friends to entertain each other (well knowing that Andy would do his part) while he absented himself to attend to some home duties, and Mrs. Scott was busy superintending the preparation for tea, &c.; and here as I find my story growing too long, I will leave them, promising that in my next I will finish the recital of one of the best Arkansas jokes that was ever perpetrated upon any OUTSIDER.

Notes

1. The setting for these incidents is shown in the 1838 U.S. General Land Office survey plat for T13S, R29W, including Judge Scott's field and the road immediately to the north that was used by the traveler. Tom Scott's household is listed immediately after Judge Scott's household in the 1850 Sevier County census, indicating that the son lived nearby. The absence of children in the account is confirmed by the census.

2. Daniel W. Fellows, of the firm of McCollum & Fellows, dry goods and receiving, forwarding, and commission merchants in Camden, which advertised in the *Washington Telegraph* because Camden on the Ouachita River was an alternative import/export point for Washington.

3. Hal (Henry) operated the Washington Hotel (during a period when hotels were referred to as taverns), as indicated by an advertisement concerning transfer of ownership in the November 6, 1844, *Washington Telegraph*. He and his younger brother Green (Greenville) became famous Red River steamboat captains, purchasing their first boat, the *South Western*, in 1842.

4. On the significance of the Arkansas Traveler motif, see the last note in Letter 36.

5. The Scott property was south of the road from Washington to Lanesport (and then to Fort Towson) that passed through Columbus and Rocky Comfort, as shown on Sidney Morse and Samuel Breese's 1845 *Arkansas*, which also shows the northern route from Washington to Lanesport by way of Paraclifta.

6. German adventurer known for exaggerating his exploits.

7. Thomas Haynie is shown as a large early property owner in T13S, R29W in the U.S. General Land Office land records. Haynie's field is shown immediately northeast of Judge Scott's field on the 1838 survey plat.

33 ✦ A Practical Joke: Part 2

The account of the practical joke perpetrated by Tom Scott is concluded in this letter.

⁂

In the conclusion of my last chapter, I left Andy Armstrong entertaining the New Yorker at the hospitable home of Colonel Scott, while their host and hostess were preparing the evening meal, and making every possible arrangement for their guests to enjoy the interval between tea time and bed time.

When at last Colonel Scott summoned the two gentlemen to tea, he detected a twinkle in Armstrong's eye, which told him, without a word of explanation, that the ground-work was all planned for suitably entertaining the stranger; and it required but a moment's conversation between the two wags, while Mrs. Scott was holding the stranger in a pleasant chit-chat before retiring from the dining room, to arrange all their plans.

After a social smoke by the three gentlemen, which between whiffs was enlivened by the relation of anecdotes of travel by Armstrong (in countries he had never visited) and the experience of Colonel Scott in the Arkansas Legislature, which was so embellished as to render it full of interest to the newcomer, who by the way was so plied with curious interrogatories calling for his impressions of the country and people that he was compelled to disgorge all he could think of. Colonel Scott proposed a "social little game of poker," and as if presuming upon the assent of his two visitors, he immediately took from the mantle and threw upon the table at which they were sitting a deck of cards which had the appearance of having done already a whole year's service. At the sight of the cards the New Yorker was horrified; and shoving his chair back from the table he begged to be excused, declaring that "for many years he had not touched a pack of cards and really knew nothing of the game proposed." But the two Arkansas friends would not listen to his protestations; they both insisted upon his joining them, and went on with their preparations for a night's sport with an air of assurance that he would at last "come to take a hand." They took their positions and each pulled out from his pocket a handful of silver coin and "stacked it up," each denomination by itself, so that no delay need occur in "making good" any bet proposed. This done, General Armstrong, (here I may as well explain that Andrew L. Armstrong, of whom I am writing, and who was familiarly known in his neighborhood as "Andy," was also dubbed "General," in accordance with the Southern usage, which, in that day, gave to every man who could claim any prominence in the community where he lived a title; and, I may add, also, that Andy Armstrong bore the honor meekly, and still he showed no lack of pride for having been, by common consent, brought into such close relationship with his illustrious prototype.)

But to return to my story. General Armstrong, as soon as his money was arranged upon the table, proceeded to draw from a belt, which was partly concealed under his coat, a huge derringer pistol, which, after having carefully examined the lock, he laid upon the table by the side of his "pile." Colonel Scott was at the same time busy in extracting from its sheath, which was fastened within the left breast of his vest, an enormous bowie knife, which, after due inspection, he coolly laid in a convenient place upon the table also.

These little preliminaries for a "social game" were so quickly gone through with that the stranger found no time to express his astonishment; but when Andy Armstrong familiarly tapped him upon the shoulder and said, "Come, stranger, you must join us," he threw up his hands, and most solemnly protested against participating in any amusement where such adjuncts as he saw before him were likely to be necessary to establish the value of "a hand" or the relative rights of the players. In short, he declined most positively to take any part in the game. Just at this moment a door opened behind him, and, as he cast a look over his left shoulder, he saw Mrs. Scott entering the room, with a young blunderbuss in the shape of a pistol in her hand, which she was critically examining as she approached; and, as she laid it down at her husband's right hand, she remarked, in her quiet way: "Husband, I think I'd put a fresh cap upon it."

"Thank you, Bettie," replied the Colonel, who was busy shuffling the cards; "I'll attend to that."

Mrs. Scott then took her seat between her visitor and General Armstrong, and entered into a commonplace conversation with the three; and turning to the stranger, she said: "You find, sir, many of our backwoods customs quite different from those of your own country no doubt, and you probably find it very difficult at times to reconcile what you meet with in your travels, with your own ideas of propriety; but, sir, we go along very smoothly, considering the disadvantages we labor under here."

The stranger assented to all of Mrs. Scott's remarks, and while he admitted the difficulty of reconciling many of the Arkansas usages and customs with those of the North and East, he "had not failed to discover wherever he had journeyed in the South, a nobleness of character seldom met with elsewhere, and, moreover, he had found so much to amuse and instruct the traveler, that his journey, although sometimes fatiguing to the body, had never yet proven tiresome to his spirits."

Here the Colonel apologized for interrupting the chit-chat between his wife and the stranger, and insisted upon commencing the "little game." Taking this timely prompting as to the part she was to play, Mrs. Scott, after admonishing the Colonel not to keep too late hours, gently alluding to the fatigue their guest must naturally feel, bade the company good night and retired through a door opening into her family bedroom.

Again the stranger was importuned to "take a hand;" and being at last forced to yield, though evidently much against his will, the game commenced "without any limit," except the "*ante*," and that being but fifty cents, the New Yorker considered that he could better afford to *ante* a few times around without betting at all, than to risk offending the two Arkansas gentlemen by refusing to join them in their evening's amusement.

After the game had run for half an hour or more, and large amounts of money had apparently changed hands, and many rough words of dispute had passed between Messrs. Scott and Armstrong, who seemingly had several times well nigh reached the point when an appeal to something more than cards or money was necessary, the stranger moved his chair back from the table and declared most positively that he could not play any longer. He pled a severe headache and a desire to retire to rest. Scott insisted upon his continuing "an hour or so longer," but when the plea of headache was made Armstrong said: "Well, Colonel, I think we must excuse the gentleman and we'll continue the game ourselves."

And so it was agreed that "the gentleman" might retire; and, after shaking "General Armstrong" by the hand, and bidding him good-night, he started, under the guidance of Colonel Scott, to what he vainly thought might prove a place of rest. He seemed to feel a special delight as he took the last look at the cards, the piles of silver coins to which he had contributed his mite, and the murderous weapons lying upon the table. But what was his surprise when Colonel Scott opened the very door through which Mrs. Scott had retired, and, pointing to a bed in a corner, where she was sleeping (?), said:

"There, sir, you will find the best bed in the house."

"But, my dear sir," exclaimed the poor, bewildered stranger; "you do not intend that I shall occupy the room where your wife is sleeping?"

"Most certainly, sir," replied Tom Scott; "that is the best bed in the house, and I *always* give the best to a stranger."

"But, *your wife!*"

"Oh, that's all right," said Scott; "Betty won't mind it. She's sound asleep now, and will be up before you wake in the morning; just go turn in there, and never you mind Betty."

But the stranger utterly refused to occupy the bed allotted to him, and retreated hastily from the open door; and throwing his saddle-bags (which he had carried upon his arm to what he supposed was his lodging-room) into a corner, he seated himself in an arm chair, and cast a look of the most perfect bewilderment upon his comrades, who by this time had resumed their "little game," Colonel Scott assuring him that the bed was at his disposal at any time when he should feel disposed to retire, and that not dreaming of any objection on his part, there had been no other bed provided for him, nor would it be possible to provide one for this night, but to-morrow Mrs. Scott would, on learning of his scruples, make other arrangements for him.

The stranger, fatigued with his travels, soon fell asleep in his comfortable chair; and when he began to snore loudly, Andy Armstrong looked up with a merry twinkle in his eye, and said: "Tom, we've got him now, and let's play it out on him." They laid down the cards, lit their pipes and with their eyes bent upon their victim, they began to contrive how most to astonish and frighten him.

After a full hour's silence, they began rattling their money on the table, and, as the tired sleeper began to nestle about and show signs of awakening, they each seized their weapons, kicked over their chairs and sprang into hostile attitudes into the middle of the room.

In an instant the traveler was awake and upon his feet. He rushed between the belligerents and cried out at the top of his voice: "Hold, gentlemen; for God's sake, hold!" and as his eyes got fairly open, he fancied he saw in Andy the most determined and murderous look, and he sprang and caught his right arm and cried: "General, spare your friend."

This was too much for Andy, and he burst into a loud laugh, which revealed to the victim a part of the joke that had been prepared for him by those two real "Arkansas gentlemen," who must have their fun, but who would not see a hair of his head harmed. Sleep was of course banished for the balance of the night, and Colonel Scott roused up a slumbering negro, who was lying on his blanket in a corner, and who was too used to his master's little jokes to be disturbed by all the noise of the night; and as he came forth, rubbing his eyes, he said: "Well, Mass'r Tom, what is it?" "Mass'r Tom" soon gave him his orders in a low tone, and as "Pete" shuffled out of the room on his errand, he looked over his shoulder and mumbled out: "Fo' God; won't Mass'r Tom nebber be done wid his jokes on poor strangers?"

In a few moments "Pete" returned with a full decanter and everything else necessary for a night's frolic. "Pete" knew just where to put his hand on "de refreshments," for they had been prepared for this special occasion by "Mass'r Tom's" orders. The door to Mrs. Scott's room was now closed, and without much persuasion, the wondering and doubting stranger drew himself up to the table as though fully determined to "do as the Romans do while he was in Rome;" and so laying all his scruples aside, he joined the convivial party, and what there was left of the night was spent without an apparent thought of weariness by any one of the party except "Pete," who was wonderfully annoyed by being frequently summoned from his corner to attend to the wants of the revelers. On one occasion, as he looked into the befuddled countenance of the "newcomer," and knew that his master and "de Genurl" were both duly sober, he was heard to exclaim: "Umph! Won't dey nebber be done?"

At an early hour Mrs. Scott summoned the three gentlemen to breakfast, and she expressed no little surprise when told that neither one of them had been in bed through the night. She reprimanded her husband for insisting upon "keeping a tired traveler up all night" simply for his own selfish amusement, and addressing herself to the stranger, but without the remotest allusion to the lodging place her husband had offered him, she said: "I will see, sir, that you have a quiet place as soon as breakfast is over where you can have a few hours of undisturbed sleep, for I am sure you must need it." The stranger bowed and smiled his thankful acknowledgement of the kind suggestion to his amiable hostess; but before he could find words to express himself, he was interrupted by Colonel Scott's proposal for a "drive" (deer hunt) in the afternoon, provided General Armstrong would delay his departure until to-morrow and join in the sport. This the General agreed to after considerable urging, and "Pete" was immediately called and instructed to have all the preparations made for "a drive," and be sure to have a certain horse (which was named) kept in the stable, "for the strange gentleman to ride."

The programme for the "drive" having been thus arranged, the breakfast party broke up, the gentlemen retiring to the room where they had passed the previous night, to enjoy a "social smoke," while Mrs. Scott went to attend to her household affairs. In the course of an hour she made her appearance among them, and reminded the Colonel of the promised rest to the stranger, and named the room prepared for him, to which he was at once conducted, and there left to sleep or ponder upon the predicament he was in as best suited him, and contrive the best and quickest way of getting out of it without offending his entertainers.

When dinner was announced he was ready, and during the meal he tried his best to excuse himself from joining in "the drive," evidently suspecting some new joke covered up among all the studied preparations for the afternoon's sport; but all his excuses were unavailing, and, before he was fairly aware of it, he found himself mounted and provided with a double-barreled gun and all the necessary accoutrements for a deer hunt.

Colonel Scott kept the best "team of hounds" in all the country, and when all were ready "Pete" and the other "boy" joined the party, bringing with them the dogs which were perfectly uncontrollable with the delight of the approaching sport; and until the hunters started off on a gallop, they kept up such a baying and howling that not a word spoken could be heard. The two negroes soon led off with the hounds, and then the necessary instructions for the hunt were given by the Colonel to his comrades; and when they came to the canebrake, General Armstrong was placed in his position or "stand," and Colonel Scott rode rapidly with the stranger to what he assured him was " the best stand in the whole drive." And as he was a novice in deer hunting, he was given special instructions to await patiently (no matter how long) the approach of the dogs; and then as their baying should betoken their earnestness in the pursuit, he might look in a direction which the Colonel pointed out for him, for the herd of deer to come bounding in their fright through the thick canebrake. "They never fail to come," said the Colonel, "but you must not be in too great haste to fire; keep cool and let one or two pass by if necessary before you get a sure aim; don't get buck fever, as most new hunters do."

With these instructions the stranger was left alone in a canebrake, so dense that the light of the mid-day sun could scarcely penetrate it, and he was not to leave his post until the hunt was over, and his companions came to pilot him back to the house.

Not until the baying of the dogs and the crackling of the cane and underbrush under the feet of the retiring horses of Colonel Scott and the two "boys" had completely died away, did our hero realize the awful stillness of the dense forest in which he was buried; and then he spent four long, weary hours without having the horrid silence once broken, except by the occasional neighing of his horse, or the hooting of an owl perched upon some tall pine. Darkness began to come on at last, and not a deer or a dog had as yet vouchsafed to startle him by their approach; and overcome by the dread of passing the night alone in the woods, he began shouting at the top of his voice. To move he dare not, for he was sure to get worse bewildered if he attempted to find his way out.

Just as he was about giving up in despair, he heard the dogs and the tramp of the horses, and he was soon delighted by the voices of the whole party of hunters, except "Pete," who had gone ahead with two fine bucks, which they had captured at least two miles from the spot the New Yorker had been watching and waiting for them.

Once at the house, and supper over, the stranger made known his determination to retire early, which he was kindly permitted to do, and on the following morning he made known his wish to proceed on his journey, instead of staying at Colonel Scott's a whole week, as he had first proposed to do. Reluctantly, and after much useless persuasion, the Colonel and his wife consented to his departure; and after breakfast his horse was saddled and brought to the door; and while "Pete" was busy adjusting his saddlebags, the poor victim of these merciless "Arkansaw jokes" attempted to offer something in the way of compensation for his entertainment, but, remembering what his Hempstead County friends had told him—that Colonel Scott would construe the offer of money into an insult and resent it as such—he was at a loss what to say. But, upon shaking hands with the Colonel and his wife and "Andy," and bidding them good-bye, he ventured to say: "I do not know, my friends, how I shall ever be able to repay you for your kindness and—" "Oh, never mind," said the Colonel, cutting him short, "put it all in your book." "Yes," said Armstrong, "put it in your book, and if you ever come to White Oak Shoals, look up Andy Armstrong, and Kittie and I will show you how we are prepared to take care of every straggling OUTSIDER."

34 ✦ At Nunnely's Landing

The *Relief* had arrived at Nunnely's Landing in Letter 31, but Withenbury interrupted his account in the next two letters to provide a description of the practical joke played by Tom Scott and Andy Armstrong. Although the present letter deals with Nunnely's Landing, much of the content is re-

lated to an incident concerning the *Concord* in 1838 when (under Jonathan Hildreth as captain and Erasmus Philley as pilot) it terminated its Upper Red River trip at Nunnely's Landing, as recounted in Letter 2. The account of the incident is derived by Withenbury from Philley in Cincinnati at the time he is writing the letters.

John Nunnely's home was at present-day Ogden, Arkansas, and he owned extensive bottom lands to the south and southwest according to U.S. General Land Office land records. The landing was to the south, a short distance above White Oak Shoals, and was a steamboat landing of modest importance. Nunnely was from North Carolina, married Mary Ann Easley (with whom he had seven children), came to the Red River about 1838, and died in 1848 at the age of 58.[1] Nunnely is mentioned occasionally as a reference in Shreveport newspaper advertisements by New Orleans cotton merchants.

⁂

In my last two numbers I have allowed myself to drift so far inland as to lose sight entirely of all steamboat matters and men; and I suppose I owe a long apology to such of my readers as feel a general interest in river matters, locate them where you will, but who, being strangers to the characters and places on which I have been dwelling so much at length, may have failed to find enough of interest to repay them for the time spent in following me in my wanderings.

Probably the best apology I can make is to go back to the Relief and "Uncle Joe Ross," at Nunnelly's Landing, to which point

I allowed them to precede me when I stopped in my narrative at Pine Prairie, lured there by the recollections of Colonel Tom Scott and Andy Armstrong and their drolleries. But before I resume the history of that long trip of the Relief, I must say a few words in explanation of the unexplained part of my last chapter.

I have said it was to this day a secret who penned the sealed letter which the New Yorker carried to Tom Scott, and so it is; but, as I heard, several years after the occurrence of the events which I have so imperfectly narrated, that the writing of that letter was attributed to Judge Field, of Hempstead County,[2] I will state that when accused of it he was able to deny it flatly and successfully, for in "the language of the law," he could prove an *alibi*. He was at that very time on one of his occasional visits "to Nashville," and so could not have been the guilty one. Those of his old comrades who may still be living will not fail to remember how completely these visits of his "to Nashville" incapacitated him for any business, or even the perpetration of a joke upon a stranger—a pastime he was particularly fond of.

But let me return to the Relief and the goodly company on board, all of which landed safely at 'Squire Nunnelly's landing long before sunset of the day on which we spent a couple of hours at McKinney's. The meeting of the Relief's crew with "the old 'Squire" was always the occasion of much real enjoyment, for the old man could not forget the landing of the "Concord," when, as I have before stated, she made his place the terminus of her first trip through the "Great Raft," commanded by Captain Hildreth, and piloted by Erasmus Philley, both of whom were now pilots on the Relief. On this particular occasion the meeting of these old friends was more than ordinarily pleasant, for Judge Smith, who was the mutual friend of all parties, and a genial soul everywhere, was with us, and by his inexhaustible fund of anecdote and reminiscence he was enabled to keep up the flow of good fellowship, even though others may have been predisposed to dullness.

Among other remembrances of the past which were duly considered, the history of the Concord's eventful trip came in for a full share; and as upon a former time I have failed to speak of one little episode in her career, I may be pardoned for bringing that pioneer steamboat in Upper Red River once more before my readers. One principal reason for her landing at Nunnelly's was the appearance of a wood pile on the bank; and as they had been running the last ten miles on fuel gathered from a drift pile, they were glad to see this first evidence of preparation for the steamers expected as soon as Captain Shreve should succeed with the Government snagboats in opening the raft; and, notwithstanding they had yet an hour and a half of daylight left, they stopped to take the wood and make the acquaintance of the people who had thus evinced the necessary forethought to prepare for their coming, and here Captain Hildreth decided to spend the night. Accordingly, the word "done with the engine" was passed to the engineer (John Henderson), and Philley, who was "on watch," left the wheel just in time to see Anderson "dampen down the fires" in the old-fashioned way, with a half dozen buckets full of water. In a few moments the engine stopped its breathings, and everybody went ashore, each as eager to place his feet first upon this new spot in Arkansas as were the fugitive children of Israel to enter the "Promised Land," when they stood on "Jordan's stormy banks," casting their wishful eyes into "Canaan's fair and happy land."

Very soon the supper-bell was heard, and Philley says he and Anderson were too tired and hungry to follow the crew very far into the woods, and so they hastened on board to supper. Anderson found something to engage his attention about the engine, and so did not reach the supper-table. Philley, however, without ceremony seated himself and commenced eating, and chatting the meanwhile with the chambermaid, who officiated as steward, cook and cabin-boy.

And now, as I am coming to the thrilling part of the story, I must be allowed to use Philley's own words (skipping a few only of the hard ones), as I remember his telling it to the crew of the Relief and 'Squire Nunnelly so many years ago, and which he repeated to me from his memory to-day, for Philley is still among us:

"You see, I had been steering all the afternoon, and as there was barely water enough for her on the shoals,[3] I had to wrestle her like d_mnation for near two hours to make about three lengths of herself in that stiff water; and by the time we landed at Nunnelly's I was ready for my supper and rest, and I didn't care to run into the woods like a d____d hound after a deer; and so when the bell tapped for supper I wasn't long in getting aboard. And says I to the chambermaid, 'Old gal, just give me my grub and don't mind waiting for the balance of 'em.'"

"I took my seat and she sot down right close to me, and poured out my coffee, and then said she: 'I b'lieve I'll just eat my supper too,' and so there we sot a' having a real cozy chat about the new country we were coming into, and wondering how much farther the old man would try to get up the river, and whether we would ever get back to Cincinnati; and just as the conversation was getting interesting, there commenced the d___dest rattling out forward I ever heard; why, it was like a young earthquake; but before I could move or speak, I saw the bulkhead[4] that was between the boilers and the cabin. (You see the cabin was on the lower deck just abaft[5] the boilers.) I say I saw that bulkhead begin to heave and set and belly out toward us, like a lateen sail in a storm, and quicker'n you could say Jack Roberson, I heard the bust up, and the whole d____d thing let go, and here came a shower of brick bats, pine knots, ashes, hot water, and bulkhead in splinters, such as no man ever dreamed of, and away went table and dishes to the after end of the cabin in a pile; and when I found myself I was piled up closer to the chambermaid than anybody had ever seen me before; and as she crawled out from under the rubbish and wiped the ashes out of her eyes, she says to me, 'Oh, for the good Lord's sake, Mr. Philley, do tell me what has happened.' But I was as much in the fog as she was, and says I, 'd____d if I know, but I guess the biler's busted by the looks of things about here.' But you bet I wasn't long in getting out forward, and there I found everything all tore to dam smash. The steps that led up on to the biler deck was lying about fifty feet from the boat, in the river, and there too was John Anderson, floundering and splashing like an alligator shot in the tail, and making better time than the Concord ever made, a' trying to get aboard of them steps. I hailed him to know if he was hurt, but d____d the word he could say. However, he soon got hold of them steps, and when I saw he was safe, I gave a whoop that would have made any Choctaw in the Nation ashamed of himself, or scared a Texas steer out of a canebrake. Either the noise of the collapsing of both flues of our starboard[6] boiler, or my yell, soon brought all hands to the scene of confusion, and poor John Anderson and a big nigger deck hand, who had been blown into the river, were soon fished out and cared for; and when we found out that nobody was hurt, and everybody badly scared, we breathed easy and went to picking up the pieces."

"But as for supper, that was out of the question on the boat, for the whole kitchen and cabin were knocked into the middle of next week; and that was just where Old 'Squire Nunnelly's strong suit came in. He raised his hands like a preacher about to pronounce a benediction on his sleepy congregation, and said, in his usual impressive tone: 'Thank God, gentlemen, you are all alive.'"

"But the difference between the old 'Squire and preachers in general was, he didn't stop at mere words, but dispatched a nigger post-haste to the house a mile or so back, with orders to have supper prepared for the whole party. God bless the old man; I hope he's alive yet. If he ain't, he's in heaven, and I know it."

Well, the short of the story is, (for I can not follow Philley's description any further,) the Concord, from some unknown cause, and after having been, as all supposed, "cooled down," collapsed the flues of one boiler, and so her trip of exploration in Upper Red River ended at Nunnelly's Landing, much to the disappointment of all concerned, most of whom were Cincinnatians.

The disabled boiler was "walled off" and the boat otherwise repaired as well as possible, and after a stay of nearly a week at Nunnelly's, she turned her head down stream, making the best headway possible with one boiler. In this plight she descended the river to the old City of Natchitoches, and no one save the crew and the people at Nunnelly's knew aught of the accident.

At Natchitoches some Frenchmen took a fancy to the Concord and proposed to purchase her, and as the ownership was fully represented on board the trade was soon made, and the sum of $2,400 was received as her full value; the purchasers knowing nothing of the collapsed flues; and Philley says, "I don't believe they ever found it out, for them Dagoes hain't no more sense than a parcel of d____d monkeys, nohow."

Had I space I would like to give Philley's description of the Concord's trip down through the raft, which to river men would be full of interest. But I must content myself with the bare mention of the fact that at Willow chute[7] she doubled her misfortunes by breaking a main shaft. Here, to use Philley's words, a "council of war" was held, and while some of the crew were disgusted and in favor of abandoning the trip "and tie the old box up and let her rot," John Anderson and Philley declared that they could mend the shaft.

Accordingly, they took it ashore and "spent a whole night in strapping and hooping (banding) it," and by breakfast time the next morning they had the shaft in its place and the boat on her way down the river, "as good as new."

In this crippled condition my patient readers must fancy they see the Concord arriving at Natchitoches, where her fame as the first boat ever put through the Red River raft so recommended her to the citizens of that old town that she found new owners who were blind to all her defects, and gladly invested their money in her; and now as Philley, who has been my reliable informant, declares that he there and then lost sight of her, we will allow her to pass into that oblivion which, with its broad pall, has since that day covered the history of hundreds of her successors.

It may be now necessary, in consequence of my many digressions, to remind some of my readers of the "day and date" of which I am now writing the history of "Uncle Joe's" Relief. I propose to do this because I am now coming to some few rather important events in the history of Upper Red River and the early steamboating thereon. So I will repeat that it was on the 5th day of February 1842, that we landed at 'Squire Nunnelly's, and where we remained till night at the old man's urgent request, in order to give him time to haul his crop of cotton—forty-nine bales—which he proposed to ship and go along himself, having waited as long as he could for General Williamson to open the raft.[8]

The river was at this time so low that "Uncle Joe" had serious doubts about getting over White Oak Shoals, five miles below; but the old 'Squire importuned him so earnestly to take his cotton, fearing it would be his last chance to ship, (and he promised to come to the shoals in the morning with his oxen and wagons and haul the whole cargo round the shoals if necessary,) that "Uncle Joe" consented, and we took the forty-nine bales on board, and then ran down to the head of the shoals to look after the stage of water and wait there for daylight. We landed alongside of a high, dry sand-bar, where we bedded our anchor, and drove several stakes to make our lines fast, fully satisfied from the indications that we would be obliged to take our entire load off in the morning in order to make the passage safely over the shoals.

At the foot of the shoals, and waiting for a rise, we found the keel-boat John Smith, loaded with emigrants, from Louisville, Kentucky, and bound for Peters' Colony,[9] at the Upper Cross Timbers,[10] in Texas. This keel-boat had come from Louisville to Shreveport, in tow of the steamboat Embassy, which had undertaken the trip with the expectation of getting through the raft; but finding it still closed they sent the keelboat through the bayous and lakes, and here the party had met their first detention, after having come some two hundred and fifty miles without the aid of steam. There were about one hundred and twenty-five souls on board, of all sizes and ages, all of whom seemed in good spirits and hopeful of arriving at their "promised land" in due time. How sadly they were disappointed, and how they eventually scattered through the country hundreds of miles short of their destination, I can not now stop to tell, as I find this chapter growing too long already. We spent some three hours of the night with them very pleasantly, learning from them all of interest that had occurred upon the trip, and all of their plans for the future. They assured us that they had everywhere met with the kindest treatment when mingling with the people along the banks of the river, and that there had been strong inducements held out to them to abandon their long and uncertain voyage, and locate nearer their old homes. These they declined, but they blessed the people who had proffered them homes among them, holding out the right hand of fellowship to one and all, notwithstanding "every mother's son and daughter" of them was, in the strictest meaning of the word, an OUTSIDER.

Notes

1. On Nunnely, see the Little River County Chamber of Commerce website and the genealogical information contained in the online "Family: John W. Nunnely + Mary Ann Easley."

2. John Field began advertising as a Washington attorney in June 1844 in the *Washington Telegraph*, and Alfred Carrigan in "Reminiscences of Hempstead County" (in *Publications of the Arkansas Historical Association*, Vol. 2, 1908) mentions Judge John Field among the prominent men of 1850.

3. White Oak Shoals, which the *Concord* had to cross to reach Nunnely's Landing moving upstream.

4. A wooden partition separating the boilers from the cabin.

5. Behind.

6. Right side of boat facing forward.

7. The upstream entrance to the old keelboat route on the east side of the river.

8. Thomas Williamson was a private contractor to the Corps of Engineers for raft removal from 1841 to 1844. Although Williamson was intermittently successful, the raft reformed in 1842, 1843, and 1844. The details of Williamson's effort are provided in my *A History of Navigation on Cypress Bayou and the Lakes*.

9. A partially successful settlement effort resulting from an 1841 grant by the Republic of Texas to 20 American and English investors led by William Peters. According to an article on the colony in the *Handbook of Texas Online*, the colony headquarters was in Louisville and the first group of immigrants left by steamboat as early as December 1841. Withenbury appears to have provided the only account of what transpired with respect to the first group of immigrants. The keelboat was towed because it was known that the immigrants would not be able to reach their destination by steamboat, and Withenbury indicates that the entire trip was made on the keelboat. A February 1, 1842, letter in the February 23 *Washington Telegraph* says that the keelboat *John Smith* arrived at Fulton on January 29 with 30 families out of 200 who left Louisville in the fall to settle at Cross Timbers, which corresponds with Withenbury's dating.

10. A narrow band of north-south woodlands separating the eastern prairies from the western prairies beginning immediately west of Dallas.

35 ✦ To Dooley's Ferry

Most of this letter is concerned with events above White Oak Shoals while the *Relief* was waiting for a rise in the river. With the rise, the *Relief* proceeded to Dr. O. S. Jones' landing, Fulton, and Dooley's Ferry, where the night was spent (Figure 10). On Dr. O. S. Jones, see the next letter. Fulton is mentioned only in passing in this letter, apparently because Withenbury was in a hurry to get down to the raft in his account. Fulton was the most important Upper Red River landing and the only one that could actually be considered a town. It had two warehouses operated by receiving, forwarding, and commission merchants and was a center for trade on the upper river and also on Little River and its tributaries. On Dooley's Ferry, see Letter 38.

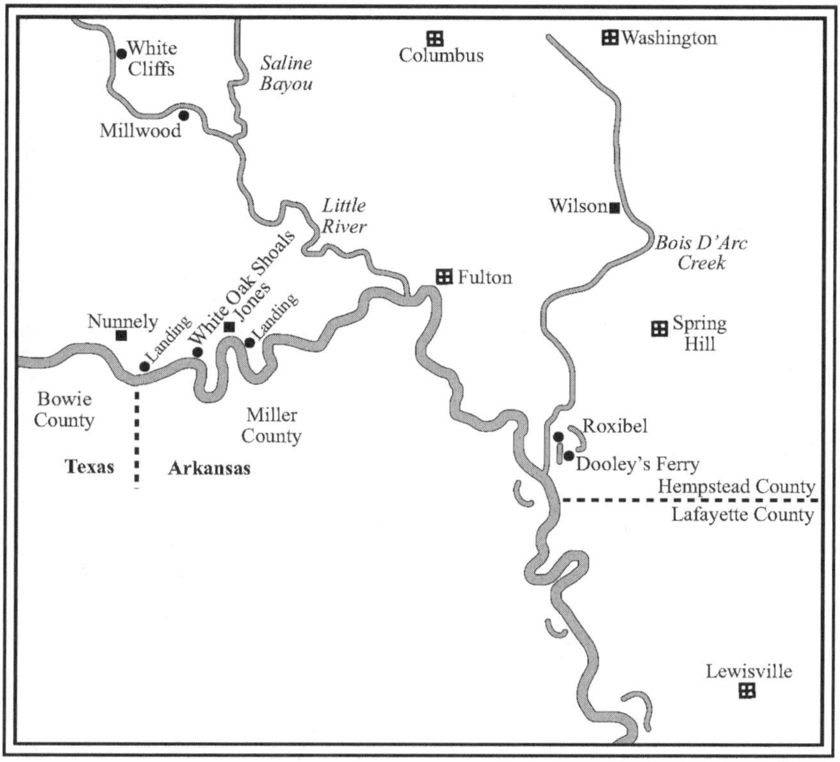

FIGURE 10: BELOW WHITE OAK SHOALS

⁂

Rather unceremoniously I left "Uncle Joe" at the head of the White Oak Shoals on the night of February 5, 1842, "staked out" to a dry sand-bar, and cut off from all communication with humanity except with the company of Kentucky emigrants on board the keel-boat "John Smith." I mean to be understood to say the Relief was "staked out" to the sand-bar, and not "Uncle Joe," for he could not endure to be staked to a dry bar, any more than a fish could live out of water.

But let me confine myself a little closer to the history of this everlasting trip of the Relief. As I said in my last chapter, the water was so low on the shoals, that the keel-boat, John Smith, with her company of impatient emigrants, was waiting for a rise in the river to enable them to ascend and proceed on their voyage. We had learned the particulars of their detention from 'Squire Nunnelly, who told us that for the last three weeks he had received daily visits from some of them, and that to relieve somewhat their impatience he had been continually prognosticating a change in the weather and a rise in the river; but now that all signs had failed, he began to fear for his acknowledged reputation as a weather prophet. And notwithstanding the fact, that for a week past he had seen such indications in the water, as had always heretofore augured and immediately preceded a sudden rise, he really began to fear that he was "fooled for once;" and so made the promise as I have before stated, to bring his "oxen and niggers" and haul our load round the shoals, if we thought the Relief could "make the riffle" in safety when light.

Of those at the head of White Oak Shoals on the night of February 5, 1842, the crew of the Relief, all except the watchman, laid down to sleep and dream of a hard day's toil on the morrow.

Just as Judge Smith (whom my readers must not forget was the guest of Captain Ross on this trip) had finished his last anecdote and had prepared to "hang up the fiddle and the bow," he reminded "Uncle Joe" of a remark that 'Squire Nunnelly made while looking at the surface of the water in the river just at sunset and while we were busy taking on his cotton.

"Oh I'll be dod durned," said "Uncle Joe," "ef I ever pay any more attention to folks guessing when the river is going to rise. One man's guess is about as good as any other man's, and I guess it'll rain before the river rises to hurt, or to do any good either, and the Lord knows I've been prayin' for rain for six weeks, and durn the drop has fell on me yet."

"But," said Judge Smith, " 'Squire Nunnelly is one of those close observers of the weather and river whose predictions are rarely at fault; and I remember hearing Captain Crooks say, last season, that while the Hunter lay high and dry upon a sand-bar, just below here, he used to visit 'Squire Nunnelly almost daily for two months, and he never got any encouragement from the old man about water until one day when he caught him looking intently, as it were, into the very depths of the river for some five minutes; and when he raised his eyes from the water, he said, 'Well, Captain Crooks, your imprisonment is about at an end, or I am very much mistaken. You will do well to get the Hunter ready for a rise, for I can see a change in the water since morning, and although it has fallen half an inch to-day, I believe it will rise a foot before morning. In fact, I am sure of it.'"

"Captain Crooks declared to me," continued Judge Smith, "that he could not discover any indications of a rise, nor could the 'Squire explain to him what he saw to give him hope; but he persisted in advising him to be ready for an immediate rise in the river. And the old Captain was glad enough to seize upon the little hope thus held out to him; and he returned to his boat, and amid the jeers of his officers and crew, who, (like 'Uncle Joe' in the present instance,) had been looking and praying for rain for six weeks, without so much as a drop falling in answer to their prayers, he ordered everything made ready for a rise; and, to the astonishment of everybody, in less than twenty-four hours the Hunter was afloat, and all hands happy." "Now," said the Judge, "I saw the old fellow looking into the water this afternoon as though he would read the hidden mysteries of 'Old Red' from the White Oak Shoals to Kiamish; and he never said a word about shipping his cotton till after he had scrutinized the river closely, and I'll be d____d if John Nunnelly would ever ship a bale of cotton if he thought it would have to be unloaded and hauled round the Shoals, only five miles below his landing; and when he promised you that he would bring his 'oxen and niggers and haul your whole load round to-morrow if necessary,' he felt d____d sure that he wouldn't have anything of the sort to do; and I'll bet liquor for all hands that he don't come here with his 'oxen and niggers' in the morning, and, moreover, that you will have plenty of water within twenty-four hours from this time. Why, I can't forget how cunning the old weather dog looked this afternoon, when he said, 'Gentlemen, I see something in the water that tells me a rise is coming, and that too not very far behind you.' Why, d__n it, he was just as sure of it as I am that I want another drink before I go to bed."

At that hint "Uncle Joe" sung out to Oliver (who was snoring as though he didn't care if there was never another inch of water in the river, so that his whisky held out); and while he was preparing the drinks, "Uncle Joe" declared that he could not go to sleep without another tune from the fiddle and one of the Judge's lively songs; and so the Judge favored "Uncle Joe," and disturbed and awakened everybody else on the boat, with

> Near the lake where drooped the willow,
> Long time ago.

* * * * *

> The bobtail bull came down the mountain
> Long time ago,
> He whet his horn on a white oak sapling
> Long time ago,
> He shook his tail and raised the river,
> Long time ago.

* * * * *

I can not say that this "refrain" found much favor with "Uncle Joe" except so far as it alluded to a rise in the river, and that was so earnestly desired, that he would willingly accept it from any source, even the shake of a bobtail bull's tail.

The Judge's potations soon overcame with drowsiness all the exhilarating effects of his music and original poetry, and a little after midnight all was quiet on board the Relief and the John Smith. But my readers may judge of the scene of confusion when about 4 o'clock our watchman ran storming through the boat, crying at the top of his voice: "Wake up everybody, for the river's rising like h_ll. The stakes are all washed up and d__n the thing is holding the boat at all but the anchor." And true enough, the rise which "the 'Squire" had foreseen had come upon us as suddenly almost as a flash, and had caught the watchman napping from the effects of a "drop too much," which Captain Ross had permitted him to take when he came up a few hours before to listen to the Judge's song. But he was now wide awake and was not long in bringing every one else into a like condition.

By the aid of the yawl, we got a line out to a large tree, and then got our anchor aboard, which by this time was entirely covered by the rapidly rising river. We then had an opportunity to observe how rapidly the volume of the river was being augmented, and we found it rising fully two feet an hour, which appeared the more wonderful and unaccountable from the fact that no rain had fallen in that locality, nor as far as we had been or heard from up the river for near two months. The next question which puzzled us was, how was 'Squire Nunnelly able to detect in the appearance of the water the approaching flood?

Judge Smith assured us that he had known the like phenomenon to occur many times before during his residence in Texas, but he had never been able, close observer that he was, to detect the premonitory symptoms of a rise in the midst of a season of drought. None could deny, however, that "the 'Squire" was a prophet; and, as "Uncle Joe" quaintly remarked, he was a "dod durned sight more profitable to him and the anxious souls on the John Smith than all them old long faces who have been on their marrow bones for the last two months a prayin' for rain, and nary a prayer answered."

All was hurry and confusion until daylight. The Relief had steam up, and ready for a brisk run to Fulton, some twenty odd miles, and was only waiting for 'Squire Nunnelly to come with his saddle-bags—carpet-bags were not known in those days—filled with clean shirts, &c., to last him on his visit to the Crescent City.[1] Before the sun was an hour high, the woods began to echo to the prolonged shouts of the 'Squire's faithful "boy," who had preceded him on his way to the boat. This "boy" told us he had been posted on the bank of the river all night, to "watch for the rise which ole massa know'd was a comin' shoo-ah;" "and now," said he, "de ole boss is jes back dere in de canebrake, and he'll be here right soon, so you can get yer bilers hot and be ready to slide."

By the time the 'Squire was among us, and we had listened to his congratulatory "God bless you all, gentlemen," we ascertained, by referring to our marks, that the river had risen eleven feet, and not a sign or sound of the shoals was to be seen or heard.

The joyous company of emigrants on board the John Smith were busy with their preparations for resuming their tedious voyage, but they would be necessarily delayed at their present landing several days longer, in order to collect together their scattered company, many of whom had wandered a long distance away landward among the Arkansas and Texas planters. A few of these truants never returned to join the "goodlie companie." Among whom I will venture to mention a young doctor from Louisville by the name of Allen. He strayed into the neighborhood where lived "Uncle Charley Moores;" [2] in Bowie County, Texas, and there he became enamored with the old man's youngest daughter.[3] But I must stop and leave him there for the present, for thereby hangs a long tale of thrilling romance, in which the doctor, "Uncle Charley," and the girl were the principal characters, and which was brought to its timely *denouement* by the prompt action—in his magistratical character—of 'Squire Nunnelly, at whose house the fugitive lovers had halted for a night's rest. Should the kindness of the printer and the patience of my readers endure long enough, I promise at some future time to take up this adventure of Doctor Allen and his charming Texas bride, and tell a "tale of real life," which shall throw fiction a long way into the shade.[4]

We landed at Dr. O. S. Jones', six miles below the shoals, took for him twenty-six bales of cotton, and then sped away down the rapid current without a single stop until we reached Fulton at noon. After a short delay at Fulton we started again, and without "let or hindrance," we reached Dooley's Ferry at dark, where we spent the night as joyously as it was possible for so weary a set of wanderers to feel while so far from kindred and home.

The pleasures of this night were wonderfully augmented by the joint musical efforts and talents of Judge Smith and the inimitable Arkansas fiddler, "Tom" Portwood, a proud Virginian by birth, but at this time the humble overseer on the cotton plantation of Captain Phineas Nash. [6]

I know there are still living in Louisiana, Arkansas and Texas a good many whose ears will tingle with the recollections of merry music, at the mere mention of the names of "Jim" Smith and "Tom" Portwood, but all that would not entitle me to bring those two "dead men" into print so far from the field of their former fame. But "Uncle Joe" and Philley and "Ed." Wilson and Elias Ehler and R. A. Holden are here among us, and they have all been there, have seen what I have seen, have heard "Jim" Smith and "Tom"

Portwood play the fiddle, and they will, if necessary, vouch for the truth of every word written by this (to some of them) unknown OUTSIDER.

Notes

1. New Orleans.

2. Charles Moores is listed in the 1850 Bowie County census as a 76-year-old planter born in North Carolina. He came to Bowie County with five of his sons in 1837 to clear land and build a home, moved his family in 1840 to the Mooresville settlement near present-day Redwater, and operated Moores' Landing and its ferry to the south on Sulphur Fork. On Moores and his family, see J. H. Atkinson, ed., "Travel In Pioneer Days" (*Arkansas Historical Quarterly*, 1961); the articles on "Moores, Texas" and "Moores' Landing" in the *Handbook of Texas Online*; the profile of his grandson Alex in the *Biographical and Historical Memoirs of Southern Arkansas*; and the online "Charles Moores & Mary Harrison Family, Texarkana."

3. Frances, who was born in 1828, married R. H. Allen, and appears to have died in childbirth in 1848.

4. Withenbury doesn't do this.

5. U.S. General Land Office land records indicate that Phineas Nash was a large early property owner in the Dooley's Ferry area. Thomas Portwood, aged 45 and born in Virginia, is listed in the 1850 Lafayette County census as an overseer.

36 ✦ Dr. O. S. Jones

The *Relief* reached Dooley's Ferry in the last letter, and Withenbury refers back to Orlando Jones, whose plantation landing was six miles downstream of White Oak Shoals. The landing is not mentioned in the newspaper re-

cords concerning steamboat movements, which is not surprising given its proximity to the White Oak Shoals landing, but is listed in the "Landings from Shreveport, La., to Preston, Texas" in *Gardner's New Orleans Directory for 1866*. According to U.S. General Land Office land records, Jones was an early large property owner with bottom lands east and southeast of the small community of present-day Temple, Arkansas (east of Ogden). He is listed in the 1840 Sevier County census and in the 1850 census as a 40-year-old unmarried physician born in Virginia.[1] Most of the letter is concerned with Jones and two merchants at Spring Hill (an interior town northeast of Dooley's Ferry) and ends with the arrival of the *Relief* at the head of the raft.

⁂

In my haste to reach our resting place at Dooley's Ferry for the night of the 6th of February, 1842, I allowed myself to quite neglect more than one prominent personage among the people of Arkansas, as well as several very interesting points in the country.

Among the characters that I have passed by in silence in my chronicle of the last day's run of the Relief, and of whom I would like to indulge my propensity to tell tales, I must just mention Dr. O. S. Jones, at whose landing I have said we took twenty-six bales of cotton.

Dr. Jones was one of those boasting "F.F.V's" [2] we have all read of, and so sure was he that men of his "stock" and culture could do no wrong that the rest of mankind had a right to take exceptions to, that he did not seem to care what he did, and his code of morals seem to have been framed more in reference to high shirt collars, red top boots, and a waxed and artistically twisted mustache, than to the wholesome teachings of the Seventh Commandment, or the views of more modern writers than old Moses, upon the requirements of a well regulated human society.

At a later date, when I knew more of the Doctor (and less of this "wicked world" than I have since learned) I used to wonder how any man bearing the evidences which he did of high intellectual attainments could content himself to lead a lonely bachelor's life upon a cotton plantation on the far western borders of Arkansas, cut off completely as he was from all the associations of his earlier life, and the endearments of home. How he could barter the holy and ennobling influences of refined and pure woman for the chances of increasing his store of "filthy lucre," and for the criminal companionship of those whom he could drive to suit his caprices, as "sheep are driven to the slaughter," was to me a puzzle.

But when, at a still later date, I visited him at his plantation, which was situated upon the borders of a beautiful little lake, once the bed of the river, but now some six miles distant from it,[3] I saw enough to convince me that the "first families" are but human at best; and then and there was forced upon me the truth of the adage, "to err is human."

But I must now leave the Doctor, his plantation and his harem, and hasten along down the river, and, possibly, at some future time I may devote a whole chapter to him and "his kind," for he was by no means "alone in his glory."

Three miles above Fulton, on the Arkansas side, a very considerable tributary, called Little River,[4] empties into Red River. This stream is navigable some sixty miles to a point called White Cliffs,[5] whenever Red River can be navigated above White Oak Shoals. The water of Little River, unlike that of Red River, is clear and pure,[6] and the current so gentle, and the curves so easy, that steamboats of, say a hundred and seventy feet length, can run the whole distance without once stopping an engine. The land immediately on its banks, though covered with an immense growth and a great variety of useful timber, is of so poor a quality that it remains to this day mostly uncultivated.

Some twelve miles back from White Cliffs is the flourishing town of Columbus, and the country round about there was settled by a thrifty race of people, who, as a general thing, would have done credit to any country.

The abundance of good white oak timber on Little River prompted Captain John Graham, an old-time Red River steamboatman, about the year 1855, to build a steamboat there. Captain Graham was a ship carpenter by trade, and had spent the early part of his life on the Cumberland River. He selected a point called Millwood,[7] for his shipyard, where a former Cincinnatian, William H. Elstner, now a merchant at Shreveport,[8] had located and built a sawmill.

After many long and vexatious delays, the boat was finished and named the "White Cliffs."[9] Her career was short and unprofitable, and since then no man has been found visionary enough to follow Captain Graham's undertaking, which proved so signal a failure to him and his friends.

Mr. Elstner soon found that Millwood and the adjacent country afforded but a poor field for the exercise of his talents, and he retired in disgust, and Millwood has long since become one of the places that were.

Now, while I am upon Little River, I can hardly resist the inclination to enter upon the recital of an incident in the life of our townsman, Edward J. Wilson, of the old firm of Harrison & Wilson; but I will pass it over for this time, with the promise that when I get into the chronicles of 1843 I will return to my theme, and write a chapter[10] entitled "The Thrilling and Chilling, and almost Killing Adventures of Ed. Wilson on an Arkansas Drift Log, in Little River." (Decidedly *in* the river.)

Now, for the sake of introducing a little Arkansas-Louisiana story, I will hurry along without stopping to take further note of Fulton or its people; postponing to a more convenient season what I would like to say of that soon-to-become-important place, [11] as the railroads now in progress stretch over the unbroken ground of Arkansas.

Ten miles back from Dooley's Ferry—where my readers must not forget the Relief was lying on the night of February 6, 1842—is the thriving village of Spring Hill, and there, in anticipation of the opening of the raft, and the consequent rapid growth of business, had settled a number of enterprising young merchants, among whom, and for a long time foremost among them, were two, who, under the auspices of business friends in New Orleans, had formed a partnership and commenced their business career at this point. But as both these men are probably now living, I will not write their names, lest one or the other might fancy himself aggrieved by my rehearsal of an old anecdote.

I will say, however, that they were both Englishmen; both single at the date of their advent in Arkansas, and that they both eventually married wives that were both the daughters of Colonel ______. There, now, I had liked to have told. Well, now, for my story. Fortune did not "smile and continue to smile" upon these adventurers "according to contract," because forsooth, the Red River raft was not cleared out according to contract, and consequently the era of "big boats" and cheap freights did not dawn upon Upper Red River as early as expected, and consequently again many of these hopeful men who had started out in the full belief that all things would be lovely with them, were soon admonished to begin to "take in sail," and prepare for a financial storm, which could be plainly seen looming up in the (not very far off) distance, and to cut it short, our Englishmen failed; not, however, until the hero of my tale had married the eldest, beautiful and accomplished daughter of a fine old Virginia gentleman then residing at Spring Hill; and there had been born to the happy and hopeful young couple a sweet little cherub of a daughter, in whom seemed centered the very soul and beauty of its doting young mother, and the pride and hope of the father.

Despite the efforts of these young merchants to keep their heads above water, the time came for their collapse; and I have no doubt that such precautionary steps were taken by them to provide for their own future wants, as most men in these more enlightened days are wont to take for a like purpose when they find themselves going under, leaving their creditors to look out for themselves as best they may.

And so one morning the hero of my tale in sadness and melancholy bade good-bye to his dear wife and sweet little daughter, then scarce two months old, and mounting the fleetest horse to be found, he, without formally notifying his business friends of his intended departure, took final leave of Spring Hill and started in a southerly direction, hoping ere another day dawned to step upon the soil of Louisiana, where he would be beyond Arkansas jurisdiction and free from the annoyance of pursuing creditors.

In his flight he was obliged to pass through the entire breadth of Lafayette County, but he took precaution to give the little town of Lewisville (the county site) a wide berth, for he knew that as soon as his sudden exit from Spring Hill should become known, his anxious friends would be in hot pursuit, and were they to learn that he had not passed through Lewisville, they would be in a degree baffled; and while they were making inquiries and enlisting the services of Sheriff Hightower[12] to continue the pursuit, he would hope to gain time and distance enough to enable him to reach another State before they could overtake him.

He soon regained the country road, and although his horse was well nigh broken down, "no grass grew under his feet," that day; but away he flew as though his life depended upon reaching his goal ahead of his pursuers. And very likely the prize to be lost or gained was of vital importance to him, for those Arkansas frontiersmen had a decidedly summary way of settling with delinquents of his class, and he had lived among them just long enough to learn their mode of doing business, and he needed no other prompting than this knowledge to urge him up to his best speed.

Just as he began to hope he was nearing the boundary of the State, he came in sight of a field where a number of negroes were at work, and he hailed the one nearest to the roadside, (who, seeing the unusual haste he was in, had halted his mule and stood in amazement, leaning upon the handle of his plow) in these words: "Boy, how far is it to the Louisiana line?"

He did not slacken his speed a whit, and consequently, before the bewildered "boy" could reply to his question, he was out of hearing and hidden entirely from sight by the cloud of dust raised by his jaded horse; and the negroes, in their amazement, began to question among themselves what could be the cause of such unusual haste in a white man.

In less than half an hour there came riding along the road at a very rapid rate, a *posse* of men, and stopping at the field the foremost rider cried out: "I say, boys, have you seen a man, on a dark bay horse, ride along here this evening?"

"Ye—yes, mas'r Hightower," answered the foremost one of them, who happened to be the same "boy" who had been questioned a few minutes before in regard to the probable distance to the Louisiana line. "Yes, dar was a man went along her jes' a whoopin; an' you orter seen him an' hearn him holler. Lord God, mas'r, dis chile nebber seen de like o' him, de way he was a gwyne an' a hollerin."

"How long since he passed, and what did he say?" asked the Sheriff.

"He's done been gone 'bout a haff hour," said the negro; "an' all he said was 'boys, how fur is it to de Loosinanna line?' but he nebber stopped, an' long 'fore I could 'a tole him he was out 'n sight; and if his horse didn't drap dead he was ober de line 'fore you got here; for you see de Loosinanna line is jes round de field dar, not mor'n foe hunerd yards; an' so, boss, you might just as well gib up de race, for you'll nebber see dat man dis side de line, 'less his horse gin out 'fore he got dar." And then the whole company of darkies shouted: "Oh, mas'r Hightower, you's done beat dis time; de white man's gone an' you can't put de dogs on his track like you does on de niggers when he's run-away. Yeah, yeah, go home, Mr. Sheriff, and tole de folks you couldn't cotch him."

And so here the chase ended; and here might my story end, also, were I not disposed to follow through an interval of some twenty years this fugitive from Arkansas, and tell how he flourished and grew great after reaching the Louisiana line, until the Spring of 1862, when, upon the approach of "Old Strabismus,"[13] at New Orleans, he again fled from the pursuer, leaving there the accumulations of the twenty years, and never resting until he reached and crossed the "Louisiana line," and landed safely at Mississippi City,[14] where, in the bosom of his largely increased family, he remained quiet until the "cruel war was over," returning at last, with numerous other braves, "not conquered," but whipped just enough to humbly beg to be restored to the possession of his abandoned home, his cotton presses, &c.

When we arrived at Dooley's Ferry, Captain Ross received word that at Spring Hill there were some ten or twelve passengers waiting for the arrival of the Relief, and so a messenger was sent to notify them that the boat would wait for them; and, if my recollection serves me right, the mule that carried that messenger was a rough traveler, and required much urging to perform the journey, and it was quite dark when the place was reached. But what added most to the tedium of the trip of ten miles and return, was the unwelcome news that the passengers had got tired of waiting for the announcement of the Relief's arrival, and had gone that very day overland, some sixty miles, to Ecore Fabre, (now Camden), on the Ouachita River, there to take a steamboat for New Orleans. This news precluded all chance for the looked-for-rest to mule and rider, and, without dismounting, I turned the animal's head toward the river again, and arrived at the boat at 9 o'clock P.M., where I found "Uncle Joe," Judge Smith and Tom Portwood, doing their best to entertain the crew, and the few neighbors who had come on board to enjoy the novelty of an evening on a steamboat.

When I made known the fruitlessness of my errand to Spring Hill, "Uncle Joe" expressed his disappointment in a very marked manner; and he came well nigh giving offense to some of the company present, who were friends of those who had disappointed him. The sudden change from the remarkable good humor he had exhibited during the whole evening, to that of evident anger and disgust, and a general consignment of the whole people of Arkansas to a region considerably below the level of Red River, required a slight backing down on his part before the representatives of that chivalrous State would be appeased; and it was right amusing to see how quickly "the Old Man" took the hint, and in the quaintest style possible, turned all his hasty words into mere pleasantries.

"Well, dod durn the luck," said he, "I'd been counting how much I'd make carrying them ten or a dozen folks down to the raft. Why, 'twould 'a been almost clear gain; for we've got mighty little on the boat that they could eat, and no show to buy anything till we reach a boat from Orleans at the foot of the raft. But it all goes in a life time, so let-er-rip. I won't have to answer for the sin of having robbed them people of their money without giving them something in return; and I'll die with a clear conscience, if I am poor."

This little speech—which, in fact, was more in the character of a soliloquy, than a sentence addressed to other parties—worked like a charm; and as soon as it was uttered, it soothed the disturbed feelings of all present except this humble writer, whose peace of mind and body was too much lacerated by that mule ride of twenty miles to be healed in so short a time.

Without being over ceremonious, "Uncle Joe" gave orders to Morrison, the engineer on watch, to "get up steam, for dang my hide," said he, "if I don't run to-night, so as to reach the raft before dark to-morrow, for I've been so long on this trip now that I've forgot when I started, and, what's more, I haven't made nary red cent yet."

The company took the hint, and a parting drink all round, and filled up the balance of the time Morrison was getting up steam, (for he had "cooled down" for the night,) by listening to the "Arkansaw Traveller" [15] as a duet performed by Judge Smith and Tom Portwood, who were both in their merriest and mellowest mood.

At 11 P.M., the adieus were said and the Relief's head turned down stream, but before she had run five miles, she ran over a snag that made "Uncle Joe" repent his rashness in attempting to run at night, and he ordered her landed, where we lay quietly till morning.

Our next day's run was uninterrupted; and we reached the "Dead Fall," (head of the raft,) where Geo. Alban held the turbulent spirits of some twenty teamsters under the most perfect control, at 11 o'clock P.M., February 7, 1842.

And now, having brought my readers to the end of this tedious trip of thirty-six days, I suppose I ought to offer some sort of apology for my many digressions from the ordinary chronicles of a steamboat career, and a steamboatman's life. But I can only say that while this scribbling has been a source of infinite pastime to me, I trust that I have not been over-tiresome in my style (if I may use that word) of laying before them a few of the incidents of my early days upon the river; and as the Relief is at last safely moored at the raft, I will promise to confine myself, in my next, to matters of history and interest pertaining to that locality and time, and will not wander from my subject to tell tales on any OUTSIDER.

Notes

1. Orlando S. Jones of Virginia graduated from William and Mary College in 1828 according to the 1855 *Catalogue of William and Mary College in the State of Virginia* and received his medical degree from the University of Pennsylvania in 1832 according to the 1877 *Catalogue of the Alumni of the Medical Department of the University of Pennsylvania 1765–1877*, with a thesis on rheumatism. Jones does not appear to have practiced as a physician. The "United States Census (Slave Schedule), 1850" (available through FamilySearch.org) indicates that he owned 37 slaves.

2. First Families of Virginia. The F.F.V. connection can be seen in "Family of Roland Jones" in the *Genealogies of Virginia Families From Tyler's Quarterly Historical and Genealogical Magazine*.

3. There are no cutoff lakes that far from the river. Jones' home was on the natural levee of Clear Lake, a relict channel of the Red River that was later reoccupied by the river and is now (from aerial photographs) once again a cutoff lake.

4. Little River was the major commercial tributary of the Upper Red River, with numerous boat returns reported in the Shreveport newspapers.

5. White Cliffs was the major landing on Little River, deriving its name from the vertical chalk cliffs on which it was located and has been designated a Natural Area by the Arkansas Natural Heritage Commission. The landing is shown on Sidney Morse and Samuel Breese's 1845 *Arkansas* and continues to appear on topographic maps.

6. John Sibley in his 1805 "Account of Red River and Country Adjacent" describes Little River as "about one hundred and fifty yards wide; the water clear as chrystal; the bottom of the river stony, and is boatable, at high water, up to the great prairies…; the low grounds generally from ten to fifteen miles wide, abounding with the most luxuriant growth of rich timber, but subject to partial inundation at particular rainy seasons."

7. This is not the present town of Millwood, but rather a landing to the northwest on a high bluff fronting the channel, which is now submerged by Millwood Lake. The lake received its name from the landing according to an article on "Millwood State Park" in the *Encyclopedia of Arkansas History and Culture*. The location of the landing is shown in backwardbranch.com's "Early Post Offices in Little River County Arkansas."

8. Elstner was one of the primary figures in Shreveport's cotton trade, advertising in the *South-Western* as a receiving, forwarding, and commission merchant at the time that Withenbury was writing.

9. The hull of the *White Cliffs* was completed on Little River in late 1854, with the launching described in the December 13, 1854, *South-Western*, and the engine installed at Shreveport in early 1856, the only year in which she was reported operational.

10. Withenbury does not do this. Harrison & Wilson were in the coffee business and are listed in the 1862 *Williams' Cincinnati Directory*.

11. Fulton became the linkage between the Cairo & Fulton in Arkansas and the Texas & Pacific in Texas when a bridge was completed across the Red River in March 1874.

12. Probably John Hightower, who owned land in Lafayette County and represented the county in the Legislature in 1844 according to Dallas Herndon, *Outline of Executive and Legislative History of Arkansas*.

13. New Orleans was occupied in May 1862 by Union forces under Gen. Benjamin Butler, who was cross-eyed (*strabismus* is the medical term for the condition).

14. A coastal community in Mississippi founded in 1838 and now part of Gulfport.

15. A popular opposing fiddle verbal exchange in which a country "rube" bests a "sophisticated" city dweller. On the motif in general, see the article on the "Arkansas Traveler" in the *Encyclopedia of Arkansas History and Culture*. A good example of the nature of the lyrics can be found in Clifton Johnson's *Highways and Byways of the Mississippi Valley*.

37 ✦ At the Raft

The *Relief* arrived at the head of the raft, where there was a company of troops for Fort Towson who had been brought from New Orleans to the foot of the raft by the *Houma*. The troops had gone around the raft by the portage road and were waiting for negotiations to be completed by the clerk of the *Houma* and Captain Crooks of the *Hunter* for transport to Fort Towson. The *Houma* had returned to New Orleans, and the clerk was aboard the *Harrisburg* at the foot of the raft. Ross and Withenbury took the portage road to meet with the clerk in an effort to take the transport contract away from Crooks.

⁂

In my effort to follow the fugitive merchant from Arkansas to the "Louisiana line," I occupied so much space in my last chapter that I made but one leap from Dooley's Ferry to the Raft, without so much as to pause to take note of a single person or point of interest in the whole distance of more than a hundred and fifty miles. And now I will say that from this omission it must not be inferred that the river and country thus passed over hurriedly, was without the usual amount of interest; but the fact of our being on the "top of a big rise" and nothing to do but to run direct to our destination, must suffice as a reason for my silence.

My anxiety to close my last chapter caused me to neglect also to mention the fact that we found the "Hunter" laying at the Raft on our arrival there. Poor old Captain Crooks and his crew had been denied all the excitement and hard steamboating which the crew of the Relief had passed through during the last five weeks, because the Hunter was of too heavy a draft of water to undertake the trip at the time we started out; and so they had been laying idle until the day before we arrived at the Raft, when the rise which overtook us at White Oak Shoals so unexpectedly had just begun to show itself, and the old man, not looking for us so soon, was taking his leisure at bargaining with the clerk of the steamer Houma for the transportation of a company of troops to Fort Towson. The Houma, Captain Joe Claiborne, had brought these troops and a considerable amount of army supplies from New Orleans to the foot of the Raft, and finding it impossible to effect a passage through, as had been expected when they left New Orleans, the troops were encamped on the bank in charge of one Lieutenant Rogers, a young West Pointer,[1] of whom I shall speak more particularly hereafter. The supplies were all in the warehouse awaiting a boat to take them up. Everything belonging to the military party was ready at a moment's notice to be put on board, as all had been hauled over the portage from the foot to the head of the Raft; and, as I said before, Captain Crooks was very leisurely driving at a bargain with the clerk of the Houma, who had been left in charge of the transportation, and was to accompany the party to Fort Towson, the Houma having already departed for New Orleans.

As soon as the Relief was well made fast to the shore on the night of her arrival, Captain Ross and myself went out to reconnoiter among the teamsters at the "Dead Fall;" and although it was near midnight, we found George Alban and several of his subordinates awake and ready to welcome us. George soon made known to us the condition of things, and said to us if we could only scareup the clerk of the Houma before daylight, we could steal a march on old Ben Crooks and pick up a right good trip; for, said he, "the old man has been flattering himself that he has 'a dead sure thing,' (not looking for you here,) and he has insisted on a greater price than the clerk is willing or authorized to give; and now I would like the best in the world to see the d_____d old fool beat at his own game. But I don't know where in the h_ll you'll find the clerk, for it's mighty uncertain where he 'holds up' at night."

Just then, one of the teamsters, who had been listening to the conversation, rolled over in his bunk as though just waking from a dream, and informed us that the clerk in question was spending the night on board the Harrisburg, then lying at the foot of the Raft with a load of Government stores from Pittsburg and bound for Fort Towson.

The distance to the Harrisburg was fully three miles by the shortest possible route for footmen in the night; and although it looked like a doubtful undertaking to make our way there, among all the prowling soldiers and negroes whom we well knew were keeping up an illicit traffic between the camp and the "quarters," we got directions regarding the route (a guide we could not get) and started for the boat fully determined to secure the only return trip "in sight" for Fort Towson, while Captain Crooks was quietly sleeping with a feeling of certainty that he could close a bargain in the morning and get the troops and "their plunder" on board and be off before the Relief would be unloaded.

The incidents and accidents of that night's tramp would of themselves make a chapter; but I must forego the "bulk of them," and content myself with telling one little story on "Uncle Joe," hoping thereby to give no offense. But a day or two before our arrival at the Raft, there had been a heavy rain in the neighborhood, and all the little gulleys and ruts in the wagon road through the woods were full of muddy water, which fact rendered it quite difficult for us to make our way; and, when over about half the distance, we sat down on a log close by the river side to rest ourselves, and to arrange our plan of attack, or rather our apology for breaking in upon the slumbers of the good people on board the Harrisburg, should we be so fortunate as to find her before daylight, which "Uncle Joe" remarked was a "little mixed."

While we were thus resting ourselves and arranging our programme, there occurred a movement in the great mass of drift wood that so completely filled and covered the surface of the water that scarce a "silvery spot" could be seen even where the moonbeams seemed creeping among the gnarled roots and entangled tree tops, striving, as it were, to convince the uncertain looker-on that the river was still there, and silently, though surely, finding its way beneath the great burthen borne upon its bosom to the unobstructed channel miles below.

The movement I have alluded to, and almost lost sight of, was caused by the sudden "swell" which the river was just now beginning to undergo; for, despite the fact that a large portion of the water of the upper river found its way through the many bayous and lagoons around the Raft, there was still enough passing under it to afford steamboat navigation from the foot of it to Shreveport, some sixty miles below, where all the waters of the river were again united.

As the Raft was being lifted by the rising river from the bed where it had laid so long, and loosened also from the shores, an immense field of it began moving down stream with a rumbling and crashing noise (or as Philley would say, "a rattling and snapping like a bear in a canebreak.") "Uncle Joe" started back, as if just awakened from a dream, or aroused from a deep and solemn reverie, and exclaimed: "How's that, 'Old Red,' are you tired of waiting for General Williamson[2] to finish his contract with 'Uncle Sam,' and so going to take the job off his hands?" And just then as a large tree was being "up-ended" by the force of the current and the weight of the moving mass, which, by its attitude threatened to fall where we were sitting, the "old man" caught me by the arm, and as we both fell back to a less dangerous spot, he said: "Look a' here, Mr. Clerk, if we intend to get them soldiers and things, we'd better jog along and get out of the way of such chaps as that," pointing to the tree just hesitating in an almost perpendicular position, whether to fall toward shore or upon the floating raft and be borne along down the current. So, without waiting to learn the decision of this defunct monarch of the forest, we resumed our walk.

The soil along here is a red clay, with an upper strata of white sand, which in heavy rains, such as had just fallen, is washed into the wheel ruts, and until again disturbed forms a very pleasant path to walk upon; and Uncle Joe was just learning to pick out these spots of ease wherever they presented themselves, and walking on them he saved himself much stumbling over the "dod durn'd grubs" in the middle of the road.

A little distance ahead there loomed up what appeared to be a smooth path of this white sand of unusual breadth; and Uncle Joe, having discovered the inviting spot, as the shimmering moonbeams lighted it up after a long interval of clouds and darkness, he made haste to reach it; and so great was his hurry that he left me just far enough behind him to halt on *terra firma* as he placed his right foot in what he supposed was the hard white sand, and sunk thigh deep in the thin white mud, and fell longitudinally into the rut, which was nearly wide enough to take in his whole body.

I ran to his aid, and much as I pitied him, I could not suppress my laughter at the ludicrousness of his predicament, for he had floundered in the rut until there was scarcely a spot of a hand's breadth on all his outer garments of its original color.

"Well," said he, "this may be 'fun for you,' as the bull-frog said to the boys, but dang me if it ain't 'death on me' and my good clothes."

He had the same coat on that was "split clean to the collar" at Smith's Landing.

"One more such dose will finish this coat anyhow; and now, Mr. Clerk, let me give you my idea of a man that will quit a good home, and a fair show for making a living at the carpenter's business, for this thing of steamboating. He's just a d____d fool."

It would be useless for me to waste words in describing the process of scraping and wringing that Uncle Joe's clothes were put through in order to render him at all presentable to the clerk of the Houma and the Captain of the Harrisburg, whom we expected to arouse from their beds before daylight. While this cleaning was going on in the stillness of the night, aided by the fitful glimmerings of light as cloud after cloud passed over the full moon, Uncle Joe paused and looked up during a moment of almost total darkness; and just as the moon began to peep from behind a black cloud, his pent up rage burst forth in these words, "Yes, you blamed jack 'o-ma-lantern, you may as well come out and stay out now, for you've got me into a pretty mess by your dod durn'd dodging in and out. This thing of leaving a fellow in the dark till his eyes begin to get used to it, and then coming out with a flash and blinding him, ain't the kind of a joke I'm fond of."

Just as we were ready to resume our tramp "Uncle Joe" said, "This reminds me of a story of an old man and his son Joe, who had been on a drunk, and staggering homeward, they both fell in the gutter, where they lay until they began to get sober and to realize their ridiculous plight, when the son, looking up in his father's face said, 'Daddy, 'spos anybody axes us how we got in the mud, what shall we tell 'em?' 'Tell 'em—hic—nothing—hic,' said the sire, 'let 'em find—hic—out as we did.' And so if anybody asks us any fool questions, let's give that old man's answer, and 'let 'em find out as we did.'"

We were not long in finishing our walk; and after running the gauntlet of a score of barking dogs which had scented us from "Jim" Mark's plantation,[3] and followed us until we came in sight of the Harrisburg's lights, we finally reached our destination in safety; and, as good luck would have it, we found the "gentlemanly clerk" of the Houma just finishing a "little game of draw," (then 3 A.M.), and so we had no need of apology for calling on him at an unseasonable hour.

We found him ready to talk business, and were not long in closing a contract for the transportation of the troops and supplies in his charge. He was quite ready (to use his own words) to "let Captain Crooks go to h__l or Fort Towson, as he liked best."

This was said in response to a remark made by Captain Smith of the Harrisburg, on behalf of Captain Crooks, whom he would like to see get the trip, because he was a "fellow Pittsburger." But there was no especial sympathy for "Pittsburgers" in the heart of the business man of the Houma. Which statement will not very much surprise my readers when I tell them that this man was none else than the veritable Captain S. W. Cooper, who has been more or less identified with Red River ever since that date.

After a short interchange of civilities with the hospitable Captain Smith and his barkeeper Byron, we started on our return tramp for the Relief. Captain Smith received much encouragement from us in regard to the river above, which he was "bound to see before the Harrisburg's head is turned down the stream," for his contract with the Government contractor was "through to

Fort Towson without reshipping." He hoped, however, to be able to make a successful claim for demurrage[4] for the many weeks lost in waiting for the Raft to be opened, as he had been assured on starting that no detention would occur at this point. The good old man, however, experienced in this case something that taught him in the future to make due allowance for the uncertainty of Government contracts.

[Paragraph left out.]

We reached the head of the Raft just at daylight, and Captain Ross immediately got all hands at work unloading our cotton, some three hundred bales; and by the time breakfast was over, the soldiers in obedience to orders began to break camp and pile their luggage close to the Relief; and this movement set old Captain Crooks to thinking and inquiring, when he soon found out that by taking his ease after we had landed alongside of him the night before he had lost the prize he had thought so securely within his grasp. And I must say that the good old man conducted himself in a slightly unamiable manner toward his successful competitors for the remaining few hours he spent with us.

At 10 o'clock the Hunter had steam up, and taking her departure left us alone in our glory; and long before midnight we had our cotton off and our cargo and soldiers and "laundresses" (eleven of the latter) on board, and ready for an early start for Fort Towson on the morning of February 8.

During the day, while we were discharging and receiving cargo, we had a visit from Captain Smith and several of the officers of the Harrisburg, and learned from them that they had been over a month out from Pittsburg; and, as the work of clearing out the Raft was going on very slowly, they were much discouraged. They received new hopes, however, from the present rapid rise in the river, which had the effect to buoy up and loosen the Raft, thus rendering the work of removing it much easier than when the water was at a low stage. Captain Smith's Red River experience on that trip of the Harrisburg was sufficient for him, and he never tried again, but left the field clear, after having finally accomplished the trip to Fort Towson,[5] and returned safely to Pittsburg, where I saw him in 1859, acting in the capacity of wharf master, and where he renewed the acquaintance and collected wharfage from this OUTSIDER.

Notes

1. Daniel G. Rogers, who graduated from West Point in 1840 according to the West Point Association of Graduates and is listed for Fort Towson in 1842 in Ancestry.com's "U.S. Returns From Military Posts, 1806–1916" (a cooperative program with the National Archives and Records Administration).
2. Thomas Williamson was removing the raft at this time.
3. According to U.S. General Land Office land records, James Marks had extensive landholdings on both sides of the river in Caddo and Bossier parishes.
4. Compensation for unforeseen delays.
5. The April 13, 1842, *Washington Telegraph* reports that the raft had been cleared and that the *Harrisburg* had departed from Fulton for Fort Towson during the previous week.

38 ✦ Near Dooley's Ferry

The *Relief* left the head of the raft and proceeded upstream. This letter actually brings the *Relief* past Fulton and McKinney's Landing and within striking distance of Lanesport; however, most of the letter is concerned with Dooley's Ferry and vicinity far downstream. Dooley's

Ferry had been a keelboat landing and was an important steamboat landing on the east side of the river in Lafayette County (but now in the southwest corner of Hempstead County) and was established at a place where branches of the Southwest Trail and Trammel's Trace intersected. George Dooley,[1] the initial operator of the ferry and the landing, appears in the 1828 tax list for Lafayette County, was coroner from 1829–1832 and sheriff from 1832–1838, and began operating the ferry in 1835. Confederate fortifications were established at Dooley's Ferry during the Civil War. The bend of the river in which Dooley's Ferry was located has now been cut off.

Much of the letter is devoted to John "Bois d'Arc" Wilson,[2] who lived on Bois d'Arc Creek north of Dooley's Ferry. Wilson was born in 1791 in Kentucky, married Jane Reaves (born 1799 in Kentucky) in 1816, and came to the Bois d'Arc Creek area in October 1817, where they had 12 children from 1818 to 1841, including one set of twins, but two of whom died in infancy. An illiterate farmer, Wilson began acquiring property in 1827, appeared in the Hempstead County tax roles in 1828, and reached 837 acres in 1844 according to U.S. General Land Office land records, with real estate valued at $3,375 and personal estate valued at $15,265 in 1860 (approximately $370,000 in today's dollars) according to the Hempstead County census.

⁂

In leaving "Uncle Joe" and the Relief to pursue their quiet way, following closely upon the heels of the Hunter, as Captain Crooks was using unusual energy to push her to the "head of the hollow" in advance of us, seemed to be rather a necessity while penning my last chapter; for I have heretofore made such frequent mention of "the Raft" as to awaken a spirit of inquiry among many of my readers, and I have found not a few of them desirous of knowing more of that time-honored pest to the whole people of Upper Red River. And now while I am offering an apology for my neglect of my old companions, I feel almost sure that I owe one also to my friends of to-day for the lame and disjointed description I have given them of the probable origin and cause of the Red River Raft.[3]

To convey a clear and intelligible idea of this remarkable obstruction in a written article of moderate length, beginning at the point where are found the first evidences of the Raft having once existed, but from which point it has so long since passed away, that we have no history of its former existence, except that of the red cedar drift wood, which is so indelibly recorded that we can no more dispute the existence there of a Red River Raft ages ago, than we can successfully deny that the Pyramids of Egypt were made by human hands, seems quite out of the question; for, unless one is somewhat familiar with the geography and topography of the Red River Valley, as we find it in these days, it would be quite impossible to understand how all the changes I have attempted to describe were possible. The lecture-room, I have often thought, would afford the only fair means of clearly elucidating this subject. And even then, unless the lecturer were assisted by a map of the Red River Valley, (I mean that part of it which is confined to the State of Louisiana,) showing all the labyrinthine water courses connected with Red River, he would find himself sadly at fault in his efforts to convey a clear idea of this mixture of land and water to his audience.

Having said this much by way of apology for my meager description of the Raft, I propose now to leave it and the hard laborers who were busy through the remaining days of February and all the month of March, 1842, working their way up to the free waters of the upper river, and follow the Relief, with her company of United States officers, soldiers and laundresses to their destination, trusting to my memory for sufficient of interesting incidents to compensate for the perusal of what I may write.

One of our pilots (Captain Hildreth) was attacked with fever and ague soon after leaving Fort Towson, on our down trip, and, despite all the remedies known throughout the country, the hateful disease held on to him with a persistency which baffled all medicines and skill, and he was thus incapacitated for attending to his duties; and as Philley had already found out that I had a natural aptitude for steering a steamboat, he was not slow to call me frequently to relieve him, and so I had less opportunity for taking note of what was going on among the crew and passengers.

We reached Fulton, Arkansas, just at daylight on Wednesday, February 9, 1842, having passed much of the interesting part of the river during the night; and I feel almost like going back as far as Dooley's Ferry to talk of some of the more noteworthy people whom I have from time to time met there—some who never ran from the Sheriff; some who never sought the Louisiana line to avoid paying their honest debts.

I have in mind now one eccentric character, who lived some eight miles from Dooley's Ferry, and about equi-distant between Spring Hill, Fulton and Washington, and so he was well known to the people of all that region round about.

Something like half a mile above Dooley's Ferry—Well, I may as well stop right here and correct myself in one particular, and give to this locality—Dooley's Ferry—its more pretending and euphonious name of "Roxo Belle;" for be it known that the proud Virginians who made up a majority of the citizens of Spring Hill in those days, had high hopes of the future greatness of this their nearest landing place upon the river bank; and not satisfied with their first encroachment upon the right of "old uncle George Dooley" to bestow his own name upon his property where he had "poled his flat" and "paddled his own canoe" across the river hundreds of times "in spite of wind and weather," they changed the name a second time from "Spring Hill Landing" to "Roxo Belle."[4] The city, however, which grew to handsome proportions in the brain of these Virginians, has never as yet crowded the forest trees out of their places, and the beautiful Miss Mary B______, who claimed the proud distinction of affixing this Spanish name to that miserable "neck of woods," has found herself, while waiting for its development into a city, grown old and gray, while the house she lived in has gone to ruin. She herself became comfortably fixed beyond the "Louisiana line," and the well deserved patronymic restored to Dooley's Ferry. "Uncle George" has long since returned to dust, and his sons, who had less of that characteristic energy which in their old father made him the peoples' favorite everywhere, have allowed the title to the land to fall into the hands of my friend Williams,[5] who is content while he reaps the profits to be known as the owner of "Dooley's Ferry."

Well, as I had begun to tell, about a half mile above this point a beautiful little stream called "Bois d'Arc Creek" pours its clear waters into the river, which my early friend Miss Mary B______ would insist upon calling "Rio Roxo"—mind you, Miss Mary "knew Spanish"—and way up many a crooked mile, on the banks of Bois d'Arc Creek, lived my old friend Wilson, of whom I had begun to write as an eccentric character. I can not give Mr. Wilson's full name, for he was so universally known as "Bois d'Arc (Bowdark) Wilson," that I never thought to inquire farther; nor do I believe that one person in a hundred who knew him intimately, could tell his first name; so if he is still living, (and I know nothing to the contrary,) he will pardon me for the liberty I take in calling him by his old familiar title.

"Bowdark Wilson" commenced life, to use his own words, "a little below the bottom rung of the ladder," and he always contended "that was a less dangersome point to start from than a higher one," and so his course was always upward, for, in other words, he never progressed backwards. When I met him last, in 1847, I found him so completely surrounded with the comforts, and what he, in his simplicity, deemed the luxuries of life, that I could not refrain from alluding, in the midst of my congratulations, to his former struggles when in the depths of the unfrequented forest he labored day after day, hewing out his fortune. He received my congratulations with due modesty, and seized upon my allusions to his former humble condition for an excuse to go proudly over his early hardships, and point out wherein was the secret of his success. "You see," said he, "when I came here I was a young man; and Jinny, thar, (pointing to his wife, who was busy patching a boy's breeches,) "she was a young gal, onusened to the ways of the world, but she was the clear grit, and without her I'd 'a been nowhar; and there wasn't a stick amiss[6] in all this country, as far as I could ride in half a day, and so you see thar was nothing to hinder me from having things pretty much to my liking ef I'd only work for it. Well, Jinny and I, we both swore we'd do our level best to make a living and be under no compliments to nobody; and so the first season we (for Jinny worked as hard as I) cleared enough for a little corn patch, and by hard licks and scant suppers we found ourselves a little ahead at the beginning of the next season. But Jinny, she was ahead of me, for she had a baby; only one, though, the first time, and that was a boy, thank God; and so I looked for'ard to the time when that boy could help to clear land and earn his living like I was getting mine; and, sir, I'm proud to say that he's never disappointed me. Wall, we went on, from little to little, still a gaining every year; and Jinny, she begun to breed like a rabbit, two at a pop every time but once since that first boy come; and I'll swear, I'll never tell you how we managed to take care of 'em all, but they kept a coming till we got eleven, five pars and an odd one."

Here Mrs. Wilson looked up from her work and put a stop to this "laying on family matters before a stranger," showing that although she was an uncultivated woman in the ways of the world, she still had enough of intuitive modesty to cause her to shrink from being paraded before strangers on account of her prolific qualifications.

But "Bowdark Wilson," determined not to be thwarted, called my attention to a couple of long poles which were suspended upon wooden hooks from the joists over our heads; and there I saw arranged in the most systematic order in reference to size and sex the clothing of all "Jinny's rabbits," save the first three. "Thar," said he, "you can see how reg'lar they come, like star steps" (alluding to the order of gradation in which the garments were arranged upon the poles.) "And all colored alike, you see, with bowdark; and Jinny's got her dye-pot all ready thar in the corner, ready for colorin for the next two if they come."

Here I will explain that the yellow wood of the Bois d'Arc (which is the Osage orange of which our beautiful hedges are made[7]) is a most excellent dye wood; and in the hands of the skillful housewife, such as Mrs. Wilson was, it produces a great variety of shades of color, from the brightest orange tint to a dark brown butternut, such as characterizes the somber garments of both men and women in many of the rural districts of Kentucky and Indiana. And all the outer garments of this family of Wilson's were colored with Bois d'Arc, which was a distinguishing mark for them, as no other family in the neighborhood made such uniform use of it.

When I asked the old man why he was known everywhere as "Bowdark Wilson," he declared that he did not know whether it was because all his clothes were "dyed yaller" or because he had first of anybody settled in the "Bois d'Arc Bottoms." The creek evidently took its name from the fact that this beautiful and valuable wood was found growing so abundantly upon its adjacent lowlands. And my friend Wilson was proud to be distinguished by the name which the beautiful clear stream had borne from the earliest settlement of the country.

My visit to "Bowdark Wilson," in 1847, was purely of an accidental character, but I never regretted the *contretemps* that brought me there. I had occasion to travel on horseback from Fulton to Dooley's Ferry at a time when Red River was on a rampage, and all the roads in the lowlands were overflown, and I was thus driven many miles out of the usual way, and at "Bowdark Wilson's" was the only crossing of the creek at that time, and I gladly availed myself of half a day and a night under his hospitable roof to study the home peculiarities of this remarkable man whom I had known for the last half dozen years only in the character of a marketer vending the products of his farm to steamboats and the hungry citizens of Fulton. And now I must bid adieu to him, his good wife, his brood of "rabbits," his broad productive fields, his deer park, his well-filled barns, his bounteous larder, and in fact, all his solid comforts and his generous hospitality as I found them in 1847, and look at him on the morning of February 9, 1842, when just at the break of day, he came bare-headed on board the Relief (then just arrived at Fulton), seeking out the steward to sell him sweet potatoes, chickens, eggs, butter, &c.

The old man had in his pocket a fine sample of his sweet potatoes, but further than that, nothing in sight. He found us in need, and the steward and myself followed him to the back of the town, (then not a great distance,) and there, under the shade of a cluster of pines, and carefully concealed from view, we found an abundant store of good things from the farm of this pioneer in the "Bois d'Arc Bottoms." But we discovered there no vehicle or other mode of conveyance for all of these things, except an old bareback mule, which stood tethered to a sapling or "staked out," and quietly picking among the dry pine straws for the few scattering blades of grass which had struggled up to the light of the sun.

Our Indian Steward, Jim Berryhill, after looking around in vain for a solution of his puzzle of "how came all these things here?" ventured to ask: "How in the name of God, old man, did you fotch all this truck here on that old jackass?" "Well now, to tell you the truth, stranger," said Wilson, "I can't afford to take another mule out'n the plow to haul this truck in a wagon, and so I jist made that old beast tote the whole load." Just then there broke out a merry cackling among a string of chickens, which the old man had secreted in a little thicket near by, and when "Jim" saw them, his astonishment knew no bounds; and he exclaimed, "My God, old man, you'll bust that donkey with another such load." "I reckon not," said Wilson, "for when I heard the old Hunter a puffin' up the river yesterday, (you see I know her cough,) I loaded up that same old mule, and beat the boat here, and Captain Crooks told me you'd be along soon, and so I went right home and loaded up again, and here I've been since midnight a waitin' for you, and the critter looks right peart yet."

We soon closed a bargain for all the mule had brought to market, except "Bowdark" himself, which load consisted of a bushel of sweet potatoes, two dozen live chickens, three dozen eggs, and a peck of corn meal; and "Jim" ordered him to "load up and bring them to the boat." "But," said Wilson, "you must find me a basket or something of the sort to tote 'em in, for I ain't got nothing." "Why, what in the name of God did you bring 'em in from home?" asked "Jim." Here the old man hesitated; but being pushed for an explanation, he was finally forced to an exposure of his novel mode of carrying truck to a market.

"You see," said he, "bags is scarce with us; and so as I was coming all the way in the night, and not many people living on the road now, I jest filled my breeches with the 'taters, and set 'em astraddle of the mule afore me, and the chickens I hung across his back behind, and they was better nor whip and spurs to keep the beast awake and jogging along; and the corn meal you see I brought in Jinny's handkercher, (a clean one, you see,) and so I came along right easy, and when I got here I emptied the 'taters out and kivered 'em with pine straw and brush, hid my chickens in the bush, tied my mule where it could feed, put on my breeches and come to your boat for a trade." But Jim was by no means satisfied until he asked, "How did you bring the eggs?" "O, fotch them in my hat," said "Bowdark;" "that was no trouble at all."

With this explanation we closed the trade, and after having thus replenished our stock of provisions and finished a little unsettled business of our former trip, the Relief left Fulton, hurrying to overtake the Hunter, if possible, before she should reach Fort Towson.

Three o'clock Thursday morning found us at McKinney's, where we were detained until daylight discharging some three thousand feet of lumber taken on at Fulton, and five hundred bushels of corn shipped by Tom Scott from Pine Prairie, during the previous night. These neighborhood accommodations, as I have before stated, were generally gratuitous on the part of "Uncle Joe" and Captain Crooks, and of course paid no direct profit; but such men as Colonel Scott and the old patriarch McKinney were never found wanting in their appreciation of services thus timely rendered by the two little steamboats. Father McKinney rather hinted that in this particular case, "Captain Crooks had shirked his duty and left the burden to be borne by the Relief alone." He did not understand the little joke the Relief had just played on the Hunter in the way of getting the soldiers at the raft until Judge Smith explained the matter to him, and "Uncle Joe" hinted that Captain Crooks was probably hurrying to Fort Towson hoping to get even with us by securing whatever business there might chance to be there for a down trip.

At McKinney's we found the river had fallen fully fifteen feet, and we lost no time, but pushed along, fearing low water before reaching our destination. We left McKinney's, aiming to reach Lanesport before dark, where we knew we must abandon running at night on account of low water and snaggy river. Our report of the condition of the work at the raft threw a damper upon the expectations of the McKinney neighborhood, for while they were amply attended to by the two steamboats already in the river, they did not pretend to deny that one and all were anxiously looking for the advent among them of some hitherto unknown OUTSIDER.

Notes

1. On George Dooley and Dooley's Ferry, see the *Biographical and Historical Memoirs of Southern Arkansas*; Carl Carlson-Drexler, "Crossroads

of Conflict: Archaeology at Dooley's Ferry, Hempstead County, Arkansas;" and the Arkansas Historic Preservation Program's "Dooley's Ferry Fortifications Historic District." The ferry and fortifications can be seen in Jeremy Gilmer's 1864 *Environs of Dooley's Ferry Ark.*, which is available online courtesy of the University of North Carolina at Chapel Hill. Dooley owned the property in Section 29 of T14S, R25W on which the landing was located according to U.S. General Land Office land records.

2. All of the readily available information on Wilson and his wife has been brought together by the professional genealogist Will Johnson in separate online inclusions for John B. Wilson and Jane Reaves. "Bois d'Arc" Wilson should not be confused with the well-known John Wilson who came to the area in 1819 by keelboat, became Speaker of the House of the Arkansas General Assembly, and killed Representative Joseph Anthony in 1837 in a knife brawl on the house floor. Many of "Bois d'Arc" Wilson's records use "B" as a middle initial, with the nickname appearing only in the probate records. John and Jane Wilson both died in Hempstead County, he in Guernsey (north of Spring Hill) in 1869 and she ten years later. There is a Wilson Cemetery in Guernsey, but graves have not been identified for John or his wife. Withenbury's description of Wilson's location places him on Bois d'Arc Creek well away from the Red River. Wilson owned all of the land in Guernsey, which is the obvious location of the cabin that Withenbury visited.

3. Withenbury presented his opinion on the origin of the Great Raft in the previous letter (which was not used). His primary contention is that Red River was once continuous with the Atchafalaya River, rather than a tributary to the Mississippi, and that the existence of cedar logs in the Atchafalaya (along which they do not grow) is the primary evidence for that contention.

4. Roxibel is shown on Sidney Morse and Samuel Breese's 1845 *Arkansas* about nine miles southwest of Spring Hill and two miles north of Dooley's Ferry (but actually closer) at the confluence of Bois d'Arc Creek with the Red River. Spring Hill Landing and Roxibel are not mentioned in newspaper accounts of boat movements. The bend of the river on which Roxibel was located has been cut off, and the location is now upstream on Bois d'Arc Creek.

5. Dooley's Ferry was operated by Robert Williams at the time Withenbury was writing according to the June 2, 1871, *Daily South-Western*.

6. No trees had been cut down to make way for agriculture.

7. Bois d'Arc, which is thorny, was commonly used for hedging before the invention of barbed wire. See Matt Turner, *Remarkable Plants of Texas*.

39 ✦ Man Overboard

With its load of soldiers picked up at the portage and bound for Fort Towson, the *Relief* was nearing Lanesport and arrived at Davis' Shoal two miles below, where an incident occurred. According to U.S. General Land Office land records, Levi Davis acquired property in 1841 along the river about two miles southeast of Lanesport. The shoal was contiguous to this property in a bend of the river that has since been cut off. Davis was one of five men appointed to select a seat for Sevier County when it was established in 1828 according to the *Acts Passed at the Sixth Session of the General Assembly of the Territory of Arkansas*, appears in the 1830 Sevier County census, and was justice of the peace in 1830 according to the March 16, 1830, *Arkansas Gazette*. Davis would have maintained a landing at his riverfront property, but it is not mentioned in newspaper accounts of boat movements.[1] The letter ends with the arrival of the *Relief* at Pecan Point on the night of February 11, 1842.

⁂

Contrary to the expectations of the whole company on board the Relief, she fell short about two miles of making the run to Lanesport, on Thursday, February 10, 1842, and in our eagerness to accomplish the whole distance, we came well nigh sacrificing a valuable human life—extra valuable because a United States soldier. And here, at the risk of boring my readers beyond endurance, I must follow my inclination to "tell a little story."

About two miles below Lanesport there is a shoal, which at certain stages of the river is a source of much annoyance to steamboatmen. It is called Davis' Shoal, named in honor, probably, not of Jeff Davis, but more likely of Dr. Davis, the compounder of a certain medicinal preparation known all over that country, in those days, as "Davis' Powders."

The curative qualities of these powders were beyond dispute, no matter what the disease, or who the patient; and I feel well assured that if Dr. Davis had lived in these days of Helmbold humbuggery and of Ridiculous Radway's Remedies,[2] he might have joined them with a fair prospect of success in the race for fame and fortune; for no medicine was ever more popular than was "Davis' Powders" from the "cross timbers" in Texas to "the Louisiana line."

But Dr. Davis was a modest, unpretending man, and he so far differed from these successors in the line of patent medicines that he was content with simply doing good to his fellow-men, and reaping therefor a very moderate reward, coupled with the high esteem of all his fellow-citizens.[3] Every steamboatman now living who may have followed Upper Red River at any time since the first introduction of steamboats there up to the present day must have had occasion more than once to bless Dr. Davis and his valuable preparation, and that being the case I need not stop to ask pardon for this most inconsistent of all my former digressions from the subject matter of my Red River narratives in thus devoting a few lines to the memory of a truly good man, who was a "Red River institution" in his day.

But let me now get back to the Relief again before I forget the difficulties that she encountered when she reached Davis' Shoal, and the little episode which caused her detention there until daylight of February 11.

It was quite dark when we began to hear the rippling of the water as it hurried among the barricades of snags which form almost a complete dam across the river just below the "slate reef" of the shoal, and Philley, in his usual nervous and slightly profane manner, began to counsel "Uncle Joe" to "lay her up below that d____d rack heap, and wait for daylight." But the old man evidently had his thoughts upon the Hunter—which boat, as we learned at Martin Glover's, a mile or two below, was more than twenty-four hours ahead of us—and he replied to Philley: "We must make Lanesport to-night if it takes 'the last button off Gabe's coat,' so work her along slow, and watch out for an opening among the chunks, and—" Just then she struck something under the water, which caused her to make a "lee[4] lurch" toward the Texas shore, and, so sudden was the interruption to her headway, that "Uncle Joe" had no time to finish giving his orders, and it was with great difficulty that he retained his position on the roof; his hold upon one of the chimney guys was all that saved him from being suddenly let down. But this was not all; for sooner than I can write it, the boat in her swinging motion to the larboard,[5] struck a huge snag whose head stood high enough above the water for the guard to receive the worst of the blow and save the hull from harm, and this "brought her up all a-standing," and in an instant the cry was heard, "Man overboard!" And then such a scene of confusion ensued as is seldom witnessed, and never fully described, every one of the crew and all the soldiers joining the cry, "Man overboard!" "throw him a rope!" "out of my way, ye bloody blaggeards!" "run for the schmall boat!" "there he goes under the wheel; och, bloody murther, but he's lost entirely, an' a good man he was as iver shouldered a musket!" This last exclamation revealed the fact that it was not one of the boat's crew, but one of "Uncle Sam's hirelings," that in the act of drawing a bucket of water, had fallen into the river, and in a moment, assisted by the rapid current, had drifted out of sight.

As soon as it became known that a soldier, and not a deck-hand was lost, there was a murmur of satisfaction heard among the crew below, and one of them, less discreet than the rest, was heard to say, "D__n the odds, let him go; he's only a soldier." But very different was the feeling among the laundresses,[6] who, by this time, were in the wildest confusion, each wringing her hands and anxiously calling out the name of her favorite; but not one of them was able to distinguish amid the shrieks whether or not a favorable response came to her inquiries, and so each continued to add her full quota to the general uproar.

In the quickest possible time the yawl was launched and manned, and "Uncle Joe," who, from the first alarm, had kept his eye on a black object which a ray of light from the engine-room revealed to him as it floated by the side of the boat, and kept dancing upon the top of the little waves caused by the boat's unsteady motion, and which was just then passing astern, and disappearing from his sight, ordered the men in the yawl to "pull for it," as he believed, "as sure as shooting the drowning soldier was under that hat."

Away went the yawl, and together with the object pursued, it was soon lost in the darkness, and so, in the uncertainty of the moment, all became quiet, and a voice was then heard, coming as it were from the very depth of the river: "Shtop the whale, shtop"—and then a gurgling sound told that he who would have fain repeated those imploring words, had suddenly gone below the surface again.

The engine was immediately stopped, and all hands were at the starboard[7] wheel with lights, ropes, planks &c., ready to assist the unlucky fellow, who, by the by, considered himself in the very best of luck as soon as the wheel (to which he was clinging like a squirrel in his cage) came to a dead stand still, and he was enabled to perch himself in an upright position and keep his head out of the water. There we found him, almost exhausted, for no sooner had he fallen overboard than he drifted under the guard and struck the wheel, which was kept slowly revolving, just to keep the boat steady against the snag where she had struck; but the motion was just quick enough to hinder him from escaping from it, and so at each revolution he went under, and as he came out of the water he had made every possible effort to cry out and make himself heard; but, to use his own words, "It was only about every third time I came out that I could get the d____d wather out of me mouth enough to shpake at all, and thin before I could repate the words, under I wint, and me mouth was full of the bloody red wather again, and just as the thunderin' noise all ye blatherskites was a makin' on deck began to cease a little, I was busy a sayin' me prayers, for I was dead sure me time had come. But I shtopped short off me prayin' and gave one more whoop for the whale to be shtopped, and be the holy saints here I am all safe again, and no thanks to any of ye's except the man that shtopped the whale."

The poor wet soldier's comrades seemed in no hurry to move him from the spot on the deck where he first felt the assurance that he was safe, and delivered himself of the foregoing impromptu speech; but he seemed to expect something more of them than the mere gratifying of their idle curiosity, and getting quite out of patience with the whole party, laundresses and all, he looked up in their faces and asked: "Is it a Crowner's jury that ye's would be holdin' on me, whin I'm not dead at all; or are ye's waiting for the nasty Red River water to be dyin' in me before ye'd sind a drop o' whisky down to make its acquaintance and bid it begone? Would ye's let Tim Daly die for the want of a little nourishment? Och! May the divil fly away wid me before I'd trate the meanest o' ye's like this."

The bare mention of whisky aroused the whole company from the bewilderment they were thrown into by the singular means of rescue which had saved their companion's life, and one and all took the hint he had just given them, and from that time through the whole night they were striving to outdo each other in their attentions to their half drowned comrade.

As soon as the word had passed to "Uncle Joe" that the man was safe on board, he tapped the bell for the return of the yawl, which had kept in pursuit of the black object floating on the surface until it was picked up, and ascertained to be nothing more nor less than the soldier's cap. When the cap was picked up and no soldier found under it, the men in the yawl concluded that the owner was forever lost, and so began pulling for the boat, and they were not many minutes in making known the fruitlessness of their search. But when they learned of the rescue of their countryman they were not slow in joining in the congratulations, and in the whisky, also; and under the ameliorating effects of the latter, they soon forgot the natural and cherished antipathy that always did exist between a soldier and a sailor, and their true warm Irish instincts took possession of the whole party.

When the yawl was hauled aboard again, "Uncle Joe," still anxious to reach Lanesport, suggested to Philley that we would try it again. But that cautious pilot's reply soon settled that question. "Now, look here, Cap'n, if you are so d____d anxious to have this boat over this 'h_ll's half acre' to-night, you just come and take the wheel, for I can see fun enough here for me in daylight; and if you'll just take my advice you'll let her flank right in to shore here on the Arkansaw side and keep cool till daylight, and consider yourself d____d lucky that all hands are not now swimming or crawling out on sandbars like a gang of alligators."

"Uncle Joe" very reluctantly gave up the chase of the Hunter for this night, and, taking Philley's advice, ordered the Relief landed in the shortest possible time at the most convenient point, which proved to be just at the foot of the first plantation below Davis' Shoal.[8]

The escaping of steam and the general confusion in consequence of our long detention, had attracted the negroes from the plantation, and long before midnight there was an assemblage upon the bank, which, by the light of an immense bonfire, presented a scene fit for the study of a Hogarth, for there was a mixture of humanity such as is seldom met with, and all from the peculiar circumstance which had called them together, were perfectly free from restraint, each acting his or her part decidedly on his or her "own hook."

The negroes were somewhat amazed at the sudden and unexpected appearance among them of so many soldiers, and for awhile they stood in awe of them. And on the other hand, the "boys in blue," most of whom were Irish, replied with threats and menaces the first advances made by "the bloody nagurs." But soon the great leveler (whisky) got to work among them, and it was truly amusing to see how quickly these opposing elements began to harmonize.

The simple-minded, honest (?) negro, however, was no match for the crafty and unscrupulous soldiers, as the sequel proved, for long before daylight the cackling of chickens and quacking of Muscovy ducks told of the success of various foraging parties who, while the unsuspecting darkies were sleeping in their drunken stupor, around the fire, had found their way to "the quarters." Nobody interfered to check the "free trade" between the negroes and soldiers. The bar-keeper enjoyed a rich harvest at the expense only of a night's sleep, and I heard him telling his "Uncle Joe" the next day, that the falling of that soldier into the river had been "a big streak of luck" to him, "and I wouldn't mind," said he, "if we could manage to duck another one before we get to Fort Towson."

I must ask a little indulgence of my readers now while I go back to Judge Smith's Landing, where, at about 3 P.M., we landed the old gentleman safe at home, amid the congratulations of his household and slaves.[9] Owing to the peculiar shape of the river there, a boat could be heard an hour at least before her arrival at the landing;[10] and the warning gave everybody an opportunity to be at the spot when the boat touched the land; and it seemed that everybody was there, and each individual, without regard to race or color, seemed anxious to be the first to manifest unusual joy at the return of one whom all loved. The Judge's wife, nor his sons and daughters, were allowed any precedence in welcoming him home, for the negroes one and all hurried to grasp his hand and say, "Howde, Mass'r Jim." Even little Mary, of the George Washington pretensions, crowded between her mistress and Miss Eliza, the eldest daughter, and was the very first to welcome him home.

Mrs. Smith insisted upon our remaining with them until morning, but the rapidly falling river admonished us to economize time, and so we were forced to leave quite too abruptly to suit our own inclinations. We were not allowed to depart, however, without being almost literally "loaded down" with the good things which always abounded at their plantation; and not until we neared the Arkansas shore in the bend above, did the multitude cease to cheer us by the waving of hats and aprons, nor did the adieus die away upon the breezes until we had steamed away out of sight.

Daylight found us all ready for the passage of Davis' Shoal, which we found no very difficult matter. But before we reached

Lanesport, Lieutenant Rodgers discovered that several of his men were missing, so we were obliged to land and send out a scouting party in the direction of the plantation where the foraging had been so extensively carried on through the night. We hurried along, after orders had been given for the soldiers to overtake us at the little town, where we would be detained an hour or so in discharging freight and taking wood.

At Lanesport we were visited by many persons, anxiously inquiring when the Raft would be opened, and they were by no means suited when we acknowledged our inability to give them the desired information. "Uncle Joe" rather abruptly answered an old fellow by the name of Goodspeed that "he'd be dod durned if he cared if it never was opened." This answer rather offended Goodspeed, and he was disposed to provoke an angry discussion with the Captain, who cut the matter short by ringing the bell and ordering the lines "let go" as soon as the truant soldiers were on board.

Having no business to transact during this day's run, we made no stops after leaving Lanesport, and night found us tied up to the Texas shore at Pecan Point Plantation, where we visited the hospitable people on shore, and in return entertained them in the best manner possible for our circumstances. Our nights, whenever we found ourselves compelled to "lay up" on account of low water, were always pleasantly spent among these frontier people, and I for one many times sighed for a cause for longer delay, and when our little craft was ready at daylight to push off and speed away, I have more than once felt an impulse to step ashore, bid adieu to my old companions and declare myself forever an OUTSIDER.

Notes

1. Davis Prairie appears on Sidney Morse and Samuel Breese's 1845 *Arkansas*, with one of his cultivated fields immediately on the river marked on the 1836 survey plat for T13S, R32W. H. M. McIver in "Water Bound In Arkansas"

(*Arkansas Historical Quarterly*, Summer 1955) says that in 1892 he spent a great deal of time talking to Henry Hawkins, who had acquired the Davis property. Hawkins said that Davis ran a trading station and bought furs from trappers and that his place was called Levi Landing. This Levi Davis should not be confused with the Levi Davis who was reportedly killed with Charles Burkham upriver in 1837.

2. Withenbury is referring to a group of nationally popular patent medicines produced by Radway & Co. (Richard R. Radway) in New York. The first was Radway's Ready Relief, which was introduced in 1849 and began advertising in the newspapers in the 1850s: "One application externally, or a few drops taken internally, will instantly free the sufferer from the most violent and terrible pains, and restore the weak, feeble and prostrate frame to strength and vigor." Radway's Ready Relief continued to be produced through the 1920s.

3. Davis' Powders were apparently not advertised in regional newspapers.

4. The side away from the wind.

5. Left side of the boat facing forward.

6. Laundresses were essential to post operations, provisioned by the military, and paid for piece work by soldiers. See the article on "Family Life at the Forts" by Mary Ramos in the *Texas Almanac 2004–2005*.

7. Right side of boat facing forward.

8. The *Relief* tied up on the Arkansas side, as recommended by Philley.

9. This, and the next paragraph, refer to events on the previous day.

10. Smith's property was upstream of a large bend with a small base. This was the bend that was cut off by Ross during his fishing expedition mentioned in Letter 29, but in a later trip by the *Relief* in May 1842. The cutoff bend was later reoccupied by the river, as shown on contemporary topographic maps.

Postscript

The letters end with the *Relief* arriving at Pecan Point on the night of February 11, 1842, only two months from its departure from Shreveport on December 10, 1841.

The *Hunter* arrived in New Orleans from Kiamichi on March 19, 1842, immediately advertised for Fort Towson, is reported at Fulton on April 13, immediately struck a snag and was grounded on a sandbar, is reported off the bar on June 29, and reported back in New Orleans from Kiamichi on July 19. The *Hunter* continued to operate on the Upper Red River through 1846.

The April 13, 1842, *Washington Telegraph* states that the raft had been opened and that the *Relief* under Capt. Ross had arrived at Fulton during the previous week. The *Relief* advertised in the *Daily Picayune* for above the raft in late April, stating that it was the only boat in the trade, reported at Fulton during the latter part of May, and arrived back in New Orleans from Fort Towson in the middle of June. The *Relief* probably went back to Cincinnati during the summer. Withenbury is shown as captain when the *Relief* arrived in New Orleans from Yazoo City, Mississippi, in early November, immediately advertised for Alexandria during a low-water period, arrived back in New Orleans at the end of the month, and immediately advertised for Fort Towson and Jonesboro.

This was the last trip of the *Relief*, which was lost on the up trip as reported in the January 14, 1843, Clarksville *Northern Standard*: "The steamboat Relief, sunk below Dooley's ferry a few days since, with 300 sacks coffee, 500 pieces bagging and a proportionable quantity of rope, on board. The freight was insured, and has been sold for the benefit of the underwriters. The loss of the bagging and rope will be seriously felt by our planters and merchants, who will thus be very much delayed in ginning and forwarding their cotton." Withenbury went back to Cincinnati, came back to New Orleans as commander of the *Waverly* in November, and arrived back in New Orleans from Fort Towson in February 1844.

After the *Relief* wrecked, Ross returned to Cincinnati and was re-elected to the city council and was engaged in a livery stable business for seven years. As a council member, he was instrumental in the development of the city's first steam fire engine (the *Uncle Joe Ross*, which was completed in December 1852) and the formation of the municipal fire department in March 1853. He ran unsuccessfully for mayor in 1853 and organized the Miami Valley Fire Insurance Company of Cincinnati in 1860, remaining its president for 11 years.

Ross died of cholera on July 6, 1875. His understanding of the meaning of his early efforts on the Red River is recounted by Withenbury in the March 3, 1871, *Cincinnati Commercial*:

> Captain Ross can hardly tell at this day what it was that so imbued him with the gift of continuance at that time of his life, and in a business, too, so full of hazard to health and pecuniary prosperity, and so totally inconsistent with a civilized man's ideas of social enjoyment and intellectual improvement. The old man now thinks he was one of the humble instruments chosen by a wise Providence to work out at its roughest stages the grand development of the fertile Red River Valley, of which his fellow-

citizens may take advantage today, with immense profit to themselves if they will; and he is content that they shall reap the full reward of his early adventures which caused him to lose well nigh his last dollar of worldly possessions, and sent him back to his brave wife and little children, to begin life again, with his health, his means and his energies sadly crippled. And his pride shall ever be, that while his own better judgment would have led him into a more profitable course of life, viewed from a purely selfish standpoint, and while his friends were so bitterly opposed to this seemingly unwise choice of a pursuit to which he was so poorly adapted, that they would not indorse even the premium notes for insurance upon the Relief, he followed, uncomplainingly, the hand of destiny which seemed to direct him and impel him onward till he could get no further.

Appendix

Withenbury's letters, with the dates referring to issues of the *Cincinnati Commercial*, are as follows:

10/8/70	Used as Letter 1. Refers back to "Bird of Passage" letter of 10/7.
10/9/70	Not used. Brief comments on Capt. Owen Franks.
10/10/70	Used as Letter 2.
10/11/70	Used as Letter 3.
10/13/70	Used as Letter 4.
10/14/70	Used as Letter 5.
10/15/70	Not used. Extended comments on the Kouns family of steamboatmen.
10/17/70	Partly used as Letter 6. Comments on *Picayune* not used.
10/18/70	Not used. Comments on Capt. Benjamin Crooks and his nephew Capt. James Crooks.
10/20/70	Partly used as Letter 7. Comments on *Picayune* not used.
10/20/70	Second letter, not used. Comments on Capt. Alex Norton and the *Grand Duke* during the Civil War.
10/21/70	Used as Letter 8.

10/24/70	Not used. Conversation with citizen of Shreveport. Comments on Capt. George Gunney and the Bon Dieu in early 1830s.
10/25/70	Not used. Conversation with Capt. Owen Franks concerning 1832 *Woodsman* trip to Ecore Fabre.
10/26/70	Not used. Comments on *James Ross* and *Napoleon* above raft in 1841.
10/27/70	Not used. Criticism of New Orleans Board of Underwriters.
10/28/70	Used as Letter 9.
10/29/70	Not used. Extensive commentary on 1848–1849 Jim's Bayou trips by *Monterey* with Withenbury as captain.
10/30/70	Partly used as Letter 10. Comments on *Picayune* not used.
10/31/70	Used as Letter 11.
11/4/70	Partly used as Letter 12. Paragraphs on Capts. Benjamin Crooks and Tom Moore not used.
11/4/70	Second letter, not used. Comments on *Southwestern*, *Frontier*, and *Ft. Towson* (Capts. Hal and Green Cheatham) and *Miami*.
11/5/70	Used as Letter 13.
11/7/70	Used as Letter 14.
11/14/70	Used as Letter 15.
11/18/70	Not used. Extensive comments on Capt. Tom Moore and improvements to western route with *Buffalo*, *Envoy*, and *Col. Harney*; also describes building of gunboat *Missouri*.
12/2/70	Partly used as Letter 16. Comments on *Picayune* not used.

12/19/70	Partly used as Letter 17. Comments on Capt. Billy Boardman not used.
12/23/70	Not used. Extensive comments on Admiral David Porter and cotton stealing on Red River during the Civil War.
12/26/70	Partly used as Letter 18. Comments on boats and captains on Upper Red River, names of some early settlers, career of Sam Applegate not used.
12/29/70	Used as Letter 19.
1/2/71	Not used. Extensive argument with *Picayune*.
1/9/71	Used as Letter 20.
1/30/71	Not used. First part on *Picayune*. Second part describes vision of outcome of Battle of Bull Run.
2/6/71	Used as Letter 21.
2/11/71	Partly used as Letter 22. First part on Red River Transportation Company not used.
2/13/71	Used as Letter 23.
2/20/71	Partly used as Letter 24. Comments on Capt. Joe Lodwick and the *Robert T. Lytle* not used.
2/23/71	Partly used as Letter 25. Comments on *Picayune* not used.
3/3/71	Partly used as Letter 26. Comments on Capt. Joseph Ross not used.
3/6/71	Used as Letter 27.
3/16/71	Partly used as Letter 28. Comments on Capt. W. R. Hoel not used.
4/1/71	Used as Letter 29.
4/28/71	Used as Letter 30.

5/1/71	Partly used as Letter 31. Comments on raft removal by Thomas Williamson not used.
5/8/71	Used as Letter 32.
5/15/71	Used as Letter 33.
6/5/71	Used as Letter 34.
6/12/71	Used as Letter 35.
6/21/71	Used as Letter 36.
6/26/71	Used as Letter 37.
7/3/71	Not used. Extensive commentary on origins of Great Raft.
7/10/71	Used as Letter 38.
7/20/71	Used as Letter 39.

Index

D

E

F

G

H

I

J

K

L

M

N

O

P

R

S

T

U

V

W